Understanding and Evaluating Prospectuses, Offering Documents, and Proxy Statements

Understanding and Evaluating Prospectuses, Offering Documents, and Proxy Statements

Thomas Robinson, Ph.D., CPA, CFP®, CFA®; David Schulte, J.D., CFA®;
Howard Marmorstein, Ph.D.; and William Trent, CFA®

The Financial Planning Association (FPA) is the membership association for the financial planning community. FPA is committed to providing information and resources to help financial planners and those who champion the financial planning process succeed. FPA believes that everyone needs objective advice to make smart financial decisions.

FPA Press is the publishing arm of FPA, providing current content and advanced thinking on technical and practice management topics.

Information in this book is accurate at the time of publication and consistent with the standards of good practice in the financial planning community. As research and practice advance, however, standards may change. For this reason, it is recommended that readers evaluate the applicability of any recommendation in light of particular situations and changing standards.

Disclaimer—This publication is designed to provide accurate and authoritative information in regard to the subject matter covered. It is sold with the understanding that the publisher is not engaged in rendering legal, accounting, or other professional service. If legal advice or other expert assistance is required, the services of a competent professional person should be sought. —*From a Declaration of Principles jointly adopted by a Committee of the American Bar Association and a Committee of Publishers and Associations.*

The views or opinions expressed by the author are the responsibility of the author alone and do not imply a view or opinion on the part of FPA, its members, employees, or agents. No representation or warranty is made concerning the accuracy of the material presented nor the application of the principles discussed by the author to any specific fact situation. The proper interpretation or application of the principles discussed in this FPA Publication is a matter of considered judgment of the person using the FPA Publication and FPA disclaims all liability therefore.

No part of this publication may be reproduced, stored in a retrieval system, or transmitted in any form or by any means, electronic, mechanical, photocopying, recording, or otherwise, without prior written permission of the publisher.

The Financial Planning Association is the owner of trademark, service mark, and collective membership mark rights in FPA®, FPA/Logo and FINANCIAL PLANNING ASSOCIATION®. The marks may not be used without written permission from the Financial Planning Association.

CFP®, CERTIFIED FINANCIAL PLANNER™, and federally registered CFP (with flame logo) are certification marks owned by Certified Financial Planner Board of Standards. These marks are awarded to individuals who successfully complete CFP Board's initial and ongoing certification requirements.

Financial Planning Association
4100 Mississippi Ave., Suite 400
Denver, Colorado 80246-3053

Phone: 800.322.4237
Fax: 303.759.0749
E-mail: fpapress@fpanet.org

www.fpanet.org

Copyright © 2006 Financial Planning Association. All rights reserved.

ISBN: 0-9753448-6-2
ISBN-13-978-0-9753448-6-6

Manufactured in the United States of America

For my parents
—T.R.

*For David C. Bayne, Emeritus Professor of Law,
The University of Iowa College of Law*
—D.S.

To Paula
—H.M.

For my father
—B.T.

About the Authors

Thomas R. (Tom) Robinson is an associate professor of accounting and director of the master of professional accounting program at the University of Miami. He also is managing director of Robinson, Desmond & Zwerner, a Florida investment advisory firm. He has a B.A. in economics from the University of Pennsylvania and a master's and Ph.D. from Case Western Reserve University. He is a Certified Public Accountant (Ohio), Certified Financial Planner™ (CFP®) certificant and Chartered Financial Analyst® (CFA®) charterholder. Tom has won several teaching awards and publishes regularly in academic and professional journals and associate editor and associate editor of *Research in Accounting Regulation*. He is a co-author of *Analysis of Equity Investments: Valuation*, published by the CFA Institute; *Financial Statement Analysis: A Global Perspective*, published by Prentice Hall; and *Tools and Techniques of Investment Planning*, published by National Underwriter.

David J. Schulte is a co-founder and managing director of Tortoise Capital Advisors (TCA), an investment advisory firm with approximately $2 billion under management. TCA manages publicly traded closed-end funds and private capital pools that invest in master limited partnerships and private companies in the energy infrastructure sector. Schulte also has experience completing acquisition and financing projects as a principal, investment banker, or attorney for growth companies in the transportation, manufacturing, retail, and service industries. Schulte is a Chartered Financial Analyst® (CFA®) and Certified Public Accountant (Iowa). He holds a B.S. in business administration from Drake University and a J.D. from the University of Iowa (member of the Missouri Bar Association). He is also a general partner and investment committee member for private equity and mezzanine funds in Kansas City and Little Rock.

Howard Marmorstein is an associate professor of marketing at the University of Miami where he teaches marketing management and consumer behavior. Professor Marmorstein received both a B.S. in economics and an M.B.A. from the Wharton School of the University of Pennsylvania. He received his Ph.D. from the University of Florida. He has also been a private investor and investment adviser for more than ten years. Professor Marmorstein won the University of Miami Professor of the Year Award in 2003. His research on consumer decision making has won two national awards and has been published in numerous academic journals. He has also served as an expert witness and business consultant for both firms and municipalities in the areas of business valuation, eminent domain, trademark infringement, and deceptive advertising.

William A. Trent has been an equity analyst since 1996, on both the sell-side and later the buy-side. Most recently, he was senior equity analyst for New Amsterdam Partners LLC, a $6 billion institutional asset manager. His experience covers all market-cap sizes and is primarily within the TMT (telecom, media, and technology) and transportation sectors. William holds the CFA® designation and earned his MBA in finance from the University of Miami. He serves on the CFA Institute Council of Examiners and various committees of the New York Society of Security Analysts. Since March 2006, he has been the senior editor of the Stock Market Beat Web site.

About FPA

The Financial Planning Association® (FPA®) is the membership organization for the financial planning community. FPA is built around four Core Values—Competence, Integrity, Relationships, and Stewardship. We want as members those who share our Core Values.

FPA's primary aim is to be the community that fosters the value of financial planning and advances the financial planning profession. The FPA strategy to accomplish its objectives involves welcoming all those who advance the financial planning process and promoting the CERTIFIED FINANCIAL PLANNER™ (CFP®) marks as the cornerstone of the financial planning profession. FPA is the heart of financial planning, connecting those who deliver, support, and benefit from it.

FPA was created on the foundation that the CFP marks best represent the promise and the future of the financial planning profession. CFP certification offers the public a consistent and credible symbol of professional competence in financial planning. And FPA benefits the public by helping to ensure that financial planning is delivered through competent and ethical financial planners.

FPA members include individuals and companies who are dedicated to helping people make wise financial decisions to achieve their life goals and dreams. FPA believes that everyone needs objective advice to make smart financial decisions and that when seeking the advice of a financial planner, the planner should be a CFP professional.

FPA is committed to improving and enhancing the professional lives and capabilities of our members. We offer a variety of programs and services to that end.

Table of Contents

Introduction 1

Chapter 1: Investor Protections: Legal and Regulatory Framework . 7

Chapter 2: Understanding and Analyzing Financial Statements . 31

Chapter 3: The Prospectus: Equity IPOs 71

Chapter 4: The Prospectus: Secondary Offerings and PIPEs ... 109

Chapter 5: The Prospectus: Mutual Funds 127

Chapter 6: The Prospectus: Principal Protected Securities 169

Chapter 7: The Proxy Statement 183

Chapter 8: Hedge Funds 205

Chapter 9: Specialized Private Equity Vehicles 217

Chapter 10: Real Estate Entities 237

Chapter 11: Investing in Real Assets 253

Appendix A: 267

Index: 285

Introduction

Nearly every day, an individual investor will drop off a large, seemingly unfathomable document with his trusted adviser, with the message that a friend said the document was for a "good deal" and asking whether the adviser would take a look at it. These "good deals" go by the formal names of prospectuses, proxy statements, offering memoranda, confidential memoranda, or even term sheets. The adviser's unenviable task is to ferret out the story, including which parties are taking which risks, and receiving which benefits. Many times these are not polished IPO prospectuses offered through brokers, but are more obscure investments that might contain contractual preferences for promoters, insiders, agents, or lenders, which can adversely affect the returns to an investor, even if the venture is wildly successful.

This book is intended as a reference tool for practicing financial planners, including financial consultants, licensed brokers, accountants, tax and estate attorneys, insurance professionals, and other financial advisers, who are trusted to provide considered advice regarding nontraditional investment options. The book is also appropriate for investors themselves. Investors are increasingly seeking to enhance their portfolios by investing in nontraditional "deals," either private or public. These investment vehicles are the subject of this book. It is designed to assist the practitioner or student in evaluating the investment materials, unlike more traditional texts that are aimed at aiding professionals in drafting investment materials.

Understanding and Evaluating Prospectuses, Offering Documents, and Proxy Statements

CAPITAL MARKETS AND ALLOCATION OF RESOURCES

In the capital markets, successful allocation of scarce financial resources is achieved through dissemination of information regarding risks and rewards, which is used by investors to determine in which economic sectors, industries, and companies they prefer to invest their capital. The United States capital markets arguably achieve the most efficient allocation of scarce capital resources in the world. Indicators of this success include the standard of living achieved in the U.S., the country's income per capita, and its evolution in response to the changing demands of its consumers.

In a free market economy, such as the U.S., pricing is the main mechanism for achieving the successful allocation of scarce resources. When making determinations about pricing, optimal disclosure about risks and opportunities by the issuer is critical. Offering memoranda prove to be one of the most sensitive sources of information used by a buyer when making pricing decisions.

The United States Securities and Exchange Commission (SEC) and various state securities regulators have established requirements that issuers of securities must meet, which enhance the quality of information provided to investors. These requirements have evolved over time and are generated and enforced by federal and state legislation, exchange regulations, rules applicable to brokers of investments, and accounting convention.[1] These regulations apply to the form—but rarely the specific content—of each offering memorandum.

There is no protection for an investor who makes a poor decision (or an adviser making a poor recommendation). When a bad decision is made, the misallocation of scarce financial resources occurs. A good example of this occurrence was the dot-com boom of the late 1990s, during which billions of dollars of capital were invested in assets that proved to be unproductive and ultimately worthless. The role of a financial adviser is to be mindful of helpful regulations, while carefully evaluating the merits and risks of the investment with your client. By performing this duty wisely, you participate in the important function of efficient allocation of financial capital.

Introduction

SPECIAL INVESTMENT CONSIDERATIONS—GOVERNANCE AND CONFLICTS

Wherever there is a separation of ownership and control, there exists potential investment risk related to the agency relationship between the fiduciary management and the owners, creditors, and other constituents. The potential for these risks to reduce investment performance is due to conflicts of interest. Some offering documents disclose known conflicts and potential conflicts, but not all are disclosed in that way. For example, the SEC is reviewing and changing the way in which executive compensation is disclosed. Executive compensation is overseen by the board of directors. This is supposed to create independent accountability to the shareholders, but governance itself may have conflicts, for example, when management selects the board of directors.[2]

Other conflicts are disclosed directly in risk factors and in certain transactions sections of IPO prospectuses, but they may not have the same scrutiny in private placement documents. While some companies and projects may have compelling economic potential, the potential for corrupt behavior is greatest where there is no scrutiny. The original premise of the U.S. securities laws was to expose to the light of day the dealings of the company with its insiders as well as its customers. The trend toward more investor transparency into dealings by companies with insiders is consistent with instilling trust in the capital markets, enabling the continued separation of ownership and control. This process relies on the functioning of many "credible intermediaries" with legal and reputational accountability for fair dealing and rigorous diligence on behalf of investors. The spectacular failures to do so have brought down some of the largest U.S. companies, audit firms, and investment banks. Keep in mind when evaluating the smaller firms, which face great pressure to perform, that conflicts and governance could lead to behavior that is not reflected in the financial statements. Be prepared to warn your client when you feel that the people involved in the business are not receptive to oversight. Look hard for the special risks that are difficult to ferret out of a disclosure document related to governance and accountability.

Understanding and Evaluating Prospectuses, Offering Documents, and Proxy Statements

ANALYTICAL TOOLS—CAVEAT EMPTOR STILL MATTERS

This book provides the tools to use in evaluating an investment offering and the related documents in order to understand the risk and returns that can be expected. The book begins by describing the regulatory framework for securities offerings in Chapter 1. By paying attention to the standard disclosures, a reader can determine whether any credible intermediary or professional firm has reviewed the disclosures for representational accuracy or suitability of risk for investors. These disclosures may appear to be boilerplate, but they assign legal liability to firms if they have not done a reasonable job. No regulatory agency will accept responsibility for review of the accuracy, however. The preliminary review of an offering document requires an understanding of how it was prepared and what level of validation has been, or has yet to be, performed by investors. Former President Ronald Reagan said it best when referring to inspections over treaty compliance, "Trust but verify." Each chapter of the book, beginning with Chapter 1, has practical examples throughout and end-of-chapter discussion questions and exercises to reinforce the concepts. Some questions relate directly to material in the chapter, while others are intended to stimulate thought and discussion on the topics covered. Suggested solutions and discussion points are provided in the appendix.

Chapter 2 provides a framework through which to analyze the financial statements and make valuation (pricing) judgments. This analysis lays bare the claims of the issuer and tempers the excitement of investors. It is essential to an understanding of the nature of the business, how it generates revenue, gross profit, and ultimately, earnings and cash flow. During the dotcom boom, one prospectus indicated that the company could not make a positive gross profit from sales, and there was no assurance that it ever would. Although this should have signaled investors to seriously consider alternative investments, the company was still successfully launched in a publicly underwritten IPO.

Chapters 3 through 11 then provide specialized tools to intelligently review distinct types of commonly available securities. These chapters provide the roadmap for a review of the material terms of which an investor should be aware, and can help you make an informed recommendation to your clients. Chapter 3 presents the analysis of a prospectus for an initial offering of equity securities. It examines the required components of a typical prospectus and the key points to examine to understand the risks and rewards of the offering. The techniques in this chapter provide the core elements for analyzing and evaluating any prospectus.

After an initial offering of securities, companies may initiate a secondary public offering or a private offering of their own securities (private investments in public entities). Chapter 4 extends the previous chapter with key points in evaluating such secondary offerings. Since the prospectus for an investment company has many unique features, Chapter 5 presents key points to consider in evaluating a prospectus for a mutual fund or other investment company. The volatility of the financial markets in recent years has led to the issuance of many types of principal-protected securities. The complicated structure of these securities deserves special evaluation. Chapter 6 presents an analysis of several typical principal-protected security issues.

Subsequent to the issuance of securities, companies of all types issue additional periodic statements in addition to the financial statements covered in Chapter 2, which require careful evaluation. Chapter 7 discusses the proxy statement and the key points to examine in determining how to vote a proxy.

Volatile equity and fixed income markets and the desire for diversification have led to increased consideration of alternative asset classes. The final four chapters of the book extend the evaluation of a prospectus presented in Chapter 3 to hedge funds (Chapter 8), private equity funds (Chapter 9), real estate investments (Chapter 10), and real asset investments, such as commodity funds (Chapter 11).

CONCLUSION

All investments, but especially new offerings, entail risks. Investors and their advisers need to be able to read, decipher, and evaluate prospectuses and other offering documents in order to assess the risks and potential opportunities involved. This book serves as a reference, highlighting key points to consider in evaluating these offering documents. It provides

Understanding and Evaluating Prospectuses, Offering Documents, and Proxy Statements

financial metrics and key points to consider for a variety of documents, including prospectuses, offering memoranda, and proxy statements.

ENDNOTES

[1] "Legal Institutions Strengthening Shareholder Rights Bring about Superior Investment Performance." Gugler, Mueller and Yurtoglu, Corporate Governance and the Returns on Investment, 47 *Journal of Law and Economics* 589, 629 (2004).

[2] Symposium on Bebchuck and Fried's "Pay Without Performance," 30 *Journal of Corporation Law* 647 (2006).

1 Investor Protections: Legal and Regulatory Framework

Investors need to have information in order to evaluate the risks and potential rewards of various types of investment securities. Issuers of securities must meet state and federal regulatory requirements that are designed to enhance the quality of the information provided to investors. The purpose of these regulations is to ensure uniformity of information quality—to make sure that the information available to make an informed decision is provided in an unbiased and appropriately detailed manner.[1]

Regulators specify the required form and content of documents provided to investors in security offerings; however, regulators do not judge the merits of the offerings. There is no protection, therefore, from an investor making a bad decision. When a bad decision is made, the resulting misallocation of scarce financial resources occurs. A good example of this was the ill-fated dot-com boom of the late 1990s, during which billions of dollars of capital were invested in assets that proved to be unproductive. The role of financial advisers is to be mindful of helpful regulations, while carefully evaluating the merits and risks of the investment for their clients.

This chapter provides background on these regulatory requirements for security offerings and discusses two types of investor documents: 1) offering documents, often in the form of a prospectus and 2) proxy statements for matters that must be voted on, such as mergers and other extraordinary events.

Understanding and Evaluating Prospectuses, Offering Documents, and Proxy Statements

A prospectus is a legal document used to offer securities or mutual fund shares for sale. The prospectus includes the terms of the sale, issuer information, objectives (in the case of a mutual fund) or planned use of the money (in the case of an operating company), historical financial statements, and other relevant information. The information in the prospectus can then be used to help qualify the investment and its suitability for a client. *Suitability* refers to the appropriateness of the risk/reward of an investment for a particular client. The role of a financial adviser is often to make this determination for clients. Licensed investment advisers and brokers face liability for failure to properly evaluate the characteristics in light of the client's circumstances.

Proxy statements for mergers and other extraordinary events are intended to solicit votes to retain or redeploy financial investments in the firm where the investor already holds an ownership interest.

FORMS OF SECURITY OFFERINGS

Securities offerings can range from small, privately negotiated transactions to large public auctions. Regulatory investor protections are based largely on the category of offering being conducted, so the first level of analysis of an offering is to determine which type of offering your client is considering.

Securities offerings can be classified as private or public, with pricing negotiated or fixed to the individual investor. Levels of regulatory protections are different for each kind of offering as depicted in Figure 1.1. The regulatory balance is an attempt to provide the most protection (high regulation) to those investors considering public offerings at fixed prices and the least to negotiated offerings with a small number of sophisticated investors (low regulation). In any case, offerings should stand up to reasonable analysis and scrutiny by the investor.

Figure 1.1: Types of Securities Offerings

	Private	Public
Negotiated Price	Low Regulation	Medium Regulation
Fixed Price	Medium Regulation	High Regulation

Chapter 1 | Investor Protections: Legal and Regulatory Framework

Private offerings are usually made by a company to a limited number of sophisticated investors who are capable of making appropriate inquiry and analysis to evaluate the investment. These offerings can be negotiated with a few investors, such as a venture capital financing, or offered to a larger number of investors with price and other terms specified by the company or underwriters. Exhibit 1.1 contains typical language that can usually be found in the opening pages of a private offering memorandum.

> **Exhibit 1.1: Sample Language from an Offering Memorandum for a Private Placement**
>
> THESE SECURITIES ARE SPECULATIVE AND INVOLVE A HIGH DEGREE OF RISK. THEY SHOULD BE SUBSCRIBED FOR ONLY BY PERSONS WHO CAN AFFORD TO LOSE THEIR ENTIRE INVESTMENT. THERE IS NO PRESENT MARKET FOR THE MEMBERSHIP INTERESTS IN THE L.L.C. AND IT IS NOT EXPECTED THAT A PUBLIC MARKET WILL DEVELOP. THE SECURITIES OFFERED HEREBY ARE SUBJECT TO RESTRICTIONS ON TRANSFERABILITY. INVESTORS MAY BE REQUIRED TO BEAR THE FINANCIAL RISKS OF THIS INVESTMENT FOR AN INDEFINITE PERIOD OF TIME. The membership interests are being offered for sale by the L.L.C. without sales commission to a select group of "accredited investors" who meet the suitability standards set forth under "INVESTOR SUITABILITY STANDARDS."

Public offerings are offered for a limited time through underwriting firms that have conducted due diligence on the assertions provided in the offering memorandum. By accepting responsibility for the underwriting of public securities, underwriters have liability associated with the due diligence on these assertions. Counsel for the underwriters also assist in the due diligence inquiry, and the offering statement usually cannot make claims that cannot be verified.

Most regulation relates only to the quality of the disclosure provided, not to the merits of the investment. The merits of the investment are what must be evaluated by investors and their advisers. Even highly regulated initial public offerings (IPOs) carry a disclaimer on the cover of the offering prospectus, such as the one from the Google offering illustrated in Exhibit 1.2.

If a highly regulated and publicly visible initial public offering such as Google's carries the above disclaimer, how can investors be confident in the regulatory process? What investor protections are these regulators actually providing? This illustration is a perfect example of why you, as an

Understanding and Evaluating Prospectuses, Offering Documents, and Proxy Statements

> **Exhibit 1.2: Language from the Prospectus of the Google Initial Public Offering**
>
> The Securities and Exchange Commission and state securities regulators have not approved or disapproved of these securities, or determined if this prospectus is truthful or complete. Any representation to the contrary is a criminal offense.

investment professional, must be confident in your ability to interpret offering documents. The purpose of the Google disclaimer is to make sure that investors are not misled into believing that the merits of the offering are somehow validated by the Securities and Exchange Commission (SEC). "*Caveat emptor*," or "Let the buyer beware," is the best form of investor protection, and a healthy skepticism regarding the offering is the best way to guide your client's investment decisions.

EVALUATING FORMS OF BUSINESS AND ENTITY AGREEMENTS

Offerings can occur for a wide variety of entities, particularly private offerings. It is necessary to understand the impact of the form of organization on the rights and obligations of the investor versus the rights and obligations of management. The separation of ownership of shares versus the control of the business creates the need for advisers to understand some legal aspects of business entities. Some legal structures have different tax outcomes, while others have different shareholder voting rights. When an investment in a firm provides the expected economic return to the investor, the form of entity is of no real interest or consequence. But if the firm goes awry, the contract that is embedded in the organizational form is critical to determining what ability your client has to recover his investment or exercise influence over management.

Proprietorship. Proprietorships are unincorporated businesses that have not been established as separate legal entities under state law and usually have single owners. State and local jurisdictions may require business licenses, but there is no other requirement to form a proprietorship since it is run by an individual, and individuals have the ability to enter into contracts and conduct business. A proprietorship is easy to form, maintain, and dissolve. However, since there is one owner who is also typically the manager of the business, a proprietorship is not used for ventures involving multiple investors and managers. Income of the proprietorship is taxed to the individual owner.

Partnership. A partnership is an unincorporated business owned by more than one person or entity. Partnerships can have very flexible terms on how profits, losses, and capital are shared. Each partner within the partnership may be entitled to differing ownership shares of assets, liabilities, profits, and losses. In some jurisdictions, partnerships can have both general and limited partners. General partners participate in management of the partnership, while limited partners do not. General partners have unlimited liability related to the partnership, while the liability of limited partners is typically limited to their investment in the business. A general partnership can be formed easily by agreement between the partners. States generally require a registration filing to form a limited partnership and usually require at least one general partner. Some states restrict the number of limited partners. Master limited partnerships (MLPs) are large limited partnerships where limited partners purchase units that are publicly traded. Partnerships are not subject to taxation; instead, their profits or losses are passed through to the partners in accordance with the partnership agreement. The partners pay taxes on their share of profits.

Corporation. A corporation is a separate legal entity that has the right to enter into contracts and transact business on its own. These entities must be created under state law and are distinct from their owners. Owners typically have limited liability related to the operations of the business (usually limited to the capital contributed). The corporation issues shares or stock certificates representing ownership interest in the entity. Most corporations are known as "regular corporations," which are subject to taxation and can have an unlimited number of shareholders. Additionally, when money is distributed to owners in the form of a dividend, this is taxable to the owners, which results in double taxation. A special type of corporation, called a Subchapter S corporation, or simply "S corporation," is exempt from most income taxes. Income flows through to, and is taxed to, the owners similar to a partnership. S corporations may only have 75 shareholders. The types of shareholders and classes of stock are also restricted. A regular corporation

Understanding and Evaluating Prospectuses, Offering Documents, and Proxy Statements

can issue different classes of common shares, which are the basic ownership type (for example, Class A and Class B), or preferred shares, each with differing rights and privileges. Corporations and S corporations are not as flexible as a partnership in terms of distributions. Partnership agreements will specify which partners are to receive allocations of profits and losses, and of cash distributions Be sure to review these flows in connection with projections of tax profit/loss allocations and character, since distributions may be allocated differently.

Limited Liability Company. Some jurisdictions have a hybrid business form that has attributes of both a partnership and corporation. With a limited liability lompany (LLC), profits and losses can be shared like a partnership, but owners have some degree of limited liability, as with a corporation. Owners are referred to as managers. Unlike a limited partnership, a general partner or member is usually not required. The type of business that can be conducted, the number of members and sales of a member's interest may be restricted under local law. For example, in many states certain professions must form a special type of limited liability company operating as a professional LLC. Tax treatment is flexible while the default is treated similar to a partnership—the entity can elect to be treated similar either to a partnership or corporation for tax purposes.

FINANCIAL CERTIFICATIONS

The financial statements of offering memoranda issuers can be of vastly different quality, depending upon the nature of the offering and the level of diligence performed before an offering is presented to potential investors. In a more detailed offering memorandum, a letter (formally presented by the issuer's accounting firm) can usually be found in the front of the financial statements describing the level of review performed of the financial statements and the type of presentation you can expect. In cases where there is no such letter, the issuer or an intermediary has most likely prepared the financial statements without review or verification. These letters should be read carefully as they have differing implications for investor protection and the ability of an investor to rely on them for accuracy.

Audited Financial Statements. The highest standard of presentation and verification is provided by *audited financial statements*. Audit firms are considered by most regulatory entities to be "experts," and by providing their expert opinion regarding the financial statement presentations, they take liability for their work. Despite some recent and very public failures on the part of a few major auditing firms (for example, within the Enron, Tyco, and Adelphia Corporation scandals), the process of financial verification by expert auditors is still considered one of the most important elements in the regulatory process.

Review. A *review*, performed by an accounting firm, provides a lower level of financial comfort in offering documents. The review process involves very superficial classification of the accounts in accordance with generally accepted accounting principles (GAAP). GAAP ensures that financial statements are prepared using similar principles to those used by other firms, enhancing comparability. However, verification procedures in a review are limited to reviewing information appearing in the financial statements for consistency, without verification of any specific accounts.

Compilation. An even lower level of financial certification is a *compilation*. The compilation is merely the presentation of the firm's financial statements in the format that the firm provides. There are usually very limited footnote explanations of the accounting policies, and there is no financial statement review or analysis for consistency.

Issuer-prepared Statements. The most suspect forms of financial statements are *issuer-prepared statements* that have no outside accounting input aside from the usual tax return presented for investor review. Issuer-prepared financial statements often lack consistency with GAAP and are of limited use in providing comparative analysis with other audited firms. Looked at over time, however, and properly understood, there is useful information that points the way to further inquiry by qualified advisers acting on behalf of investors.

Successful investments are made on the merits of the opportunity and the risk/reward tradeoff associated with the investment. Financial comfort is one element of risk reduction, but alone is not an indicator of value or merit of an investment. Private equity firms will sometimes make investment decisions based upon issuer-prepared financial statements. They will generally do so only if they have the opportunity to engage expert accountants to perform an "agreed upon procedures" review of key figures to provide additional confidence in those amounts.

Financial statements prepared in accordance with GAAP follow a standard of presentation consistent with established practice for companies with similar operations. Further, statements that are audited in accordance with "generally accepted auditing standards" have the highest level of assurance as to accuracy and consistency in presentation, and are required in public offerings registered with the Securities and Exchange Commission (SEC).

Higher-quality offerings will provide investors with management's discussion of the financial statements and provide commentary on trends. This is a requirement in public offerings, but many private offerings also have insight from management regarding the trends in historical financial statements and the relevance to expectations for future performance.

STATE "BLUE SKY" REGULATION

For offerings of securities not registered with the SEC, state regulations provide some compliance requirements intended to protect investors. Most states do not provide independent regulation of public offerings conducted in their territory. However, when their regulations do apply, they can be more protective of investors than federal securities regulation.

Jurisdiction. Jurisdiction refers to the geographical area over which a court or government body has the power and right to exercise authority. States have jurisdiction over all offerings occurring in that state. State laws do, however, have exceptions regarding offerings and there are a variety of offering types that are not subject to state regulation; so, while all offerings are subject to state jurisdiction, not all are subjected to state regulation. Nevertheless, all states make it illegal to provide misleading disclosure to investors in the state. Most exemptions from state regulation fall into two types: large offerings (which are registered with the SEC) and small offerings (either in dollar amounts or in terms of the number of investors solicited). Each offering memorandum will contain information in the front about the special rules that must be followed for the state in which the offer is made.

Chapter 1 | Investor Protections: Legal and Regulatory Framework

Merit Regulation. The state of origin of securities regulation was Kansas, where laws were passed to protect ranchers and farmers from being offered the "clear blue sky" in an offering. Kansas pioneered a merit-based regulatory system—the "blue sky" regulation—that was adopted by many other states, although not in a uniform fashion. The goal of merit regulation was to require strict adherence to a set of guidelines designed to prohibit offerings that were not of regulatory "merit," regardless of their disclosure regarding risks and opportunities. Until recently, these merit rules applied to all offerings in the state, even public offerings. The result was that some offerings could not satisfy merit regulations and would not be available in Kansas or other "merit" states. There are now exemptions for such offerings.

Merit regulations provide a useful guide to measuring information that has been used in the past to exploit investors and are believed to be areas where offerings are unfair to investors. These regulations limit options to insiders, dilution to new investors based on the financial contributions of previous investors and founders, and require minimal levels of profitability of the issuing firm. While useful for questioning any offering, these rules are based on concepts of value rooted in accounting measurements rather than capital market acceptance. Particularly for firms such as software and technology innovators, merit regulation restricts valuation and terms, acting essentially on behalf of investors.

For offerings not subject to SEC registration, the states are the only source of quality regulation, and in most states there is no merit regulation; rather, there is some kind of disclosure regulation. Some states have integrated their rules with federal rules, and in some private offerings, state rules still do not apply. These are offerings to a limited number of investors or offerings to sophisticated investors. Ironically, the definitions of wealth used for the exemptions include wealth based upon real estate holdings, so the original set of investors who were to be protected by merit regulation in Kansas have been exempted from regulation on disclosure and merit!

Private Offerings. Private offerings are characterized by their small offering size or the sophistication (measured by wealth) of the offerees. Typical language describing this limitation is presented in Exhibit 1.3. (Attorneys

Understanding and Evaluating Prospectuses, Offering Documents, and Proxy Statements

> **Exhibit 1.3: Typical Language Associated with Offering Limitations**
>
> THESE SECURITIES MAY ONLY BE OFFERED TO INVESTORS BELIEVED BY THE ISSUER TO BE "ACCREDITED" UNDER THE SECURITIES LAWS. NO INVESTMENT MAY BE ACCEPTED FROM AN INVESTOR WHO IS NOT ACCREDITED, BASED UPON REPRESENTATION MADE BY THE INVESTOR IN THE SUBSCRIPTION AGREEMENT FOR THE OFFERING.

usually use all capital letters to emphasize the importance of the restriction.)

By limiting private offerings to such investors, issuers can provide non-audited financial statements and other relaxed provisions. In some cases, issuers need not provide financial information, but need only comply with antifraud statutes and provide investors with access to information that can be obtained with reasonable effort and expense. These offerings put a high burden on the investor and adviser to research for relevant information and assemble it in a useful way. There have been many venture capital fundings based upon this kind of offering, where the financial information and operating history are less relevant to the investment decision than the technology being developed and assessed by experts at the venture fund. These offerings, while appealing to an investor's sense of adventure and risk-taking, are suitable only for individuals who can tolerate the loss of their entire investment and who understand the nature of the risk being taken.

Private offerings are the type of offering that investment professionals are most likely to be invited to review on behalf of their clients. These offerings can be from any industry or issuer, can be large or small, can be debt or equity, and can generally be offered to an unlimited number of qualified institutions or to up to 99 accredited investors. The rules and definitions can vary by jurisdiction, and investments that involve investors in different states come under the purview of the SEC. Exhibit 1.4 discusses the debate over state or federal securities regulation. The SEC defines an accredited investor as any one or combination of the following:[2]

1. A bank, insurance company, registered investment company, business development company, or small business investment company
2. An employee benefit plan, within the meaning of the Employee Retirement Income Security Act, if a bank, insurance company, or registered investment

adviser makes the investment decisions, or if the plan has total assets in excess of $5 million
3. A charitable organization, corporation, or partnership with assets exceeding $5 million
4. A director, executive officer, or general partner of the company selling the securities
5. A business in which all the equity owners are accredited investors
6. A natural person who has individual net worth, or joint net worth with the person's spouse, that exceeds $1 million at the time of the purchase
7. A natural person with income exceeding $200,000 in each of the two most recent years or joint income with a spouse exceeding $300,000 for those years, and a reasonable expectation of the same income level in the current year
8. A trust with assets in excess of $5 million, not formed to acquire the securities offered, whose purchases a sophisticated person makes

In private offerings, minimum investment size can range from under $100,000 to over $1 million per investor. In some cases, these offerings may also be made to as many as 35 nonaccredited investors provided that all investors are given an offering memorandum with the same type of information provided to investors in a registered offering. These can be negotiated or fixed-price offerings. In each case, the financial adviser must assess the most significant risks, ask questions of management to help assess those risks, and review the opportunity and risks with the investor.

In cases where nonaccredited investors are offered securities, investors must be provided with a "purchaser representative," paid for by the issuer, to help investors understand and interpret the information. In this way, the exemption from registration is conditioned upon the investor, alone or with his or her representative, being financially sophisticated.

These private offerings lack an essential element of a public offering, which is a future option to sell the investment if the investor desires to convert the investment to cash (See Exhibit 1.1 for typical disclosure about the market for private securities). Assessing the risk of an "exit" from a private offering is one of the key elements to valuing the offering.

Understanding and Evaluating Prospectuses, Offering Documents, and Proxy Statements

> **Exhibit 1.4: State or Federal Securities Regulation**
>
> "Theoretically, states could enforce a mandatory disclosure system. The [school of thought advanced by professors at the University of Chicago] views competition among states for corporate charters as analogous to competition among exchanges for listed firms: both are primarily influenced to set rules that benefit investors. Like easily shifting investment out of the NYSE, for example, an investor can shift investment among firms chartered in different states. Firms then have an incentive to incorporate in and, thus, abide by the rules of the state which is most likely to attract investment dollars because of investor-favorable rules....The [school of thought advanced by professors at Harvard University] believes that states are unable to enforce restrictive corporation statures...much like the NYSE is unable to promulgate and enforce effective disclosure rules. [Firms] have economic interests in nondisclosure. Additionally...state blue sky laws failed miserably to either prevent fraud or enforce disclosure rules. State blue sky [securities regulatory] officials supported federal regulation [by the SEC] because they were powerless to prevent fraudulent securities sales made across state lines."
>
> *Source:* Schulte, "The Debatable Case for Securities Regulation", 13 *Journal of Corporation Law* 535, 545–546 (1988).

GOVERNANCE REGULATION

One characteristic of a firm seeking public investor capital is limited involvement between investors and issuer management. The original purpose of the limitation was to remove investors from liability, beyond the investment amount, for potential expenses of the business. However, by reducing liability, the investors also necessarily reduce their ability to affect the actions of management. In order to provide management oversight, a board of directors is required to represent the interests of investors and oversee the management of the business.

The identity of the directors, their independence from the officers, and their duties to act in the best interests of investors all provide a measure of protection for investors.[3] There is a long history of common law regarding the duties of directors, two of which include loyalty to the corporation and

Figure 1.2: Corporate Governance Structure

Investors → Vote to elect → Board of Directors → Hire/regulate → Management taking care to act responsibly. Often, directors are selected by the officers, diminishing their perceived independence. Even directors elected solely by investors are dependent upon officers to provide them with information to make decisions. The strength of these directors and their ties to management bear evaluation, since it is rare that a director will be held liable for shareholder losses.[4]

Since the demise of Enron and the string of corporate scandals that followed, the duty of care of directors and the independence of directors has received scrutiny from Congress, accountants, financial analysts, and investors. The Enron Board of Directors included highly regarded members of the academic community as well as respected business leaders. Yet, these directors have been accused of failing to exercise their duties of oversight and care. They believed that they were performing their jobs as directors, but actually they did not understand the extent of conflicts of interest of the officers and one another. The board of Enron was sued for its neglect, and the claim was settled for $168 million, $13 million of which was to be paid personally by the directors.[5]

Thanks to Enron and other similar corporate scandals, the current corporate environment has placed an increased level of demand upon public company boards of directors. There is no legal basis in state common law for public versus private companies relating to the basic duties to investors of care and loyalty. Whether your client is considering a private placement or public offering, the identity and activity of the directors is an important consideration.

The state with the most evolved common law regarding investor rights, and director and officer duties, is Delaware.[6] Many other states follow Delaware precedent. If the issuer is a Delaware corporation, an investor can be assured that director duties have been reviewed by courts and that attorneys are well aware of the rules of conduct.

NASD REQUIREMENTS
Public and private offerings conducted with the assistance of brokers have additional protections for investors. Brokers offering securities are required to conduct a reasonable investigation into the issuer before the offering is

made to clients. The SEC requirements for public offerings are discussed in the next section. Brokers offering private placements are subject to rules of conduct enforced by the National Association of Securities Dealers (NASD).

> **Exhibit 1.5: From the NASD Home Page (www.nasd.com, March 14, 2006)**
>
> "As the world's largest private-sector regulator of financial services, NASD touches virtually every aspect of the securities industry. By law, every securities firm doing business with the American public must register with NASD. Today, about 5,200 brokerage firms and more than 668,000 stockbrokers and registered representatives fall under our jurisdiction. We register securities firms, write rules to govern their behavior, examine them for compliance and, when necessary, bring enforcement actions against those who break those rules."

Direct Participation Programs. The NASD rules define a direct participation program as one that has tax flow-through characteristics—generally, partnerships and LLCs—which are engaged in any business activity. This requirement captures investments that straddle between being public and private. They are publicly offered but not tradable in any aftermarket. These offerings are required to be suitable for the investor, due to the lack of liquidity, and the brokerage firm must conduct an investigation of the offering memorandum with due care. This is a very common type of offering to wealthy investors.

Exhibit 1.6 presents NASD due diligence guidelines for brokers. These guidelines have been in place for decades and represent the best practices of the NASD member firms in protecting their clients. There are major national offerings and small regional offerings. The diligence on the major offerings is usually undertaken by a lead brokerage firm from one of the national brokerage firms, whereas, regional offerings usually require a more thorough investigation by the broker's staff. The diligence officers can be questioned as to the procedures that they conducted, which must be documented and retained in a file.

The investigation processes described above are also undertaken by reputable brokers before offering any nontradable offering to its clients. The standard of due care that is often recited is that the person responsible for conducting the investigation should use the same prudence that he would

Exhibit 1.6: Due Diligence Guidelines for Brokers (NASD Manual, Section 2810)

(1) Application

No member or person associated with a member shall participate in a public offering of a direct participation program or a limited partnership rollup transaction except in accordance with this paragraph.

(2) Suitability

(A) A member or person associated with a member shall not underwrite or participate in a public offering of a direct participation program unless standards of suitability have been established by the program for participants therein and such standards are fully disclosed in the prospectus and are consistent with the provisions of subparagraph (B).

(B) In recommending to a participant the purchase, sale, or exchange of an interest in a direct participation program, a member or person associated with a member shall:

(i) have reasonable grounds to believe, on the basis of information obtained from the participant concerning his investment objectives, other investments, financial situation and needs, and any other information known by the member or associated person, that:

a. the participant is or will be in a financial position appropriate to enable him to realize to a significant extent the benefits described in the prospectus, including the tax benefits where they are a significant aspect of the program;

b. the participant has a fair market net worth sufficient to sustain the risks inherent in the program, including loss of investment and lack of liquidity; and

c. the program is otherwise suitable for the participant…

(3) Disclosure

(A) Prior to participating in a public offering of a direct participation program, a member or person associated with a member shall have reasonable grounds to believe, based on information made available to him by the sponsor through a prospectus or other materials, that all material facts are adequately and accurately disclosed and provide a basis for evaluating the program.

(B) In determining the adequacy of disclosed facts pursuant to subparagraph (A) hereof, a member or person associated with a member shall obtain information on material facts relating at a minimum to the following, if relevant in view of the nature of the program:

(i) items of compensation;
(ii) physical properties;
(iii) tax aspects;
(iv) financial stability and experience of the sponsor;
(v) the program's conflict and risk factors; and
(vi) appraisals and other pertinent reports.

undertake in the management of his own affairs. It provides risk reduction that the information is false, but it does not substitute for a judgment as to the merits of the offering by the investor versus other alternatives.

SEC REQUIREMENTS

In the United States, equity markets are regulated by the SEC and governed by several securities-related acts passed by Congress. The Securities Act of 1933 (Securities Act) requires an initial filing of a registration statement for new securities offerings (unless an exemption exists as discussed further below) and disclosure of material facts necessary for investors to make an informed decision. The Securities Exchange Act of 1934 (Exchange Act) requires annual and quarterly disclosures in subsequent years regarding operating and financial results.

Offerings to the public that are tradable on an exchange or on NASDAQ are subject to SEC mandatory disclosure requirements. The offering memorandum, called a prospectus, has audited financial statements, and the underwriting brokerage firms have conducted an investigation of all material factual representations in the prospectus. The prospectus has been vetted by counsel expert in the Securities Act of 1933 representing the issuer, and similarly experienced counsel representing the underwriters. Experts are named in the prospectus in order to add credibility and shift liability for errors to these outside firms. This risk sharing helps investors feel confident that the accounting firm named in the prospectus, and other experts, such as engineering firms, which provide opinions, have conducted a reasonable examination of the disclosure covered by their opinions. Finally, the prospectus is usually vetted by the SEC for conformity with their interpretations of disclosure rules (which can include requests for confirming data from third parties).

Brokers acting as underwriters in the offering are liable for misrepresentations, if any, in the prospectus unless they undertake a reasonable investigation of the information. Accounting firms assist the process for representations that are derived from financial records of the company, such as revenue per transaction for a retail company. The underwriters' "due diligence" results in the information presented being factual and not hype or promotional.

Federal disclosure rules and liability for failure to conduct a reasonable diligence investigation are designed to provide "disinfectant sunlight"[7] on the investment. These factors allow investors to make an informed decision as to the pricing. It is well-informed pricing that results in optimal allocation of scarce financial resources to firms. The information content of the prospectus has resulted in increased efficiency of the capital markets,[8] due to enhanced investor confidence and the resulting willingness to invest capital in new firms and new offerings.

Exemptions. There are a number of exemptions that permit the offering of securities for sale without registration with the SEC. All offerings, however, are subject to antifraud provisions of federal securities law. Further, there are still requirements for providing offering documents and annual financial statements to investors.

Section 3(a)(11) of the Securities Act exempts certain intrastate offerings for the financing of local businesses where they are incorporated in that state, carry out a significant amount of their business in that state, and make offers and sales of securities only to residents of that state. Such offerings are subject to state regulation.

Section 4(2) of the Securities Act exempts certain private offerings where there is not public solicitation of advertising in connection with the offering. All purchasers must be "sophisticated investors," having enough knowledge and experience to evaluate the risks and merits of the investment, have access to information normally found in a prospectus, and agree not to resell or distribute the securities to the public.

Regulation A of the SEC exempts certain small securities offerings under Section 3(b) of the Securities Act. Such offerings must not exceed $5 million in any 12-month period. An offering circular, similar to a prospectus, is required.

Regulation D of the SEC provides several exemptions. Rule 504 of Regulation D exempts offers of up to $1 million of securities in any 12-month period where there is no advertising and where resale of the shares is restricted. Rule 505 provides an exemption of sales of up to $5 million of securities in any 12-month period to an unlimited number of accredited

Understanding and Evaluating Prospectuses, Offering Documents, and Proxy Statements

investors and up to 35 other persons. Resale is also restricted and advertising may not be used. Rule 506 is similar to 505, but permits raising of more capital. However, all investors must be "sophisticated."

Continuous, Integrated Disclosure Rules. The federal securities laws anticipate that there will be trading in the aftermarket that should be based upon fully informed decisions as well as in the market for initial public offerings (IPOs). The confidence that investors have in the public filings post-IPO, regulated by the Securities Exchange Act of 1934, will translate into a greater willingness to participate in IPOs. The ability to sell the investment at any time is a vital component of reducing the risk of making the investment in the first place, and thus reduces the required return of investors allowing for less costly capital market access for companies. Evaluating the possibility of an exit from the investment is one of the most important criteria for entering an investment in the first place.

Sarbanes-Oxley. Investor confidence was substantially damaged in the aftermath of Enron's demise. To restore public confidence in the financial markets, Congress passed the Sarbanes-Oxley Act in 2002 (SOX). By more strictly regulating corporate governance, internal and external audit controls, and management responsibility for corporate fraud, SOX more clearly defined the rules under which public companies function and created harsher penalties associated with breaking those rules. The impact of SOX is still being measured by corporations and studied by commentators. The most costly compliance effort is driven by Section 404 (see Exhibit 1.7), which requires a documentation of internal control procedures and a finding regarding material weaknesses in the system.

STOCK EXCHANGE REQUIREMENTS

Each listing place for the trading of securities in the United States—the New York Stock Exchange, the NASDAQ, and the American Stock Exchange—promulgate rules of conduct for companies listing securities. These exchanges have varying degrees of automation and varying regulations applying to board governance and disclosure of events affecting the companies. It has long been thought that the NYSE had the most stringent requirements, and that the blue chip corporations would list their securities

> **Exhibit 1.7: Case Study—SOX Impact on Global Securities Markets**
>
> "On December 15th, Air China joined the growing ranks of Chinese companies listed on western stock exchanges…The national airline chose to land at the London Stock Exchange rather than in New York. One reason is thought to be that listing in America has become increasingly burdensome since Congress passed the Sarbanes-Oxley Act in 2002, in the wake of accounting scandals at Enron, WorldCom and elsewhere….The most onerous part of the act is Section 404 which came into effect November 15th…The number of controls that big companies must test and document can run into the tens of thousands, down to who signs company cheques. J.P. Morgan Chase says that it has 130 employees working fulltime on compliance with the rule.
>
> "There is no cost-benefit analysis that would make this work," complains the chief executive of a Fortune 500 company. This may be harming American exchanges' ability to compete with European rivals for new listings. Of course, against the expense and lost business must be weighed the benefits of better auditing and more trustworthy accounts. Though more difficult to quantify, they are no less real… "There is something to be said for listing on the exchange with the highest listing standards," said [an NYSE representative]. The NYSE thinks that European corporate-governance regulation is already tightening too, thus reducing the competitive gap. For listed companies, there may be no escaping the paperwork."

Source: "404 Tonnes of Paper", *The Economist* (December 18, 2004, p. 142)

there. The market capitalization of NASDAQ now is larger than that on the NYSE, and, as a result, NASDAQ now has many rules and regulations associated with its listings. Many of the more innovative, new public companies choose to list on NASDAQ, while many more conventional funds tend to choose listing on the NYSE.

The growth and automation of NASDAQ make it a much more investor-friendly trading network than it was several years ago, when dealers would maintain markets by telephone conversations and electronic trading. Probably the most efficiency-enhancing regulation was the change from fractions to decimals in trading. The spreads between bid and ask prices on securities narrowed considerably, and firms began using the small order execution system (SOES), an automated order matching system, more frequently. Recent evidence that NYSE member firms used the antiquated cry-out system to claim excess profits from investors led to a bonus to its former chairman of over $100 million in a single year. The NYSE is now studying ways to automate, like NASDAQ, certain of its trades.

Understanding and Evaluating Prospectuses, Offering Documents, and Proxy Statements

As a reviewer of an offering memorandum, equal comfort can be drawn from listing standards on the exchanges. They are fierce competitors for new listings and have adopted regulations that may impose more stringent investor protections. The exchanges attract investor capital and provide more liquidity for investors seeking to recover their investment and redeploy it into new opportunities.

PROXY STATEMENTS

The rise of the corporate form of business and public capital markets resulted in a separation between the ownership of the firm and the control of the firm.[9] Investors provide investment capital but do not have control over the operations of the firm. In many entities, this separation is mandated by the form of organization. For example, in a limited partnership, the general partner has control over operating and other decisions while limited partners have no say in management decisions. In fact, participation in management can create unlimited liability even for a limited partner. In entities that are closely held, control often rests with management or a small group of shareholders. In a widely or publicly held company, the owners' interests are represented by the board of directors.

Managers may run the firm but have relatively small ownership percentages. This separation of ownership from control can lead to agency costs—costs incurred because managers (the agents) may have interests in conflict with those of the investors (the principals). For example, managers may take actions that increase their compensation or personal wealth but not necessarily the value of the owners' investment, such as through lavish expense accounts or other perquisites. Agency costs can be reduced by monitoring of the managers and similar activities. Depending upon the organization form, investors may have various levels of influence over management, such as oversight by the board of directors. Some matters require a vote of shareholders, depending upon the type of organization and legal jurisdiction.

The SEC requires that companies subject to the Securities Exchange Act of 1934 follow certain rules regarding the solicitation of shareholder votes. The SEC requires that shareholders be provided with a proxy statement discussing management compensation, stock options plans, employment agreements, stock performance charts, and the matters that are subject to vote. For example, proxy statements will provide biographical information on directors up for election or re-election. Review and analysis of proxy statements are an important part of the monitoring process of an investment, which is essential both in evaluating the performance of management and making decisions on matters subject to a vote.

CONCLUSION

State and federal regulators, as well as self-regulatory organizations, have rules in place that are designed to protect investors. These rules primarily require that certain disclosures are provided to investors. The level of disclosure depends upon the nature of the offering and the sophistication of the investor. The regulatory organizations do not pass judgment on the investment merit of any offerings. The regulations are instead designed to provide disclosure deemed necessary for the investor and investment advisers to evaluate the potential risk and rewards of the offering. Investors and advisers must examine these disclosures and perform additional due diligence to evaluate the offering. Subsequent chapters describe how to evaluate offering documents and proxy statements.

ENDNOTES

[1] Hannes, "Comparison Among Firms: (When) Do They Justify Manditory Disclosure?" 29 *Journal of Corporation Law*, 700 (2004); Schulte, "The Debatable Case for Securities Disclosure Regulation," 13 *Journal of Corporation Law* 535 (1988).

[2] Securities and Exchange Commission, Regulation D, Rule 501.

[3] There is a sphere of board control and a sphere of shareholder control. Shareholders' primary roles are to vote for directors and buy or sell their shares, or the entire corporation. Paredes, "The Firm and the Nature of Control: Toward a Theory of Takeover Law," 29 *Journal of Corporation Law* 103, 125–126 (2003).

[4] Engen, "Worried About Shareholder Suits? Fuhgedaboudit!," *Corporate Board Member* (March/April 2004). (www.boardmember.com/issues/archive.pl?article_id=11825, March 14, 2006).

[5] *Wall Street Journal*, January 7, 2005.

[6] *MM Cos v. Liquid Audio, Inc.* 813 A2d 1118, 1126 (Del 2003).

[7] Louis Brandeis, *Other People's Money*, Chapter 5. New York, 1914.

[8] The strongest evidence for a mandatory disclosure system may be efficiency-based. Empirical data strongly suggests that the adoption of a mandatory disclosure system reduced price dispersion and thereby enhanced the allocative efficiency of our capital markets. Loss and Seligman, *Securities Regulation* (3rd) 170, 217–219.

[9] See Berle and Means 1932, and vol. 32 (2) of the *Journal of Law & Economics* in 1983 celebrating the 50th anniversary of Berle and Means.

Understanding and Evaluating Prospectuses, Offering Documents, and Proxy Statements

DISCUSSION QUESTIONS

1. Why are public securities offerings more highly regulated than private offerings?
2. What would be the advantages of using a limited liability company (LLC) as opposed to a partnership or corporation for an investment venture using many investors?
3. The chapter discusses some examples of agency costs that may occur when there is a separation of ownership and control in an investment entity. What are some other potential costs of this separation of ownership and control?
4. What actions could investors take to reduce potential costs related to the separation of ownership and control?
5. How can state and federal regulations reduce potential costs related to the separation of ownership and control?

EXERCISE

The SEC requires electronic filing for most issuers of securities. These filings can be viewed on the SEC's EDGAR filing system.

1. Go to the SEC's Web site at www.sec.gov.
2. Click on Description of SEC forms under Filings and Forms (EDGAR).
3. What types of forms are used for filing of initial registration statements?
4. From the main SEC Web site page, click on Search SEC filings. Search for a company IPO prospectus (Form S-1). Review the prospectus and briefly list and discuss its contents.

RECOMMENDED READING

SEC v. Howey—The 1946 U.S. Supreme Court case that defined the characteristics of an investment contract. See McDonald, "Toward Consistent Investor Protection Under the Securities Laws," 32 Sec. Reg. L. J. 68 (2004) (Discussing Howey and post-Howey developments).

Adolf A. Berle, Jr. and Gardiner C. Means, *The Modern Corporation and*

Private Property, The Macmillan Company, New York, 1932.

Corporations and Private Property: A Conference Sponsored by The Hoover Institution, *The Journal of Law & Economics*, vol. 26.

2 Understanding and Analyzing Financial Statements

In addition to mandatory disclosures to meet legal requirements, issuers provide a great deal of useful information in the prospectus about their financial condition and performance. This information is designed to influence prospective investors' assessments of the potential rewards and risks associated with the securities. Understanding and analyzing financial statements, which is the subject of this chapter, entails the application of tools and techniques that enable the readers of the prospectus to make more informed decisions about the offering.

During periods when investor sentiment is exuberant, firms with little more than a new concept or promising technology may seek funds from the capital markets. In these cases, financial statement analysis may not be the most valuable approach for evaluating the offering. These early-stage firms may have little in the way of revenues or assets, let alone profits, for the investor to examine. In more typical markets, however, firms that seek to raise a considerable amount of capital have operated businesses that own assets and have generated revenue for several years. This track record can provide an excellent foundation for the prospective investor, who is interested in estimating the return that the issuing firm will generate on its new capital. Financial statement analysis can yield considerable insight under these circumstances.

In this chapter, we will begin by presenting the fundamental financial statements that often appear in a prospectus.[1] We

Understanding and Evaluating Prospectuses, Offering Documents, and Proxy Statements

will also address underlying assumptions and inherent limitations of this financial information. We then introduce a set of analytic tools for examining financial information that is commonly known as ratio analysis. As that name implies, this fundamental technique focuses on the ratio of various line items that appear in any firm's financial accounts to assess specific aspects of that firm's condition or performance. Looking ahead, examples of widely used ratios that we'll consider in this chapter are metrics such as return on equity (that is, net income/shareholders' equity) and asset turnover (sales/assets). The former ratio is an important indicator of a firm's performance while the latter ratio provides one indication as to why this firm is delivering a superior, average, or substandard rate of return.

The next-to-last section of this chapter shows how a set of five individual ratios, which initially are examined individually, can be used collectively to decompose a firm's performance more precisely. This decomposition of return on equity (or ROE) often reveals strengths and weaknesses of a company's business model; these insights can be vital to the investor who seeks to arrive at a decisive opinion about the offering's attractiveness.[2]

Ultimately, the decision to purchase a security hinges upon the investor's assessment of its valuation. Therefore, the chapter concludes with a discussion of the application of ratio analysis to valuation. While a comprehensive treatment of valuation techniques is beyond the scope of this book, our presentation of the market-multiple approach provides the investor with a valuable perspective and starting point for assessing the attractiveness of an offering.[3]

UNDERSTANDING FINANCIAL STATEMENTS

The quality of the accounting for a company's transactions since its inception underlies the integrity of the financial information on which all of our analyses will be based. Fortunately, ongoing efforts to refine the accounting rules (for example, recent rules regarding the expensing of stock options) and increased adherence to those rules (for example, Sarbanes-Oxley, 2002) provide considerable assurance about the resulting financial statements. Nonetheless, it is vital that the user of the financial information contained in any prospectus not only understands the financial statements but also appreciates the limitations that are inherent to the accounting data.

There are three primary financial statements of concern to potential investors. These are the income statement, the balance sheet, and the statement of cash flows. The income statement reflects the profitability of the enterprise over a given time period (for example, for the year ended December 31, 2004). The balance sheet shows the financial position at a given point in time. Finally, the statement of cash flows shows the sources and uses of cash over a given period of time.

Income Statement. Exhibit 2.1 presents the income statement for Google Inc., which accompanied their 2004 prospectus. Note first that the heading of the income statement is titled "Consolidated Statements of Income." The term *consolidated* means that the income statement reflects the results of the parent company as well as any subsidiaries controlled by the parent company. The heading also indicates that amounts are denominated in thousands. So the net revenues reported for 2003 of $961,874 represents $961,874,000, or over $961 million.

Net revenues reflect the amount that Google charged to customers for services rendered during the fiscal year net of any returns or allowances. Revenues are reported when earned, rather than when they are collected from customers. This is known as the accrual basis of accounting. The cash collected from customers is also important but is not reflected on the income statement. Instead, it is a component of the statement of cash flows, which is discussed below.

After net revenues, the company lists the expenses incurred in generating those revenues. Expenses are recorded when incurred as opposed to when the cash is paid, similar to the treatment of revenue. Cost of revenues, sometimes referred to as cost of goods sold reflects the direct cost of delivering goods and services such as materials, labor, and some overhead. Often a company will present a subtotal on the income statement called "gross profit," which is net revenues less cost of revenues. Research and development (R&D) expenses are listed separately, since this is an important category, particularly for technology-related companies. While spending more money on R&D reduces current profits, it can be a signal of potential for increased revenues in the future.

Exhibit 2.1: Example Income Statement:

Google Inc. CONSOLIDATED STATEMENTS OF INCOME (In thousands, except per share amounts)

	Year End December 31,		
	2001	2002	2003
Net revenues, costs and expenses	$86,426	$347,848	$961,874
Cost of revenues	14,228	39,850	121,794
Research and development	16,500	31,748	91,228
Sales and marketing	20,076	43,849	120,328
General and administrative	12,275	24,300	56,699
Stock-based compensation	12,383	21,635	229,361
Total costs and expenses	75,462	161,382	619,410
Income from operations	10,964	186,466	342,464
Interest income (expense) and other, net	(896)	(1,551)	4,190
Income before income taxes	10,068	184,915	346,654
Provision for income taxes	3,083	85,259	241,006
Net income	$6,985	$99,656	$105,648
Net income per share: basic	$0.07	$0.86	$0.77
Diluted	$0.04	$0.45	$0.41
Pro forma basic (unaudited)			$0.51
Number of shares used in per share calculations: basic	94,523	115,242	137,697
Diluted	186,776	220,633	256,638
Pro forma basic (unaudited)			208,825

Source: Google Inc. prospectus, dated August 18, 2004.

Sales and marketing expenses include internal and external expenditures such as sales staff or outside advertising. General and administrative expenses reflect the cost of supporting the organization such as accounting, finance, and human resource departments. Stock-based compensation reflects an estimate of the value of stock and stock options granted to employees and spread out over the period over which employees must perform services related to the options. All of these expenses are typically referred to as operating expenses. After subtracting these from net revenues, the company presents a subtotal for income from operations.

After income from operations, companies present non-operating income and expenses, such as investment income and interest expense (unless the company is a financial institution, in which case these are operating items). Income before income taxes reflects the pre-tax profit from both operating and non-operating activities of the enterprise during the period. Provision for income taxes is the amount of income taxes the company expects to pay on the reported pre-tax income. As with other expenses, the income tax provision may not reflect the cash taxes paid for the year.

The bottom line, net income or loss, reflects the after-tax profit of the enterprise. This amount accrues to the owners and may be paid out as a dividend at some point in time. Since shareholders own varying amounts of shares, the company must present net income on a per share basis. Basic earnings per share is net income divided by the average number of shares that were outstanding during the year. Diluted earnings per share reflects the potential impact on earnings per share of stock options and similar potentially dilutive securities. In the case of Google Inc., they also present a "pro forma" earnings per share figure that reflects the potential impact of convertible preferred stock that is antidilutive (increases diluted earnings per share).

Balance Sheet. Exhibit 2.2 presents the balance sheet for Google Inc. As with the income statement, the balance sheet is consolidated and is presented in thousands of dollars. The balance sheet, sometimes referred to as the statement of financial position or condition, presents the assets of the business and the claims against those assets. The claims include those of owners, referred to as owners' or stockholders' equity, and others, referred to as liabilities.

Some balance sheets segregate current assets from long-term assets (the long-term section is not labeled—it is all assets other than current assets). Current assets are those expected to be used up or converted into cash in

Understanding and Evaluating Prospectuses, Offering Documents, and Proxy Statements

Exhibit 2.2: Example Balance Sheets:

Google Inc. CONSOLIDATED BALANCE SHEETS (In thousands, except par value)

Assets	Year End December 31, 2002	Year End December 31, 2004
Current assets:		
Cash and cash equivalents	$57,752	$148,995
Short-term investments	88,579	185,723
Accounts receivable, net of allowance of $2,297, $4,670, and $5,611	61,994	154,690
Deferred income taxes	12,646	22,105
Prepaid revenue share, expenses, and other assets	10,825	48,721
Total current assets	231,796	560,234
Property and equipment, net	53,873	188,255
Goodwill	—	87,442
Intangible assets, net	96	18,114
Prepaid revenue share, expenses, and other assets, non-current	1,127	17,413
Total assets	$286,892	$871,458
Liabilities, Redeemable Convertible Preferred Stock Warrant, and Stockholders' Equity		
Current liabilities:		
Accounts payable	$9,394	$46,175
Accrued compensation and benefits	14,528	33,522
Accrued expenses and other current liabilities	10,810	26,411
Accrued revenue share	13,100	88,672
Deferred revenue	11,345	15,346
Income taxes payable	25,981	20,705
Current portion of equipment leases	4,350	4,621
Total current liabilities	89,508	235,452
Long-term portion of equipment leases	6,512	1,988
Deferred revenue, long-term	1,901	5,014
Liability for stock options exercised early, long-term	567	6,341
Deferred income taxes	580	18,510
Other long-term liabilities, commitments, and contingencies	—	1,512
Redeemable convertible preferred stock warrant	13,871	13,871

Chapter 2 | Understanding and Analyzing Financial Statements

Stockholders' equity:		
Convertible preferred stock, $0.001 par value, issuable in series: 166,896, 164,782, and 164,782 shares authorized at December 31, 2002 and 2003, and March 31, 2004; 70,432, 71,662 and 71,662 shares issued and outstanding at December 31, 2002 and 2003, and March 31, 2004; no shares issued and outstanding pro forma; aggregate liquidation preference of $40,815 at March 31, 2004	44,346	44,346
Class A and Class B common stock, $0.001 par value: 700,000 shares authorized, 145,346, 160,866, and 163,541 shares issued and outstanding, excluding 3,281, 11,987, and 10,946 shares subject to repurchase (see Note 9) at December 31, 2002 and 2003, and March 31, 2004; and 235,203 shares outstanding pro forma	145	161
Additional paid-in capital	83,410	725,219
Note receivable from officer/stockholder	(4,300)	(4,300)
Deferred stock-based compensation	(35,401)	(369,668)
Accumulated other comprehensive income	49	1,660
Retained earnings	85,704	191,352
Total stockholders' equity		
	173,953	588,770
Total liabilities, redeemable convertible preferred stock warrant and stockholders' equity	$286,892	$871,458

Source: Google Inc. prospectus, dated August 18, 2004.

the near term (usually one year). Within current assets, assets are typically listed in order of liquidity (how quickly they are expected to be converted into cash or used up). The most liquid current asset includes cash and cash equivalents. This amount represents the amount held on that day in petty cash, bank accounts, short-term certificates of deposit, and other near-cash investments with maturities of less than 90 days. Short-term (and sometimes long-term) investments listed separately represent other investments such as stocks, bonds, and other investments. In most cases, these are listed at their current market value; however, some bond investments or nonmarketable investments are listed based on their historical cost.

Accounts receivable, net of allowance, reflects the amount owed to the company by customers reduced for any expected bad debts. Deferred income tax assets appear when the company has been required to report net income for tax purposes before it is reported on the financial statements. Essentially, this is a prepayment of taxes. Other prepaid assets may include prepaid rent, insurance, and similar items. For example, a company may pay its insurance policy at the beginning of the year. This is initially recorded as a prepaid asset. Later, as time passes, this amount is recorded as an expense on the income statement. Some prepaid assets are listed in current assets; others are listed under long-term assets.

In long-term assets, the most common assets are property and equipment, which includes land, buildings, equipment, furniture, and similar items. These are recorded initially at cost. In the case of property and equipment other than land, this amount is reduced each year by an estimate of how much the asset has depreciated. The annual depreciation is recorded among the expenses on the income statement.[4]

Goodwill is an intangible asset that represents the cost of an acquisition in excess of the value of the other underlying assets. It only appears on the balance sheet when the company has acquired another company. It may reflect the good name, location, or other unspecified intangible assets acquired when one company purchases another. Intangible assets, net, represent specifically identifiable intangible assets such as patents or copyrights. These intangible assets are amortized over their useful life (a process akin to depreciation of property and equipment).[5]

Total assets represent the total resources of the business from an accounting standpoint. Some resources, such as human capital or internally generated goodwill, are not reflected on the balance sheet.

Liabilities represent claims against the enterprise such as those of suppliers, employees, banks, or other creditors. As with assets, liabilities are often classified into current liabilities and long-term liabilities. Current liabilities are those expected to be paid or otherwise extinguished in the near term (usually one year).

Accounts payable are the amounts owed to suppliers for goods and services acquired by the enterprise. Accrued expenses include amounts owed to employees and others for things like salaries, bonuses, commissions, or revenue-sharing amounts owed to others, health care benefits, and the like. These are accrued as expenses on the income statement and liabilities on the balance sheet when they are incurred. The liability is reduced when amounts are actually paid.

Deferred revenue represents revenue that has been collected in advance. This amount represents a liability until the enterprise has delivered the required goods or services, at which time it is transferred to the income statement. Some deferred revenue is listed under current assets and amounts received further in advance are listed under long-term liabilities.

Most companies would also report bank debt or bonds payable in liabilities. The amount due within one year would be listed under current liabilities with the remainder under long-term liabilities. In the case of Google Inc., the company has entered into equipment leases that have been classified as purchases of equipment for accounting purposes. The obligations related to these leases are reflected in current and long-term liabilities.

Google Inc., also has a long-term liability related to some employee stock options where the company allowed the employee to exercise the options prior to vesting. This amount represents payments received by the company from the employee and is essentially a deposit toward the purchase of the stock. Over time, this liability will become part of stockholders' equity.

Deferred income tax liabilities represent taxes the company expects to pay in the future related to net income that has been reported for accounting purposes but not yet reported for tax purposes. Other long-term liabilities include all other obligations payable in more than one year.

The redeemable convertible preferred stock warrant represents the estimated amount of a right held by another party to purchase preferred stock at a specified price.

Stockholders' equity represents the amounts invested by the owners in the firm. These can include common stock (the basic unit of ownership typically with voting rights), preferred stock (stock with certain preferences such as liquidation or dividend preferences), and earnings retained in the business. It can also include some items of gains or losses that have not yet been reported on the income statement. Essentially, stockholders' equity is a residual claim: the owners are entitled to what is left of the assets after paying other claims (liabilities).

Cash Flow Statement. Exhibit 2.3 presents the cash flow statement for Google. The cash flow statement shows the net inflows and outflows of cash for the enterprise. While the income statement presents the profits for a period of time, it is prepared using the accrual basis. Net income is important but is not the same as cash. Cash is necessary to pay suppliers, employees, and others. It is therefore essential to examine the cash flow statement in addition to the income statement.

The cash flow statement separates the cash flow into three categories: operating, investing, and financing activities. Operating cash flows are those arising from operating the business and are usually presented by starting with net income and making adjustments for all the accruals to arrive at cash flow provided by (or used in) operating activities. For a mature company, this should be the major source of cash. Some companies present this section of the cash flow method using a direct format that shows the cash received from customers, cash paid out to suppliers, and so on. This method is more useful to the reader, but is not presented by many enterprises. In viewing a more typical indirect format cash flow statement, the reader should not spend too much time examining the accrual adjustments. Rather, it is useful to examine the overall cash from operating activities to see if it is positive and whether it is sufficient to grow the business and ultimately repay investors and creditors. For a start-up company, operating cash flow may be negative initially, but before investing in any business, the investor needs to be comfortable that operating cash flow will turn positive and grow as time passes.

The investing section of the cash flow statement shows where the company is investing its cash flows, such as in equipment, other companies, or other investments such as bonds. The financing section of the cash flow statement shows where the company has raised its own capital, either issuing stock, bonds, or borrowing funds from other entities. This section also reflects repayment of debt, dividends paid to shareholders, and any repurchases of stock by the company. The sum of these three categories, along with the impact of exchange rates, shows the overall flow of cash during the period.

Statement of Owners' Equity. In addition to the income statement,

Chapter 2 | Understanding and Analyzing Financial Statements

Exhibit 2.3: Example Cash Flow Statements:

Google Inc. CONSOLIDATED STATEMENTS OF CASH FLOWS (In thousands)

	Year End December 31,		
	2001	2002	2003
Operating Activities			
Net income	$6,985	$99,656	$105,648
Adjustments to reconcile net income to net cash provided by operating activities:			
Depreciation and amortization of property and equipment	9,831	17,815	43,851
Amortization of warrants	4,157	10,953	4,864
Amortization of intangibles	194	215	6,334
In-process research and development	—	—	11,618
Stock-based compensation	12,383	21,635	229,361
Changes in assets and liabilities, net of effects of acquisitions:			
Accounts receivable	(11,736)	(43,877)	(90,385)
Income taxes, net	2,398	11,517	(6,319)
Prepaid revenue share, expenses and other assets	(22)	(5,875)	(58,913)
Accounts payable	1,643	5,645	36,699
Accrued expenses and other liabilities	4,207	15,393	31,104
Accrued revenue share	—	13,100	74,603
Deferred revenue	1,049	9,088	6,980
Net cash provided by operating activities	31,089	155,265	395,445
Investing Activities			
Purchases of property and equipment	(13,060)	(37,198)	(176,801)
Purchase of short-term investments	(26,389)	(93,061)	(316,599)
Maturities and sales of short-term investments	11,460	20,443	219,404
Acquisitions, net of cash acquired	—	—	(39,958)
Change in other assets	(1,102)	99	—
Net cash used in investing activities	(29,091)	(109,717)	(313,954)
Financing Activities			
Proceeds from issuance of convertible preferred stock, net	1,042	—	—
Proceeds from exercise of stock options, net	988	2,262	15,476
Payments of notes receivable from stockholders	34	—	—
Payments of principal on capital leases and equipment loans	(4,503)	(7,735)	(7,386)
Net cash provided by (used in) financing activities	(2,439)	(5,473)	8,090
Effect of exchange rate changes on cash and cash equivalents	—	—	1,662

Net increase (decrease) in cash and cash equivalents	(441)	40,075	91,243
Cash and cash equivalents at beginning of year	18,118	17,677	57,752
Cash and cash equivalents at end of year	$17,677	$57,752	$148,995

Source: Google Inc. prospectus, dated August 18, 2004.

balance sheet, and cash flow statement, enterprises present a fourth financial statement. This is the statement of owners' equity. This statement provides a reconciliation of activity for the equity section of the balance sheet from the beginning to the end of the period. This fourth statement can be useful in understanding the balance sheet.

Accounting Conventions. Three important accounting conventions that affect, and in some cases limit, the interpretation of financial statement information are the reliance on historical cost for some assets, the accrual basis of accounting, and the need for accounting estimates.

The principles of objectivity and conservatism underpin the use of historical cost-based accounting. This approach requires companies to record and maintain many valuable assets at the original (that is, historic) cost at which they were purchased or produced. Consider the following example. XYZ Corporation purchased 100 acres of land on which to locate its corporate headquarters and first manufacturing plant in 1935 for $10 million. Assume that this same tract of land is now worth $100 million. On the company's balance sheet dated December 31, 2005, the land will continue to be listed as a long-term asset at an amount of $10 million. Wouldn't XYZ prefer to report the land more accurately and favorably at its current market value? In general, companies are not permitted to revalue upward the amount at which their property and equipment are recorded.[6] Only when the asset is sold will the appreciation of this land be reflected on the company's financial statements. This approach eliminates the company's need to have the asset subjectively appraised each year and compels use of an objective basis, through an arm's length transaction, in accounting for the asset.

Interestingly, the aforementioned principle of conservatism also compels companies to write-down (that is, re-value downward) assets that decline in value in most instances. This "mixed-model," in which some assets are listed at fair value while others appear at historical cost, complicates the analysis process and limits the interpretability of conclusions in some cases. Note, in addition to purchased assets, that assets produced or generated internally by a firm can also be understated. Intangible assets, such as patents that were obtained by means of the company's own research and development efforts, are valued at the cost of the *inputs* that preceded their approval or completion. In successful instances, the market value of a patent often greatly exceeds and bears little relation to its historical cost.

With increasing globalization of trade and flow of information, more investors seek to compare the valuation of U.S. firms' offerings to those of overseas companies in which they could also invest readily. Examination of the data provided in the financial statements is one sensible method of assessing the relative attractiveness of any U.S. offering to a domestic or foreign competitor. A nontrivial type of limitation of which the investor must be aware arises because accounting rules and regulations vary across jurisdictions.

In the U.S., corporate accounting follows generally accepted accounting principles (GAAP) as determined by the Financial Accounting Standards Board (FASB). In the European Union and many other developed nations, the International Accounting Standards Board (IASB) is responsible for establishing international accounting standards. While these two sets of rules are converging over time, some differences remain. Within U.S. GAAP, there can also be differences in the accounting methods that companies use, such as over what period of time they depreciate their assets, as discussed below. The footnotes that accompany the financial statement must provide a summary of accounting methods used so the reader can determine if two companies are using similar methods.

Another limitation faced by users of financial information stems from the need for accounting estimates for items ranging from depreciation to bad debt expense. Suppose, for example, that a semiconductor manufacturer invests $50 million to acquire a piece of equipment on the first day of its fiscal year. Naturally, it records this long-term asset at its historical cost. How much of that investment should it record as an expense in its income statement in that fiscal year? As a general rule, the portion of the asset that will be consumed this year will be expensed while the remainder will remain on the balance sheet as an asset. It seems reasonable that the

Understanding and Evaluating Prospectuses, Offering Documents, and Proxy Statements

answer to this question depends upon the expected life of the asset (and its salvage value, if any).

Perhaps an accounting regulation could specify the depreciable life for this type of asset, thereby ensuring that the firm's accounting is appropriate and comparable to other firms that use similar equipment? Unfortunately, the very same piece of equipment can be used by different firms at varying intensity or even for different purposes. As a result, the most valid estimate of the rate at which this equipment should be expensed (that is, depreciated) can best be determined by each firm that owns it. The consequence is that firms can make idiosyncratic estimates of the annual expense for such long-term assets. Later in the chapter, we will suggest a method by which the reader of a prospectus can gauge the reasonableness of a company's pattern of such estimates.

For similar reasons, each company's recognition of bad-debt expense entails an estimate. Again, one might wonder why any estimate is required to record the amount of a company's receivables that were not paid on time during the past year. What could possibly be more straightforward than accounting for this expense? The origin of the need for estimation in this case, much like the situation for depreciation, is found in the accounting convention of accrual accounting. Accrual accounting requires that revenue be reported when it is earned regardless of when it is received.

The logical consequence of this accounting convention is that firms must expense an estimate of bad debts for sales made in one year, while the actual losses will not be known until the following year. And, as was the case with depreciation, each firm's experience with uncollectible accounts will differ as a function of its industry, target customers, and even its terms of sale. The upshot is that each firm is required to use a rational, consistent approach in arriving at such estimates from year to year; but there is no absolute standard with which they must comply. Clearly, the reader of the prospectus must be cautious when making comparisons across firms or of a single firm's performance over time.

In sum, there are noteworthy pitfalls in the path of the financial analyst. But, as we'll see next, the insights that can be gleaned from ratio analysis and other financial statement analysis techniques often enable the reader to make better-informed decisions than would otherwise be possible.

Chapter 2 | Understanding and Analyzing Financial Statements

COMMON SIZE AND RATIO ANALYSIS

What's so special about ratios, and why are they instrumental for evaluating whether a new company's forthcoming shares should be purchased? Suppose a fictitious company called Newco achieved revenue of $15 million in its initial year. Assume further that, and we believe that, it will grow its sales to $20 million this year and the funds derived from the offering will finance new products and expansion sufficient to achieve revenue of $50 million within five years. How could we go wrong with an investment in Newco?

Ratio analysis will inject a healthy dose of reason into our appraisal of investment opportunities such as this one. We will use ratios to determine the likelihood that a company will be able to meet its short-term need for cash (that is, liquidity) and long-term obligations (that is, solvency), which could be critical impediments to the success that might otherwise be attained. Additional ratios will help us assess the efficiency and effectiveness with which a company is deploying its existing assets, which are often predictive of its future returns on investment and stock movement. Ultimately, the set of ratios that we compute and analyze will enable us to decide if the valuation of a company's securities, relative to both its industry peers and the market overall, renders it an attractive investment at this time.

In making comparisons of a company to peer companies, many differences will be found due to differences in size and, in some cases, currency. By creating ratios, size and currencies are removed as factors permitting comparisons between companies or over time. The simplest form of ratio analysis is common size financial information. Rather then comparing expenses such as general and administrative expenses in dollar terms over time, all expenses on the income statement can be converted to a percentage of sales for that year. Exhibit 2.4 shows Google's general and administrative expenses as a percent of sales (common size data) for 2001 to 2003. This demonstrates that as the company has grown, many of these fixed administrative costs have been spread out over a higher volume of sales, improving the ultimate profitability.

Common size data can also be created for the balance sheet by dividing all balance sheet accounts by total assets for the same year.

Understanding and Evaluating Prospectuses, Offering Documents, and Proxy Statements

Exhibit 2.4: Google Inc. General and Administrative Expenses

Year	Percentage of Sales
2001	14.20%
2002	6.99%
2003	5.89%

Source: Computed from Google Inc. prospectus, dated August 18, 2004.

In addition to creating ratios using data from a single income statement, such as common size data, ratios can be created by using information from several financial statements. In view of the limitless number of ratios that could be computed from financial statement information, the challenge faced by the prospective investor is to identify the measures that will be most relevant to the decision at hand. This section presents some of the more popular and useful ratios.

Liquidity Ratios. One of the obstacles that can prevent a promising company from reaching its potential is a shortage of liquidity. In this context, liquidity refers to a company's ability to meet its short-term cash obligations. Growing companies, which are the type in which we generally seek to invest, need funds to promote new products, open additional channels of distribution, recruit more staff, and so on. Along with these cash requirements are the ongoing needs to service existing debt (if any); conduct research and development activities; cover selling, general, and administrative (that is, S, G, & A) expenses; and meet any unexpected expenses that arise in the normal course of business (for example, legal settlements). If a firm is unable to pay for these items as they come due, then it will either need to raise more capital (potentially impacting its stakeholders) or fail. Accordingly, analysts have developed a set of ratios that can be computed from the information in a prospectus to assess whether the firm in question is secure in terms of liquidity.

We will explain three widely used measures of a firm's liquidity and illustrate their application to the information contained in the financial statements associated with Google's 2004 prospectus.

Current Ratio. This ratio is defined as the sum of a company's total current assets relative to (that is, divided by) the sum of its current liabilities. Current assets are typically comprised of cash, short-term investments, receivables, inventory, and other current assets. Each item on this list qualifies as a current asset by virtue of the fact that it either is cash or is readily converted to cash within the current year or a company's operating cycle (whichever is longer). Therefore, these amounts are available to meet the company's current liabilities, which are claims on the company over the corresponding time horizon.

Of its $232 million in current assets in 2002, Google reports about $58 million in cash. Short-term investments are about $89 million. Google does not list any inventory. Since inventory refers to goods held for sale or work-in-progress, the absence of inventory for this service provider is not surprising. Accounts receivable are about $62 million. Other current assets of about $23 million are listed.

Total current liabilities of about $90 million are composed of accounts payable, accrued expenses, deferred revenue, taxes payable, and short-term debt related to leases. The current ratio (current assets/current liabilities) results in a figure of 2.59 as of December 31, 2002. The fact that it well exceeds one is positive. This indicates that Google has sufficient current assets to meet those short-term obligations that are shown on the balance sheet. The analyst might also note, however, that this figure is slightly lower as of December 31, 2003, at a level of 2.38. The ratio still indicates that Google has sufficient current assets to meet current liabilities.

At this early stage in our presentation of ratios, a discussion of the purpose of using a ratio, rather than a difference, as an analytic tool is warranted. Suppose, instead, that we had computed the difference between total current assets and total current liabilities to ascertain if it is above zero. By definition, the aforementioned difference is known as working capital. Wouldn't this provide the identical information and conclusion? The answer is sometimes.

Briefly consider the following hypothetical numeric example:

	XYZ Corporation	
	2005	2004
Current Assets	1000	150
Current Liabilities	950	100

Note that this company's working capital (that is, difference between current assets and current liabilities) is unchanged in 2005 from the prior year at +50 (that is, 1000 − 950). However, its current ratio has declined from 1.5 to 1.05 along with our confidence that its level of liquidity is more than adequate.

Returning now to Google, if we sought to compare its liquidity to that of a much smaller (or larger) competitor, our preference for the ratio-based approach should now be evident. The current ratio might well detect a difference in the margin of safety that absolute working capital would overlook.

Quick Ratio. In some cases, the analyst is interested in taking a more stringent view of a company's ability to meet is short-term obligations. The quick ratio, also known as the acid test ratio, provides such a view and is defined as follows:

$$\frac{\text{Current Assets} - \text{Inventory} - \text{Prepaid Expenses} - \text{Other Current Assets}}{\text{Total Current Liabilities}}$$

The rationale for deducting inventory from the numerator is that this asset cannot be used to meet cash needs until it is sold and the revenue is collected, which may require a period of months. Prepaid expenses cannot truly be applied toward cash expenses at all; rather, as noted above, they represent future costs that will not require any cash outlay. Other current assets are also removed unless detailed (that is, footnote) information about their liquidity is presented and compelling. These reduced short-term assets, known as quick assets, are then compared to the company's total current liabilities. This amount typically includes cash, accounts receivable, and short-term investments. If the ratio exceeds one, then it appears that the subject company is readily able to meet its short-term need for cash. In the case of Google, we find that the quick ratio is 2.33 for 2002 and 2.08 for 2003. These figures are not much lower than those for Google's current ratio because neither inventory nor "other" current assets represented a major portion of its current assets. In many other cases, however, the quick ratio will depart significantly from the current ratio.

Defensive Interval Ratio (D.I.R.). A third, more comprehensive way to gauge a firm's liquidity makes use of the defensive interval ratio. This ratio is more encompassing than either of the preceding two ratios in that it includes expenses that are expected to be incurred in the immediate future. It can be defined as follows:

$$\frac{\text{Cash + Short-term Investments + Accounts Receivable}}{(\text{Operating expenses including costs of revenues})/365}$$

Note that the numerator of this ratio captures the same "quick" assets that we just discussed. For 2003, this amounts to about $489 million for Google. The denominator now captures the set of ongoing costs of ordinary operations that the company will incur; specifically, this formula measures the average daily costs of normal operations in the current period. In the case of Google, this is about $1.068 million per day for 2003. The resulting ratio reveals the number of days of costs that can be met with quick assets on hand. In Google's case, the result is about 458 days for 2003. Because companies that manufacture or distribute physical goods require working capital for inventory, this measure takes on greater importance for such firms.[7]

Solvency Ratios. The preceding set of ratios helps us to assess whether a company's liquidity is likely to be adequate to meet its existing short-term obligations without difficulty. Clearly, that is just one prerequisite for making an investment in the issuer. A second hurdle that merits examination concerns the company's ability to meet its long-term obligations. These obligations may appear on the face of the balance sheet (for example, bonds payable) or exist only "off balance sheet" (for example, long-term lease payments).[8]

Two basic categories of solvency ratios that we'll discuss focus on the company's capital structure and "coverage" of its fixed obligations. There are numerous ways that measures within each of these two categories of ratios could be formulated. For each category, we'll define and illustrate specific ratios that are revealing and therefore widely used in practice.

Capital Structure Ratios. What is a firm's capital structure, and how might it affect our willingness to invest in a firm's securities? Capital structure refers to the breakdown of the firm's financing of its assets. As depicted by the fundamental accounting equation that can be derived from the balance sheet, Assets = Liabilities + Owner's Equity, companies must finance their assets either through the equity of owners of the firm or issuance of debt to nonowners (that is, creditors). In the simplest case, the firm's shareholders contribute all of the capital necessary to fund the firm. In addition to the simplicity of this capital structure, it is also less "stressful" on the firm and reduces the volatility of its earnings and cash flow. When a business does well, the firm can reward its shareholders with dividends and share repurchases. In a year when the business fails to earn a profit or its liquidity is under stress, the firm is under no obligation to make payouts to shareholders or incur any annual cash outflows for financing expense.

In contrast, consider the situation where a firm has issued long-term debt to obtain capital. Irrespective of whether a corporation's operations are profitable, bond holders are legally entitled to receive periodic (usually semiannual) interest on the funds they have loaned to the firm. As noted above, the inevitable consequences of including long-term debt in its capital structure are reduced flexibility and heightened volatility of its earnings.

Under these circumstances, one might legitimately wonder why a firm's owners would willingly elect to complicate the situation and add stress to their own business's existence by issuing long-term debt? From an investor's perspective, debt is less risky than equity. As just noted, investors in debt such as bonds have a contractual right to receive interest payments. Equity investors have no such right. As a result, investors in equity securities demand a higher rate of return. It is therefore often cheaper for a company to borrow money rather than raise equity capital. Further, interest is generally tax-deductible while dividends are not.

Firms that have made moderate (or no) use of debt in the past retain greater flexibility to raise funds to capitalize on both unexpected opportunities that arise and meet unanticipated obligations. One ratio that is designed to measure the proportion of a firm's assets financed through debt is called the debt ratio, which is defined as:

Debt Ratio = Total Liabilities/Total Assets

For Google, the debt ratio as of December 31, 2003, was 0.3244 or 32.44 percent (282,688/871,458). This is down from the prior year level of 39.37 percent, indicating a higher level of solvency. In general, this ratio will be less than 1.0. Only in the "special" case where a company has achieved negative equity can the ratio exceed one. Companies that have cumulative net losses since inception may reflect negative equity on their balance sheet.

The debt ratio presented above includes all of the firm's liabilities in the numerator, not all of which are interest bearing (for example, accounts payable). As a result, the debt ratio is sometimes modified to exclude non-interest bearing liabilities from the numerator. The ratio can also be expressed by replacing total assets in the denominator with total stockholders' equity, referred to as the debt-to-equity ratio. The most important factor is the ratio is computed consistently between companies or over time.

Coverage Ratios. The debt ratio provides an excellent start toward assessing a company's solvency. Yet, the investor might still be unaware of important aspects of the strength of the firm's finances. Recall from our discussion of liquidity ratios (for example, quick ratio) that the measure informed us about the "slack" of the firm in regard to quick assets versus its short-term obligations. In the context of a firm's long-term contractual obligations, we are seeking an analogous gauge.

Among the ratios that are designed for this purpose is the interest coverage ratio (also known as times interest earned), which is defined as follows:

$$\frac{\text{Earnings before Interest and Tax Expenses}}{\text{Interest Expense}}$$

For Google, data from its footnotes for 2003 indicates that interest expense was $1.931 million. Earnings before interest and tax expense was $348.585 million, indicating that the interest coverage ratio was 180.5. Since this number is well in excess of one, it indicates that Google would not be expected to have any difficulty meeting their interest payments.

Numerous modifications of the preceding coverage ratio have been devised for specific purposes. For example, in industries as divergent as retailing and air travel, long-term leases may constitute as onerous a long-term obligation as interest expense. In such cases, the following coverage ratio (fixed-charge coverage) can lend greater insight into a firm's solvency:

$$\frac{\text{EBIT + Rent Expense}}{\text{Interest Expense + Rent Expense}}$$

Together with analysis of a firm's capital structure, coverage ratios provide a great deal of information about a firm's ability to meet its long-term obligations as well as its capacity to obtain additional financing.

Activity Ratios. The preceding two sets of ratios, which examined liquidity and solvency, focused on the capacity of the firm to survive. Of equal or greater interest to prospective investors is whether the subject company is likely to thrive and generate high returns. Activity ratios examine the efficiency with which a firm is managing both its working capital and its overall asset base. For marketers of physical goods, whether the firm is a manufacturer or a retailer, the efficiency of inventory management is an important determinant of profitability. If a company does not manage to deliver a sufficient quantity of the right goods to the right place at the right time, then customers encounter stockouts. The firm then incurs the opportunity cost of lost sales as well as the loss of customer goodwill from its unreliable inventory management. If excessive inventory is carried by a firm to ensure a good level of customer service, then high inventory carrying costs (that is, spoilage, warehousing, insurance, capital) will hinder profitability. Two related measures of the efficiency with which a firm is managing this aspect of its operations follow.

Inventory Turnover Ratio = Cost of Goods Sold/Average Inventory

The denominator is typically computed by summing the firm's inventory at the beginning and end of year and dividing by two. The numerator measures the cost to purchase all of the goods that were sold. The resulting quotient provides an estimate of the number of times that inventory was acquired and subsequently sold during the year. Again, the absolute number is less revealing than the trend in a company's performance or a comparison to its direct competition. Clearly, we would expect an operator of grocery stores (for example, Safeway) to manifest a higher level of inventory turnover than an operator of jewelry stores (for example, Zales); so, the fact that the two companies have inventory turnover ratios of over eight in one case and less than one in the other does not indicate that one is superior to the other in terms of inventory management. Rather, it merely confirms that these industries and the firms therein have differing business models.

A closely related measure of a company's efficiency in this area of its operations is called days inventory, which is defined as follows:

$$\textbf{Days Inventory} = 365/\text{Inventory Turnover}$$

As your intuition should suggest, this captures the average number of days of inventory that a company typically has on hand. A lower number over time is indicative of a favorable trend, provided that it is not accomplished at the detriment of increased revenues.

Similar ratios can be computed to assess the ability of the company to collect amounts due from customers in a reasonable period of time.

$$\textbf{Accounts Receivable Turnover Ratio} = \text{Sales/Average Accounts Receivable}$$

$$\textbf{Days Receivable} = 365/\text{Accounts Receivable Turnover}$$

Comparing days receivable over time can indicate whether a company is having problems with collections from customers or is collecting more quickly.

A broader indicator of the efficiency of a company's asset utilization is provided by the following ratio:

$$\textbf{Total Asset Turnover} = \text{Sales/ Average Total Assets}$$

For Google, this ratio is 1.66, indicating that they generate $1.66 in revenue for every dollar of assets. The higher the number, the more efficient a company is at generating revenues.

Profitability Ratios. The astute reader may have noted an important "limitation" of each of the activity ratios that we have examined thus far. While they may help us to diagnose the efficiency with which a company is using its working capital and noncurrent assets, these ratios are mute on the question of the company's profitability. In fact, the apparent limitation is by design. It avoids confounding a company's level of turnover (that is, sales) with the profitability of those sales. This decoupling enables an elegant and useful decomposition of a firm's return on investment, which will be explained in the next section. Among the most memorable lessons of the dot-com era is that valuations based on sales alone are suspect; ultimately, shareholders are interested in profit and cash flow. In the absence of an expected stream of profit, share prices decline.

Analysts and investors can use a set of ratios to assess the profitability and rate of return generated by a firm. The most straightforward, summary measure of a company's net profit margin, also known as return on sales, is defined as follows:

$$\textbf{Net Profit Margin} = \text{Net Income/Sales}$$

For Google, the net profit margin is 0.1098 or 10.98 percent for 2003, indicating that the company generates $10.98 of profits for every $100 in revenues. Note that for the same period, Yahoo!, a competitor, had a net profit margin of 14.64 percent, indicating that Google is a bit less profitable.

Note that this measure gauges return on sales after taxes and/or any non-operating gains (or losses). Similar ratios can be computed on operating income and/or before taxes as we'll see shortly in our decomposition of a firm's rate of return. Those ratios can help pinpoint areas where performance is changing, substandard, or otherwise in need of further scrutiny by the analyst.

Two further methods of measuring a firm's profitability make the distinction between return on total assets and return on equity, respectively. From the standpoint of the debt holder, who has a prior claim to the assets

Chapter 2 | Understanding and Analyzing Financial Statements

and cash flows, it is the return on total capital that is of concern. Return on assets (ROA) is defined as:

Net Income/Average Total Assets

For Google, return on assets was 18.24 percent, based on 2003 data.

In some situations, investors may wish to focus on return on assets before interest and taxes. This is computed as earnings before interest and taxes relative to average total assets or EBIT/Average Total Assets.

Of particular interest to shareholders is the rate of return generated on the firm's internal (that is, equity) capital. Return on equity (ROE) is computed as follows:

ROE = Net Income/Average Total Equity.

For Google, return on equity was 27.70 percent based on 2003 data. This is quite good, indicating that the company generated $27.70 in profits for every $100 invested in the company by the shareholders.

An investor in common stock may prefer to measure the return on only the portion of net income that is available to common stockholders. Since preferred stockholders receive their dividends, if any, prior to common stockholders, then return on common equity (ROCE) can be computed as:

(Net Income − Preferred Dividends)/Average Equity)

As you would expect, a higher ROE is better. Moreover, a firm's ability to grow and generate good returns for shareholders is directly related to its ROE. Does a high (for example, 20 percent) ROE ensure a high return to the investor that holds such a stock for the long term? Unfortunately, there are at least two good reasons why that is not the case. First, the firm's ROE may decline. In fact, industries in which participants are able to earn high returns usually attract more competitors. As a result, the supranormal returns are difficult to sustain. Second, as we will discuss again in the final section on valuation, it is rare in the modern era that an investor can purchase a stock at "book value" (that is, Price per share = Total stockholder's equity per share). In recent years, the S&P 500 has generally traded in excess of 500 percent of book value. Therefore, even if the firm in question continues to earn a high ROE (for example, 20 percent), the investor who paid five times book value is not necessarily earning a return of 20 percent per year on the amount that he or she paid per share. If the price-to-book value that the market accords to the stock declines during the investor's holding period, then the investor will not earn the same return at which the firm's equity is increasing.

Decomposing a Firm's Return on Equity. To briefly recap our progress to this point, we began by examining potential impediments to a company's success. Ratio analysis was used to assess the adequacy of a firm's liquidity in the short term and its solvency over the long term. We then focused on the efficiency with which a firm was managing its working capital and its overall asset base. Lastly, we analyzed whether the firm was achieving the observed level of activity in a profitable fashion. Measures such as net profit margin revealed whether the firm's business model was capable of delivering positive returns on investment.

An additional type of analysis that can provide useful input to the investment decision process entails a decomposition of the firm's return on equity into a set of three to five components. This holistic look at the firm can help the analyst to decide whether the competitive strengths that management has articulated are likely to be brought to fruition as additional capital becomes available for deployment and the proceeds are used in the purported fashion.

This framework for analyzing ROE enables us to examine the interrelatedness of the firm's capital structure, efficiency, and profitability. Specifically, this analysis highlights the fact that these components interact (that is, combine in a multiplicative, rather than additive way) to determine a firm's ROE. One implication of this realization is that poor management of one aspect of an enterprise is often enough to prevent a firm from achieving the level of performance that investors are seeking.

Let us first examine the relationship between ROA and ROE. Consider two firms that are identical in all respects except for their capital structure. Both firms obtained $10 million in capital at the start of the year to purchase long-term assets. Firm U has no long-term debt. Firm L's capital structure includes $5 million in long-term debt along with $5 million in stockholder equity. Both firms have just completed their first year in existence and were pleased to report earnings before interest and taxes of $2 million. Firm L's bonds outstanding were issued at face value at a coupon rate of interest of 7 percent. Therefore, it incurred interest expense of $350,000. Both firms were taxed at a rate of 40 percent. Neither firm paid any dividends this year. Abbreviated income statements for the respective firms appear below.

	Company U	Company L (leveraged)
Revenue	20,000,000	20,000,000
Operating Expenses	18,000,000	18,000,000
EBIT	2,000,000	2,000,000
Interest Expense	--------	350,000
Income before Tax	2,000,000	1,650,000
Net Income	1,200,000	990,000

Measures of Return:
Return on Assets (ROA)
 For Company U: Net Income divided by Average Assets for the year = 1,200,000/((10,000,000 + 11,200,000)/2) = .113 or 11.3 percent

 For Company L: Net Income divided by Average Assets for the year = 990,000/[(10,000,000 + 10,990,000)/2] = .094 or 9.40 percent

Return on Equity (ROE):
For Company U, Net Income divided by Average Equity for the year = 1,200,000/[(10,000,000 + 11,200,000)/2] = .113 or 11.3 percent

For Company L, Net Income divided by Average Assets for the year = 990,000/[(5,000,000 + 5,990,000)/2] =.180 or 18.0 percent

Three observations merit emphasis. First, Company L (L is for leverage) has a lower net income than Company U (U is for unleveraged) because it incurs interest expense. Since ROA measures net income relative to the firm's assets during the year (that is, average assets), ROA is also lower for Company L. Finally, our primary point here is that ROE is markedly higher for Company L than for Company U (18.0 percent vs. 11.3 percent) despite its lower net income. Since the amount of equity outstanding is much lower for the leveraged firm, the rate of return on the *owners'* equity is much higher in this case. This explains, in large part, why owners are willing to tolerate the earnings volatility and related stress associated with use of long-term debt in the capital structure.

This financial leverage is beneficial if the company can borrow at a lower rate than it expects to earn by investing the proceeds in their business. While ROA may be lower, ROE can be higher. The relationship between ROE and ROA can be expressed algebraically as:

ROA = Net Income/Average Total Assets
ROE = Net Income/Average Total Equity
Leverage = Average Total Assets/Average Total Equity

ROE = ROA x Leverage

Further insight can be gleaned by breaking ROA into two components:

ROA = Net Profit Margin (or Profitability) x Asset Turnover (hereafter called Efficiency)
Recall that Profitability = Net Income/Sales, while Efficiency = Sales/Average Total Assets

Viewed in this light, a firm can increase its ROA either by increasing the efficiency of its asset utilization or increasing profitability. The breakdown of ROA also highlights that the decision to use leverage to enhance ROE can be seen as a separate financing issue for the firm.

Applying the foregoing formulae to data for 2003 for Google, we find:

ROA = (Net Income/Sales) x (Sales/Avg. Assets)
ROA = (16801/487190) x [487190/(837119/2)]
ROA = 10.98 percent x 1.66 = 18.24 percent

To increase ROA, a firm might improve the net profit margin by using expense control. Alternatively, increasing efficiency might be accomplished.

How has leverage affected Google's ROE? Recall that leverage substitutes debt for equity financing and thereby reduces the denominator of this ratio. But, at the same time, leverage decreases net income because additional interest expense is incurred. As long as the pre-tax return on the assets in which a firm has invested exceeds the pre-tax cost of interest on the debt, then leverage will elevate ROE above what would otherwise have been achieved.

Proceeding with our decomposition of ROE, we can separate ROE into three components:

ROE = Profitability x Efficiency x Leverage
ROE = (Net Income/Sales) x (Sales/Avg. Assets) x (Avg. Assets/Avg. Equity)
ROE = 10.98 percent x 1.66 x 1.52 = 27.70 percent

An even more detailed breakdown of ROE recognizes that taxes have a profound impact on ROE and that management's actions can influence the firm's effective tax rate. For example, tax credits are available periodically for investments of specific types (for example, energy-saving devices or pollution-control equipment). Additionally, as international operations play an increasing role for many firms, the location of manufacturing plants and intracompany transfers of goods and services from one tax jurisdiction to another can lower (or raise) tax obligations. Likewise, decisions to acquire other firms with tax-loss carryforwards affect a firm's tax situation.

Along with taxes, one might also seek to isolate the effect of financing from a firm's operations on its profitability. To do so, one can decompose profitability as follows:

Profitability = (NI/EBT) x (EBT/EBIT) x (EBIT/Sales) = Net Income/Sales

Or:

Net Income/Sales = (Net Income/Earnings before Taxes) x (Earnings before Taxes/Earnings before Interest and Taxes) x (Earnings before Interest and Taxes/Sales)

The firm's net profit margin has now been disaggregated into three separate components. This more refined model shows how operating profit is attenuated by tax and interest costs.

This expanded look at profitability can then be incorporated into a five-component decomposition of ROE by restoring efficiency and leverage back into the full model. Among the practical applications of this model is the examination of the *trend* in the company's performance in each of these areas over time. Depending upon the perceived relevance of the historical information, which is a function of the pace of change in the industry and structure of the company, the analyst might look at trends for up to five years. Exhibit 2.5 shows a breakdown of Google's ROE for 2003.

Note that the tax burden indicates the amount of profits the company gets to keep after taxes (1 − the tax rate). Google therefore had a very high effective tax rate for 2003, which detracted from their profitability. The high tax rate was related to the use of stock-based compensation. In spite of the high effective tax rate, Google generated a high ROE, largely due to the high operating profit margin, their efficiency, and the use of leverage.

Exhibit 2.5: Breakdown of Google's Return on Equity (ROE)

	2003
ROE	27.70%
Tax Burden (NI/EBT)	.30476
Financing Burden (EBT/EBIT)	.99446
Operating Profit (EBIT/Sales)	36.24%
Turnover (Sales/Average Assets)	1.66
Leverage (Average Assets/Average Equity)	1.52

Source: Computed from Google Inc. prospectus, dated August 18, 2004.

Chapter 2 | Understanding and Analyzing Financial Statements

VALUATION

In the preceding sections, we have applied ratio analysis to assess a firm's operations and decompose its firm's return on equity. We now consider ratios that describe the market's valuation of a firm. When our objective is to determine whether a given security is underpriced, and therefore attractive, we can compare the security's valuation to that of its competitors or the overall market. To do so, all of the information gleaned from our prior analyses can now be brought to bear. For example, if a firm was trading at a discount to its peers and we believed that its future performance was going to be superior, then this would provide an indication that its security was priced attractively. The market-multiple approach to valuation, which we introduce here, provides a perspective and a set of specific metrics for gauging how a firm's offering is priced relative to the securities of its competitors and/or the overall market. A discussion of four ratios that are widely used to assess the relative valuation of a security follows.

Price-to-Earnings Ratio (P/E). Probably the most widely cited measure of a company's valuation in the marketplace is its price-to-earnings ratio. The P/E ratio is defined as price per share divided by earnings per share. From this definition, which is simply a company's price per share divided by its earnings per share, it is apparent that this "multiple" is merely another name for a ratio. It indicates how much the investor must pay for each dollar per share that a company is earning. Holding earnings and all other characteristics (for example, growth, risk) constant, we would prefer to buy a security that has a lower P/E ratio (that is, lower valuation).

A second perspective on the meaning of a P/E ratio can be gleaned by considering what a rational investor would pay for a security where earnings are expected to remain constant at the current level forever. If a company earned $1 per share and we were sure that it would continue to do so, this stream of income could then be defined as an annuity of $1 per year. Its present value to the investor would be equivalent to this annuity discounted by the required rate of return on this security: its value would be given simply by $1/r$ where r is the required rate of return. So, for example, if $r=10$ percent, then the value of the stream of income would equal $1/.1 = \$10$ per share. If the market price of this security were greater than $10 per share, this would imply that the market expected the earnings of this firm would grow over time, rather than remain constant at $1 per share.

Interestingly, the reader will encounter two variations of the P/E ratio with almost equal frequency, so we'll note and illustrate them both. The most objective computation of the P/E ratio, which was reflected in the preceding paragraph, uses a firm's prior 12-month earnings in the denominator. This is referred to as a trailing P/E. A variation of this same ratio that analysts often apply is based upon the expected earnings for the next four quarters. This is known as a leading P/E. Clearly, this approach injects a great deal of subjectivity into the valuation since analysts' earnings estimates have been found to be imprecise. If the purpose, however, is to predict what the price of a security will be in 12–18 months, then it is reasonable to incorporate expected earnings in the valuation.

Price-to-Sales Ratio (P/S). Another market-multiple approach to valuation that has become more popular in recent years examines the price of a company's stock relative to its revenues. The P/S ratio is defined as: Price per Share/Sales (or Revenue) per Share. The fundamental logic underlying use of this ratio to evaluate the attractiveness of a security is similar to that for the P/E ratio. It assumes that the firm or industry will ultimately trade at some "normal" level of price-to-sales. If a firm is currently trading below that level on this metric, then its security may be attractive.

One reason why a firm may trade at a below-average price-to-sales ratio and thereby attract investors stems from the very fact that its profitability is low. The attractiveness of such a stock hinges on the following rationale. It would not be unreasonable for a prospective investor to expect one of two favorable events to occur. Ideally, the firm's management would improve its operations and net profit margin, in which case the market would likely accord the normal price-to-sales valuation to the firm and its security would appreciate. Alternatively, if the firm's management lacked the expertise to achieve greater profitability, another firm might see the potential to buy these operations (and sales) cheaply and improve its margins, thereby unlocking the latent value. Again, the investor who purchased the share when they were trading at a "discount" to the industry's price-to-sales ratio would benefit.

Why did this valuation approach become much more popular toward the end of the last millenium? First, it had worked reasonably well over the long term. Moreover, the previous discussion highlighted the logic of this valuation tool and some scenarios that could unfold favorably for the investor. Unfortunately, investors who applied this tool indiscriminately over the past five years learned (the hard way) a conceptual limitation of the tool and its promoters. Because investment firms were motivated (that is, underwriting fees) to recommend purchase of their offerings, they needed to find a justification for high stock valuations and "buy" ratings of companies that had no income or near-term likelihood of significant earnings per share. Some Internet firms had cumulative losses and negative cash flow from their inception. Clearly, the (negative) P/E ratios on such firms could not serve the basis for favorable recommendations. On the other hand, analysts could allude to the high price-to-sales ratios at which competing e-commerce firms were trading to suggest the appreciation potential of the securities to be offered.

Beyond reminding the investor about the need to retain a healthy skepticism when consuming others' research, this discussion highlights a limitation of the price-to-sales ratio along with all of the market multiple methods of valuation. Note that they are all relative, rather than absolute, measures of value. At any given point in time, it is possible that all of the companies in an industry or even the overall market are overvalued or undervalued. Therefore, this approach should be used carefully.

Price-to-Book Ratio (P/B). This ratio is defined as Price per Share/Book Value per Share. Book value is defined as net assets or total assets minus total liabilities. The denominator of this ratio is then computed as net assets divided by shares outstanding. This ratio was used successfully for decades by value-oriented investors and was popularized by Graham and Dodd in their classic, *Security Analysis* (1940). If an investor could find companies that were priced by the market at less than their net assets, it was clear that the market was not according much, if any, value to the cash flow that the company might generate from its operations. If the performance of the firm then exceeded these low expectations, then the market value of the firm could rise substantially. If the firm was unable to deliver much in the way of operating performance, then investors who purchased shares below book value had a "margin of safety" on their investment. Additionally, it was possible that the carrying value of the assets (for example, land) on the company's books was an understatement of their true market value in the event of liquidation. This increased the likelihood further that the investor would ultimately recoup most of the price paid per share even if the company's performance remained lackluster.

In fact, research supports this theory and indicates that investing in a diversified basket of such firms produced good results when measured in terms of risk-adjusted performance. Regrettably, in the current age of free-flowing digital information, mispriced securities of this nature are much more difficult to find than in decades past. As noted above, the S&P 500 Index trades at over 500 percent of book value. Some thinly traded securities (for example, smaller firms or those with high family ownership and resulting low float) can still be found trading at a discount to net asset value. Note that when the price-to-book ratio for a firm is found to be lower than for its peers or the overall market, this information might still indicate that the market's expectations for the firm are relatively low. If a prospective investor believes that the fundamental outlook for the firm is good, then the stock might be an attractive candidate for further research and/or investment. Additionally, if the investor believes that the assets are undervalued on the firm's books and the price-to-book ratio is not far above unity, then the downside risk associated with this security might be assessed as relatively low.

Price-to-Cash Flow Ratio (P/CF). This ratio is defined as Price per Share/"Cash Flow" per Share. This measure of valuation is analogous in structure to each of the three preceding price-multiples and closest in content to the P/E ratio. Because of the need to apply accounting conventions and make numerous estimates that affect a company's reported income, it is often useful to assess a company's valuation in terms of cash flow. While it might first seem that the same accounting decisions that affect a company's income would also influence its reported cash flow (rendering the P/CF ratio redundant), we will soon see that is not necessarily the case. Therefore, the primary purpose of this discussion is to explain several important differences between a company's cash flow and its earnings. In addition to describing the computation of cash flow and highlighting its importance to prospective investors, we hope to motivate and encourage the reader to continue exploring the ever-changing domain of financial statement analysis after completing this book.

The first step toward understanding the distinction between cash flow and earnings is necessarily to define three measures of cash flow that the investor will encounter. In some contexts and publications (for example, Value Line Investment Survey), the term cash flow is computed as net income plus depreciation expense. Because depreciation involves the allocation of the cost of past expenditures that are expected to benefit a company for more than one period, the annual expense for depreciation does not represent any current cash outflow. The actual cash outflow occurred at the time that the investment in a long-term asset, such as a physical plant or equipment, was made. Therefore, one seemingly reasonable way to arrive at a company's annual cash flow is simply to add back the reported depreciation expense.

Among the most common measures of valuation that the investor will encounter in the media is the following ratio: Enterprise Value/EBITDA. EBITDA is earnings before interest, tax, depreciation, and amortization expense. A company's enterprise value is defined as the market value of its stock plus its outstanding debt. The market value (or market capitalization) of a stock equals: number of shares outstanding times the market price.

The denominator of this cash-flow-oriented ratio is EBITDA. The logic of adding back interest, taxes, depreciation, and amortization is that the cash flow available to a third party who would acquire the target firm would be its net income, plus its noncash expenses, plus interest on its debt, which would no longer be incurred after the acquirer purchased the target firm's outstanding securities (both debt and equity) in the open market. For firms that have made a number of acquisitions and/or have significant amounts of other intangible assets on their balance sheets that require amortization, the annual expense for amortization can be large. Note that, parallel to depreciation expense, this reduces reported income without any corresponding effect on the company's actual cash flow. EBITDA is designed, in principle, to provide an alternative measure of cash flow for prospective investors that reported earnings.

Understanding and Evaluating Prospectuses, Offering Documents, and Proxy Statements

Another measure of the cash being generated by a firm is called operating cash flow from the cash flow statement. In contrast to net income-based measures of cash flow, such as the first one that was considered in this section, this metric recognizes that there are transactions that affect a firm's net income that do not alter its cash flow. Additionally, there are transactions and events that affect cash flow that are not reflected in net income. Finally, there are transactions that affect a firm's cash flow in a given year that are not expected to recur regularly and therefore not especially relevant to predicting a firm's future (operating) cash flows. While a more arduous set of computations is required to reconcile a firm's net income to its operating cash flow, fortunately, this reconciliation is required of publicly traded firms along with its financial statements. Our immediate focus can therefore be to provide a better understanding of each of the aforementioned types of discrepancy between income and cash flow. You will then be more able to decide whether a cash flow-based multiple should be used for evaluating the attractiveness of an offering or a simpler earnings-based multiple will suffice.

There are a number of types of items beyond depreciation and amortization expenses that impact a company's net income without affecting cash flow. Suppose that Company X had a patent listed on its balance sheet at a value of $2 million. Suppose further that Competitor Y developed a new technology that obsolesced the value of the patent entirely so that its value at year-end was nil. Company X would write-down the value of this long-term asset on its balance sheet and record an expense of $2 million on its income statement. Note that this write-down did not entail any outflow of cash. In this case, Company X's income would understate its operating cash flow by $2 million.

Consider next that factors such as the company's terms of sale (for example, "buy now, no payment required until 2006") affect the company's earnings but result in no current cash flow. How is this possible? In our discussion of accounting conventions, we noted the important accrual basis of accounting by which sales and the related gross profit were recorded at the time of sale rather than when the receivable was collected. Similarly, a company could be expanding its inventory in a reckless fashion without recording a corresponding direct expense (since the direct cost of the inventory will not be expensed until the goods are sold). Consequently, a company can report a healthy net income and return on assets while consuming, rather than generating, impressive amounts of cash.

Finally, there are transactions that affect a firm's cash flow in a given year that are not expected to recur regularly and therefore not especially relevant to predicting a firm's future (operating) cash flows. Suppose, for example, that an operator of cinemas decides to sell off one of its theaters in a city where it no longer expects to achieve its desired return on this investment. Even if this facility is sold for an amount that is less than or equal to its book (or carrying value), the transaction will generate cash flow but not income. Once again, the informed user of financial statements is fortunate in that the required cash flow statement of a firm must be subdivided into three sections: Operating Cash Flow, Investing Cash Flow, and Financing Cash Flow. Sales (and purchases) of long-term assets, such as the theater in the preceding example, would be listed in the computation of investing cash flow, rather than operating cash flow. This helps to maintain the "purity" of operating cash flow, which is more likely to account for, and be predictive of, a firm's recurring ability to generate (or consume) cash.

CONCLUSION

For companies that have been operating for some time, it is important to examine their past performance and current financial position to assist in evaluating the potential risks and rewards of making an investment in the company. For new ventures, forecast or pro forma financial data should be examined. The investor or adviser should examine these past or forecast financial statements and compare performance and financial position to other companies in the industry. Cash flow should be considered in addition to net income. Valuation ratios are particularly important to determine whether the offering is priced reasonably compared to other potential investments.

ENDNOTES

[1] Often, the prospectus financial information is abbreviated, but full financial statements may be included in associated filings.

Understanding and Evaluating Prospectuses, Offering Documents, and Proxy Statements

[2] Among the earliest documented users of this approach to decomposing corporate ROE were financial analysts at the DuPont Corporation. As a result, decomposition of ROE is often labeled DuPont analysis.

[3] This chapter adopts the perspective of an investor in equity securities. Subsequent chapters consider other types of securities' offerings and the issues associated with their valuation.

[4] Note that appreciation is not recorded and property and equipment other than land are depreciated even though they may increase in value or retain their value.

[5] At one time, goodwill was also amortized. Under current accounting standards goodwill is not amortized. It remains on the balance sheet unless the company determines at some later date that its value had been impaired. At that time, a loss or expense would be reported on the income statement.

[6] Companies are required to re-value some assets, such as investment securities and derivative securities.

[7] The reader may also have encountered another measure of liquidity that is examined for start-up ventures and many biotechnology firms—the "cash burn" rate. Like the defensive interval ratio, the intent of that measure is to help determine the length of time that a firm with minimal profit, or even revenue, can sustain normal operations with its current level of liquid assets.

[8] A firm may have substantial long-term obligations, such as leases, that do not appear on the face of the balance sheet. Only in the footnotes to the firm's financial statements, if at all, are these obligations disclosed.

DISCUSSION QUESTIONS:

1. What insight might an investor hope to glean by computing a liquidity ratio (for example, current ratio) for a firm that would not be readily apparent from the firm's level of working capital (that is, current assets − current liabilities)?
2. Under what circumstances might it be important for a prospective investor to examine a firm's defensive interval ratio?
3. What are the advantages and disadvantages of the historical cost convention of accounting that is reflected in companies' financial statements? For which industries would you expect the impact of this convention on companies' balance sheets to be most? Least?
4. What inferences can safely be drawn when an analyst report indicates that a firm "capitalized" $50 million of R&D expenditures in its most recent year? Would it be more conservative for a firm to capitalize or expense its development expenditures?
5. Explain how a firm can have a debt-to-asset ratio that exceeds 1.0.
6. At present, the P/E ratio of XYZ, Inc., is 25 while the P/E for the S&P 500 Index is 22. What does this suggest about the market's expectations for XYZ relative to the market?

Chapter 2 | Understanding and Analyzing Financial Statements

EXERCISE:

A decomposition of Dell, Inc.'s ROE is presented below for five recent years. Explain the main drivers of Dell's trend in ROE.

	2003	2002	2001	2000	1999
ROE	47.43%	44.36%	24.16%	39.84%	43.68%
Tax Burden (NI/EBT)	71.03%	70.10%	71.98%	68.16%	67.97%
Financing Burden (EBT/EBIT)	105.08%	106.43%	96.76%	119.94%	108.31%
Operating Profit (EBIT/Sales)	8.55%	8.03%	5.74%	8.35%	8.96%
Turnover (Sales/Average Assets)	2.38	2.44	2.31	2.56	2.75
Leverage (Average Assets/Average Equity)	3.12	3.03	2.61	2.28	2.41

RECOMMENDED READING

Analysis of Equity Investments: Valuation, John Stowe, Thomas Robinson, Jerald Pinto, and Dennis McLeavey, CFA Institute, 2002.

Security Analysis: The Classic 1940 Edition, Benjamin Graham and David Dodd, McGraw-Hill, 2002.

Additional information on ratios and common size analysis can be found at www.financial-education.com.

3 | The Prospectus: Equity IPOs

Public companies come into being through an initial public offering (IPO). An IPO is the first time shares are offered for sale to the public. The offering entity could be a private company that desires to raise additional capital, or it could be a new venture. IPOs could represent an equity interest in operating companies, mutual funds, or other investment companies. Since this is the first time the entity will be publicly traded and have outside investors, it is imperative that investors be aware of the potential risks and rewards of the venture before investing. Advisers can assist investors in identifying the risks and rewards through an evaluation of the prospectus. In this chapter, we will focus on key points to consider in evaluating the prospectuses of equity IPOs.

INITIAL PUBLIC OFFERING PROCESS

Why do companies go public? There are a variety of reasons:[1]

- Companies may desire to raise additional capital to expand operations, and sufficient debt or equity capital is not available at attractive costs from private sources.
- Founders, venture capitalists, and other investors in a private company may desire to "cash out" all or part of their equity investment, either at the time of the IPO or in the future.

Understanding and Evaluating Prospectuses, Offering Documents, and Proxy Statements

- The company may desire to make acquisitions using publicly traded securities for payment.
- The company may desire to establish an external measure value for the firm.
- The company may desire to have a liquid market for shares that can be issued to employees and others for services provided to the firm.

Once a company decides to go public, it enlists the assistance of an investment bank or several investment banks to serve as underwriters. In the case of multiple investment banks, one will serve as the lead underwriter. The underwriter will advise the company on the steps necessary to go public, price the offering, and market the offering to individual and institutional investors.

Before securities can be offered to the public, the company must file a registration statement with the relevant authorities. Most initial public offerings are registered with the Securities and Exchange Commission (SEC) with the filing of Form S-1, Registration Statement under the Securities Act of 1933. Form S-1 sets out the information that must be included in a registration statement in accordance with Regulation S-K. Part 1 of the registration statement is the prospectus. Part 2 contains additional information that is not required to be provided to prospective investors, but which is available by viewing the SEC filing. Regulation S-K specifies, in some cases, where in the prospectus the required information is presented. While Form S-1 is the most common form of the registration statement, other forms are used in the case of certain filers such as small businesses or foreign issuers. The contents of the prospectus will be similar for the various forms.

Once the registration statement is filed, the company may distribute the preliminary prospectus. The preliminary prospectus is also referred to as a "red herring," due to the cautionary language printed in red on the cover page and the fact that certain information is not known, such as the price and number of shares to be issued. During this period, the SEC reviews the filing for compliance with regulations. Note, however, that the SEC does not evaluate the investment merits of the offering. Registration becomes effective in 20 days unless the SEC requests changes or additional information from the company. The period up to the effective date is known as the waiting period, and no sales of securities can be made during this period.

The underwriter will assist the company with determining the price of the shares to be offered. This process may involve comparison of price multiples (such as the P/E ratio discussed in Chapter 2) of similar peer companies and other valuation methods, such as a discounted cash flow analysis. In a "firm commitment" underwriting, the underwriter purchases the entire issue from the company at a discounted price and then resells it. The difference in the price the underwriter pays the company and the price at which the securities are sold to the public is known as the spread, and is typically around 7 percent. Another type of offering is a "best efforts" underwriting, where the underwriter does not purchase the securities but pledges to make his or her best effort to sell the offering. In this case, the underwriter receives a commission.

The underwriter must perform a reasonable investigation of the offering. This typically includes steps such as: interviewing company officials, customers, distributors, industry organizations; reviewing the company's financial statements, budgets, and financial models; meeting with the company auditors and attorneys; and retaining consultants as necessary to understand the company's business.[2]

The underwriter will also participate in a "road show" with management, where presentations are made to groups of individual and institutional investors. During the road shows, the parties can gauge the potential demand for shares of the offering as well as provide information to potential investors.

Before securities are sold, the company must file a final prospectus with the SEC, which would now include the price and number of shares to be issued.

EVALUATING THE PROSPECTUS

As noted above, in order to provide some measure of protection for the investing public, regulations require that offerings of equity securities provide an offering memorandum or prospectus to prospective investors. The prospectus is the primary document from which the investor can learn fundamental aspects of the potential risks and rewards of the investment and must be evaluated carefully.

The prospectus must contain certain disclosures as specified by the SEC or other relevant authorities. For this section, we will examine the required components of the prospectus that must accompany SEC Form S-1 (item numbers in parentheses are the items specified by the SEC and found in SEC filings).

Forepart of the Registration Statement. Certain information is required to be presented on the outside front cover of the prospectus. The information includes the name of the firm, type of securities, price, risk factors, and other items as detailed further below. Some of the information may be left blank in the early stages, to be completed later. In such a case, the prospectus "subject to completion" legend will appear in red along the top or left side of the page. The outside front cover page of Google's "red herring" or preliminary prospectus is shown in Exhibit 3.1, and the final prospectus is shown in Exhibit 3.2.

Name. The name of the entity must be provided. If the name could be confused with another well-known company, information must be included to eliminate any confusion with the other company. If the name indicates a line of business in which the company is not engaged or is engaged only to a limited extent, information must also be provided to avoid misleading readers. For example, if the company's name is Miami Restaurant Group, but is no longer in the restaurant business, this fact must be disclosed. In some cases, the company may be required to change its name to properly reflect its current operations. For some, the name can be an important signal of business strategy. Dell Computer, Inc., recently changed its name to Dell, Inc., to reflect its expanding line of products and services.

Title and amount of securities. The title refers to the type of security being issued. For example, Google's IPO offering pertained to Class A common stock. Common stock is the basic unit of ownership for a corporation. A company may have different classes of stock (A, B, etc....) with differing rights (such as voting privileges). A company may also issue preferred stock, which is typically nonvoting and is entitled to a stated dividend, whereas common stock pays a dividend at the discretion of the board of directors.

The amount is the number of shares being offered. In the case of

Chapter 3 | The Prospectus: Equity IPOs

Exhibit 3.1: Google "Red Herring" Prospectus Cover Page:

The information in this prospectus is not complete and may be changed. We may not sell these securities until the registration statement filed with the Securities and Exchange Commission is effective. This prospectus is not an offer to sell these securities and we are not soliciting any offer to buy these securities in any jurisdiction where the offer or sale is not permitted.
Prospectus (Subject to Completion) Dated April 29, 2004

Shares: Google Class A Common Stock

Google Inc. is offering ___ shares of Class A common stock and the selling stockholders are offering ___ shares of Class A common stock. We will not receive any proceeds from the sale of shares by the selling stockholders. This is our initial public offering and no public market currently exists for our shares. We anticipate that the initial public offering price will be between $___ and $___ per share.

Following this offering, we will have two classes of authorized common stock, Class A common stock and Class B common stock. The rights of the holders of Class A common stock and Class B common stock are identical, except with respect to voting and conversion. Each share of Class A common stock is entitled to one vote per share. Each share of Class B common stock is entitled to ten votes per share and is convertible at any time into one share of Class A common stock.

We expect to apply to list our Class A common stock on either the New York Stock Exchange or the Nasdaq National Market under the symbol "___."
Investing in our Class A common stock involves risks. See *"Risk Factors"* beginning on page 4.

Price $___ A Share

	Price to Public	Underwriting Discounts and Commissions	Proceeds to Google	Proceeds to Selling Stockholders
Per Share	$	$	$	$
Total	$	$	$	$

Google has granted the underwriters the right to purchase up to an additional ___ shares to cover over-allotments.

The price to the public and allocation of shares will be determined primarily by an auction process. As part of this auction process, we are attempting to assess the market demand for our Class A common stock and to set the size and price to the public of this offering to meet that demand. Buyers hoping to capture profits shortly after our Class A common stock begins trading may be disappointed. The method for submitting bids and a more detailed description of this process are included in "Auction Process" beginning on page 25.

The Securities and Exchange Commission and state securities regulators have not approved or disapproved of these securities, or determined if this prospectus is truthful or complete. Any representation to the contrary is a criminal offense.

It is expected that the shares will be delivered to purchasers on or about ___, 2004.

Source: Morgan Stanley, Credit Suisse First Boston, ©2006. Edgar Online, Inc.

Understanding and Evaluating Prospectuses, Offering Documents, and Proxy Statements

Exhibit 3.2: Google Final Prospectus Cover

Prospectus (Subject to Completion) Dated April 18, 2004

19,605,052 Shares: Google Class A Common Stock

Google Inc. is offering 14,142,135 shares of Class A common stock and the selling stockholders are offering 5,462,917 shares of Class A common stock. We will not receive any proceeds from the sale of shares by the selling stockholders. This is our initial public offering and no public market currently exists for our shares. We anticipate that the initial public offering price will be between $85.00 and $95.00 per share.

Following this offering, we will have two classes of authorized common stock, Class A common stock and Class B common stock. The rights of the holders of Class A common stock and Class B common stock are identical, except with respect to voting and conversion. Each share of Class A common stock is entitled to one vote per share. Each share of Class B common stock is entitled to ten votes per share and is convertible at any time into one share of Class A common stock.

Our Class A common stock has been approved for quotation on The Nasdaq National Market under the symbol "GOOG," subject to official notice of issuance.

Investing in our Class A common stock involves risks. See "Risk Factors" beginning on page 4.

Price $ A Share

	Price to Public	Underwriting Discounts and Commissions	Proceeds to Google	Proceeds to Selling Stockholders
Per Share	$	$	$	$
Total	$	$	$	$

The selling stockholders have granted the underwriters the right to purchase up to an additional 2,940,757 shares to cover over-allotments.

The price to the public and allocation of shares will be determined by an auction process. The minimum size for a bid in the auction will be five shares of our Class A common stock. The method for submitting bids and a more detailed description of this auction process are included in "Auction Process" beginning on page 34. As part of this auction process, we are attempting to assess the market demand for our Class A common stock and to set the size and price to the public of this offering to meet that demand. As a result, buyers should not expect to be able to sell their shares for a profit shortly after our Class A common stock begins trading. We will determine the method for allocating shares to bidders who submitted successful bids following the closing of the auction.

The Securities and Exchange Commission and state securities regulators have not approved or disapproved of these securities, or determined if this prospectus is truthful or complete. Any representation to the contrary is a criminal offense.

It is expected that the shares will be delivered to purchasers on or about August ___, 2004.

Source: Morgan Stanley, Credit Suisse First Boston, Goldman Sachs & Co., Lehman Brothers, JP Morgan, Citigroup, Allen & Company LLC, UBS Investment Bank, WR Hambrecht + Co, Thomas Weisel Partners LLC, ©2006. Edgar Online, Inc.

Google, shares were being offered both by the company and by existing stockholders (founders and early investors). The proceeds from the shares offered by the company will belong to the company and be used for corporate purposes. Proceeds from shares offered by existing stockholders will go to those stockholders and will not be available for corporate purposes. The prospectus must clearly distinguish between shares offered by the company and by existing stockholders. The preliminary prospectus cover in Exhibit 3.1 does not contain the actual number of shares being offered, but that information is required to be disclosed prior to the offering date as shown in Exhibit 3.2. In addition, underwriters typically require issuers to provide an over-allotment option, under which the underwriter may purchase additional shares at the offering price should investor demand exceed the primary allotment. Such arrangements must be disclosed. For Google, any over-allotments will be provided by the selling stockholders rather than the company. Finally, any unusual attributes of the stock, such as partial voting rights, should be described briefly. In Google's case, the Class A shares receive one vote (as is normal), but investors are informed that the Class B shares are entitled to ten votes each.

It is important to understand the rights of the class of shares being issued. A purchaser of Class A shares must understand that control over the board and major decisions will rest largely with the Class B shareholders in this case.

Offering price of the securities. The price of the securities, the underwriter's discounts and commissions, the net proceeds to the company, and any selling shareholder's net proceeds must be disclosed on both a per share or unit basis and for the total amount of the offering. In some cases, offerings may be conducted on a minimum/maximum basis. In such cases, the prospectus should show the total minimum and total maximum amount of the offering. The information may be presented in a table, term sheet format, or other clear presentation that fits the design of the cover page and is not misleading.

For the preliminary prospectus (red herring), the details of the offering price need not be disclosed. In such cases, the prospectus must provide a bona fide estimate of the range of the maximum offering price and the maximum number of securities offered. If this is not practical, the prospectus must explain the method by which the price is to be determined. Google's red herring states that both the number of shares to be offered and the offering price will be determined by an auction process; the investor is referred to page 25 of the prospectus for a detailed discussion of the auction process.

From the investors' perspective, it would be preferable to have a larger amount of proceeds going to the company as opposed to underwriters and selling shareholders. While it is normal for some shares to be sold by existing shareholders, and they are certainly entitled to "cash out" part of their holdings, prospective investors would like to see that the selling shareholders maintain a significant financial interest in the company indicating their faith in the future of the company. Additionally, any proceeds going to selling shareholders are not available for use in company operations. A lower underwriting commission or spread also means more money to operate the company. Notice that, in Google's case, the underwriters' commission is only about 2.8 percent (2.3839/85).

Market for the securities. The prospectus should list whether any national securities exchange or the Nasdaq Stock Market will list the securities offered and identify the trading symbol(s) for the securities. For example, Google's Class A common shares trade on the NASDAQ market under the ticker symbol "GOOG."

Risk factors. The cover page provides a cross-reference to the risk factors section, including the page number where it appears in the prospectus. Such reference must be in prominent type. Risk factors are a very important factor in evaluating an investment, which is highlighted by the reference on the cover page. Google references the list of risk factors that can be found on page four of the prospectus and is discussed further below.

State legend and commission legend. A blanket statement is required that neither the Securities and Exchange Commission nor any state securities commission have approved or disapproved of the securities or passed upon the accuracy or adequacy of the disclosures in the prospectus, and that any contrary representation is a criminal offense.

The cover page should also include any legend or statement required by the law of any state in which the securities are to be offered. If no separate state legend is listed, then none was required by the state of incorporation.

The majority of U.S. companies are incorporated in Delaware, but can be incorporated anywhere. Delaware is favored by companies due to its well-developed corporate statutes and case law. The state of incorporation will determine laws and regulations that must apply, such as procedures for determining the board of directors and other matters subject to shareholder vote.

Underwriting. This section identifies the lead or managing underwriter(s) as well as the nature of the underwriting arrangements. In Google's case, the auction process provided for a firm commitment. Other types of offerings include:

1. **Best efforts.** The underwriters are not required to sell any specific number or dollar amount of securities but will use their best efforts to sell the securities offered.
2. **Best efforts, minimum-maximum.** The underwriters must sell the minimum number of securities offered if any are sold. The underwriters are required to use only their best efforts to sell the maximum number of securities offered.

If the securities are offered on a best-efforts basis, the description should include the date the offering will end, any minimum purchase requirements, and any arrangements to place the funds in an escrow, trust, or similar account. If no such arrangements were made, the effect on investors should be described.

Date of prospectus. The date the prospectus was prepared.

Prospectus "subject to completion" legend. This is the statement that appears in red on a preliminary prospectus, giving it the nickname "red herring." Usually, this statement follows the boilerplate language seen at the top of Exhibit 3.1.

Inside Front and Outside Back Cover Pages of Prospectus (Item 2). On either the inside front or outside back cover page of the prospectus, the issuer must provide a reasonably detailed table of contents. It must show the page number of the various sections or subdivisions of the prospectus and include a specific listing of the risk factors section. The table of contents must immediately follow the cover page in any prospectus delivered electronically.

Understanding and Evaluating Prospectuses, Offering Documents, and Proxy Statements

On the outside back cover page, the issuer must advise securities dealers of their obligation to deliver a prospectus when effecting transactions in the securities. Investors should not consider an investment in an IPO without receiving and evaluating the prospectus.

Summary Information, Risk Factors, and Ratio of Earnings to Fixed Charges (Item 3). *Summary Information.* The summary provides a brief overview of the key aspects of the offering in clear, plain language. If it is not included on the cover page, the summary section must contain the complete mailing address and telephone number of the company's principal executive offices.

Google's prospectus summary begins with a description of the company, its position within the industry, and the fact that it provides information freely to anyone with an Internet connection. It describes its various programs to generate revenue through advertising and states the company's mission to "organize the world's information and make it universally accessible and useful."[3] It also states that the company believes the user experience drives long-term revenue growth, and that the company will not compromise the user experience for short-term gains. The address of the company headquarters, along with a description of registered and unregistered trademarks held by the company, is also included.

Google's summary also reiterates the details of the offering and the market for the securities, elaborating on the information provided in the cover page. In particular, the total shares that will be outstanding following the offering, as well as a description of the selling shareholders, are provided. Of importance in the case of Google is the number of Class A and B shares that are expected to be outstanding after the offering:

Class A	33,603,386
Class B	<u>237,616,257</u>
Total Common Stock	271,219,643

Note that while Class A shares will represent 12.4 percent of the total common shares, their voting power is much lower since each Class B share is entitled to ten votes. Further, the summary notes that these amounts do not include warrants and options outstanding for both Class A and B shares. Exercise of these warrants and options will result in further dilution of the ownership of investors.

Google's summary also refers to the unusual auction process that was used to determine the number of shares and offering price, known as a Dutch auction. The procedures are described in more detail later in the prospectus.

Finally, Google's summary provides a summary of the historical results of operations (income statement) and the current financial position (balance sheet). The balance sheet is presented both as actual and on a pro forma basis adjusted to present the data as it would appear following the completion of the offering. The information in the summary section is very abbreviated. Full financial statements for analysis are found later in the prospectus. Chapter 2 of this book describes analysis techniques for this financial information using Google's financial statements as an example.

Risk factors. This section provides a discussion of the most significant factors that make the offering speculative or risky, and should be read carefully by the investor and his or her representatives. The SEC provides the following guidelines for the risk factors section.[4]

> This discussion must be concise and organized logically. Do not present risks that could apply to any issuer or any offering. Explain how the risk affects the issuer or the securities being offered. Set forth each risk factor under a subcaption that adequately describes the risk. The risk factor discussion must immediately follow the summary section. If you do not include a summary section, the risk factor section must immediately follow the cover page of the prospectus or the pricing information section that immediately follows the cover page. The risk factors may include, among other things, the following:
>
> (1) Your lack of an operating history
> (2) Your lack of profitable operations in recent periods
> (3) Your financial position
> (4) Your business or proposed business or

(5) The lack of a market for your common equity securities or securities convertible into or exercisable for common equity securities

Google provides *22 pages* describing risk factors in its prospectus. Some of these risks, such as "we occasionally become subject to commercial disputes that could harm our business by distracting our management from the operation of our business, by increasing our expenses and, if we do not prevail, by subjecting us to potential monetary damages and other remedies," appear to fall under the category of "risks that could apply to any issuer or any offering" and thus could have been eliminated from the prospectus. However, Google's lawyers likely wanted them included to provide additional protection from shareholder lawsuits.

Other risks noted in the risk factors section are more noteworthy, and offer investors real insight to the risks they face when buying Google stock. For example, consider in aggregate the following four factors (from the many listed in the prospectus).[5]

- *We generate our revenue almost entirely from advertising, and the reduction in spending by or loss of advertisers could seriously harm our business.*
- *We rely on our Google Network members for a significant portion of our revenues, and otherwise benefit from our association with them. The loss of these members could prevent us from receiving the benefits we receive from our association with these Google Network members, which could adversely affect our business.*
- *New technologies could block our ads, which would harm our business.*
- *If we fail to detect click-through fraud, we could lose the confidence of our advertisers, thereby causing our business to suffer.*

The first factor sets the stage that the company depends almost entirely on advertising for its revenues. The second states that third-party content providers host Google ads on their Web sites. Such content providers could choose ads from other sources such as Yahoo!, or could develop their own ad sales if they became successful enough. Google specifies that 43 percent of its revenue in the latest period was generated through such third-party content providers. The third factor simply states that Internet users may begin to deploy ad-blocking technology (such as pop-up blockers) to avoid being exposed to advertising. This would obviously undercut Google's business. Finally, Google's Web-based ads are valued by advertisers because presumably only interested consumers will click through to the advertiser's site. However, since content providers are paid by the click, they may be tempted to generate revenue by clicking on the ads themselves, or having others do so. Alternatively, competitors may click on the ads to increase the advertiser's expenses. If click-through fraud becomes pervasive, advertisers would likely pay much less per click or seek other advertising outlets, and Google would suffer. These risk factors point to the core of Google's business and provide investors a realistic assessment of the associated risks.

Perhaps a more compelling case for investors to read the prospectus thoroughly is the recent example of Refco, a commodities brokerage. Their prospectus disclosed the following risk factors.[6]

- *We are subject to an SEC investigation, which could adversely affect our business.*
- *Our auditors reported to us that, at February 28, 2005, there were two significant deficiencies in our internal controls over financial reporting.*
- *Our business may be adversely affected if our reputation is harmed.*
- *Our substantial indebtedness could adversely affect our financial health, harm our ability to react to changes to our business, and prevent us from fulfilling our obligations under our indebtedness.*

Investors who carefully read the prospectus may have avoided significant losses. According to an Associated Press article:[7]

> Weighed down by an accounting scandal, a former chief executive under indictment and the possibility of serious trouble with the Securities and Exchange Commission, commodities broker Refco Inc. appears to be struggling to hold on to as many customers—and as much cash—as possible....Credit rating agency Standard & Poor's said the situation was getting so bad, the company was likely to default on its debt payments due to a lack of cash....Refco said Friday it would begin

"winding down" its stock, bond, and credit portfolios within its Refco Securities LLC subsidiary, selling all its holdings to pay off its customers and, hopefully, preserve some of its capital to potentially use to help keep the company going.... Refco is busy trying to keep customers from fleeing the company and taking their money with them....The SEC on Friday compounded Refco's problems by barring Refco Securities LLC and another Refco subsidiary, Refco Clearing LLC, from moving more than 30 percent of excess net capital to any shareholder, employee, partner or affiliate for the next 20 days....Twenty days could be too long to wait for the nation's largest independent futures broker, which went from one of Wall Street's rising stars to scandal and a looming cash crisis in the space of five days. On Monday, Refco said Bennett would go on leave after paying the company $430 million, plus interest, to account for bad debts hidden in another entity under Bennett's control. That made Refco's revenues appear much larger than they actually were, since it was unlikely that the company would ever collect on those debts. It also may have misled investors in the company's initial public stock offering, just two months ago. The stock has lost more than 70 percent of its value since its Oct. 7 close.

Investors must realize that all businesses have risks. The risk section of the prospectus can be compared to other investments under consideration so the investor can determine whether the risks are appropriate given their expected return from the investment.

When analyzing the summary and risk factors, investors should try to understand the company and its industry. Specific questions include:

1. How does the company generate revenue?
2. How much profit is generated from operating revenue (versus non-operating activities)?
3. Who are the competitors?
4. Do I understand the risks and opportunities?
5. How serious/likely are the potential risk factors?
6. How do these compare with those of other potential investments?

If the investor cannot answer these questions based on the prospectus alone, he or she should seek the information from trusted sources or avoid the investment altogether.

Ratio of earnings to fixed charges. For debt or preferred equity offerings, the issuer must show a ratio of earnings to fixed charges, including preferred dividends. The ratio for each of the last five fiscal years and the latest interim period for which financial statements are presented must be included. If the proceeds from the offering will be used to repay any existing debt or retire other securities and the change in the ratio would be 10 percent or greater, a pro forma ratio showing the application of the proceeds will be included. The pro forma ratio may only be shown for the most recent fiscal year and the latest interim period. The ratio is effectively the amount of operating income divided by fixed charges, such as interest. A ratio in excess of one indicates that the company has sufficient operating income to cover these fixed charges.

If the fixed charge ratio indicates less than one-to-one coverage (Earnings/Fixed charges < 1), the company must disclose the dollar amount of the deficiency. Foreign private issuers must show the ratio based on the figures in the primary financial statement, and based on the figures resulting from the reconciliation to U.S. generally accepted accounting principles if this ratio is materially different.

Note that the investor should not necessarily be comfortable even if the ratio exceeds one, since in an economic downturn, the company may not be able to make interest payments. Further, the ability to make interest payments does not inform the investor of the ability to repay principal. The higher the ratio, the more comfort the investor would have in the ability of the company to withstand a downturn. The investor should compare this ratio to other companies in the industry to assess the risk of nonpayment.

Use of Proceeds (Item 4). Issuers must tell potential investors how they intend to use the money raised through the offering. If there is no specific plan for the proceeds, or a significant portion thereof, the registrant must say so and discuss the principal reasons for the offering. When there is more than one stated use, management should indicate how the competing

Understanding and Evaluating Prospectuses, Offering Documents, and Proxy Statements

uses will be prioritized and discuss the company's plans if substantially less than the maximum proceeds are obtained. The discussion need not be detailed. For example, saying that $1 billion would be used to build a new plant and the remaining proceeds would be for general corporate purposes could be sufficient. If the current offering is insufficient to accomplish the purposes, the company should state the sources and amounts of the remaining funds needed. However, the following uses must be specifically disclosed:

- Any proceeds being used to reduce existing indebtedness.
- Any assets to be acquired, with specific disclosure if the assets are being acquired from parties related to the company.
- Any proceeds that may, or will, be used to finance acquisitions of other businesses. If known, the identity of such businesses should be disclosed. If not known, the company should disclose the nature of the businesses to be sought.

Google described their use of proceeds as follows:[8]

We estimate that we will receive net proceeds of $1,163.6 million from our sale of the 14,142,135 shares of Class A common stock offered by us in this offering, based upon our initial public offering price of $85.00 per share, after deducting underwriting discounts and commissions and estimated offering expenses payable by us. We will not receive any of the net proceeds from the sale of the shares by the selling stockholders.
    The principal purposes of this offering are to obtain additional capital, to create a public market for our common stock, and to facilitate our future access to the public equity markets.
    We currently have no specific plans for the use of the net proceeds of this offering. We anticipate that we will use the net proceeds received by us from this offering for general corporate purposes, including working capital. In addition, we may use a portion of the proceeds of this offering for acquisitions of complementary businesses, technologies, or

other assets. We have no current agreements or commitments with respect to any material acquisitions.

Pending such uses, we plan to invest the net proceeds in highly liquid, investment-grade securities.

Investors should consider a number of factors related to the proceeds and how they are being used. For example, is the amount being raised appropriate? If it is not enough to accomplish the company's purposes, how soon will they need to raise additional funding? Many start-up businesses lose significant amounts of money for quite some time, and an IPO should provide them with enough money to fund the business for several years or until they become profitable. If market conditions are poor when the company needs money again, they might not be able to raise it and the company could fold. Alternatively, is the amount raised too much? Companies with more cash than they need may be tempted to use the money frivolously. Is the money being used appropriately? Selling shares to pay off debt could be a good thing—improving the company's flexibility—or a bad one—simply raising new funds to pay off existing investors in a Ponzi-like cycle.

Investors should have had the following concerns about Google's IPO, and been sufficiently comfortable with the implications, before investing:

1. A good portion of the proceeds were going to selling shareholders rather than the company. Are you comfortable investing in the company in order to allow other people to cash out?
2. The company does not appear to need the money. They are generating cash and have no plans for the proceeds. Although it is common practice for technology companies to have a "war chest" to tide them through bad times, facilitate any opportunities that may arise, and thwart takeovers, is this an appropriate strategy?
3. Is the company going public just to create a tangible value for employees exercising options, and if so, is the investor comfortable with this?

Determination of Offering Price (Item 5). Because no prior market has existed for shares sold in an IPO, the value of the shares is fairly subjective.

Understanding and Evaluating Prospectuses, Offering Documents, and Proxy Statements

The prospectus must outline how the company and underwriters arrived at the offering price. In many cases, the underwriters or other qualified experts may offer a "fairness opinion" with regard to the offering price.

When analyzing the offering price, consider whether the method used seems appropriate. Common methods are projecting future cash flows and discounting those to the present. This involves a great deal of estimation and does not consider current market prices of peer companies; however, it is the method preferred by acquirers in business takeovers and has been found to be an effective valuation method. Another method is to value the company based on price-multiples such as P/E ratios. The ratios of similar publicly traded peer companies are evaluated to arrive at a relative valuation of the subject company. This method considers current market prices of similar companies, but assumes that these companies are fairly valued under current market conditions. The investor should evaluate the assumptions used and whether good peer companies are available for comparison. If a risky start-up is being compared to established competitors, perhaps a lower multiple would be justified to offset the risk. In most cases, the underwriters will set the offering price somewhat low to ensure that the shares are all placed and the first day of trading is positive.

The investor should consider the P/E multiple they are paying in relation to current market conditions, alternative investments, and the risk factors for the subject company. In Google's case, the Dutch auction process was used to determine investor interest in terms of both number and price of the shares to be offered. Effectively, the market determined the offering price.

Dilution (Item 6). In many ways, the act of taking a company public signals that it has been successful as a private company. Because of its past success, the officers, venture capitalists and other early investors in the company likely paid a far lower price for their shares than the public shareholders will. Public shareholders must be informed of this disparity, and explicitly shown the net tangible book value per share before and after the distribution; the amount of the increase in such net tangible book value per share attributable to the cash payments made by purchasers of the shares being offered; and the amount of the immediate dilution from the public offering price that will be absorbed by such purchasers. Tangible book value is the total tangible assets (such as land or buildings but excluding certain intangible assets such as goodwill) of the company minus liabilities. Think of this as the amount that could be distributed to shareholders if all of the company's assets were sold for the amount listed on its balance sheet and the liabilities were paid off. This is then divided by the number of shares to obtain the tangible book value per share.

Google's dilution disclosure is presented in Exhibit 3.3. Google's tangible book value prior to the offering was $913.2 million, or $3.55 per share. After the offering, the tangible book value rises to $2,076.8 million, or $7.66 per share. So the $85 per share investors contribute has a tangible value that is only $7.66 per share, for dilution of $77.34 per share. In other words, if the company were liquidated immediately, the new shareholders would suffer a loss with that value shifted to the shareholders existing before the offering. However, a company is typically worth much more as an operating, going concern as opposed to liquidation, particularly one with a large number of intangible assets.

Google's disclosure also indicates that existing stockholders paid an average of $0.35 per share, compared to the $85 that will be paid by new investors. Prior to the public offering, the existing stockholders had provided 100 percent of the capital and owned 100 percent of the shares. Due to the substantial appreciation in value between the existing stockholder's price and the price offered to new stockholders, after the offering new stockholders will have contributed 93.1 percent of the capital but will own only 5.2 percent of the company.

Is this deal fair to the new stockholders? Apparently, they believe it is, because they are willing to pay the $85 per share (and profited handsomely from the post-IPO appreciation). In addition, early investors risked their capital when Google had not yet proven its business. Founders and early employees worked for low salaries (in exchange for large stock option grants) in the hope that the company would indeed be successful and the options would not expire worthless. In addition, new stockholders are passive investors whose only contribution to the health of the company is financial. By contrast, employees and venture capitalists can be considered to have provided "sweat equity" in the form of their labor and intellectual contributions to

Understanding and Evaluating Prospectuses, Offering Documents, and Proxy Statements

Exhibit 3.3: Dilution Information Contained in Google Prospectus

DILUTION

If you invest in our Class A common stock, your interest will be diluted to the extent of the difference between the initial public offering price per share of our Class A common stock and the pro forma as adjusted net tangible book value per share of our Class A and Class B common stock immediately after this offering. Pro forma net tangible book value per share represents the amount of our total tangible assets less total liabilities, divided by the number of shares of Class A and Class B common stock outstanding at June 30, 2004 after giving effect to the conversion of all of our preferred stock into Class B common stock, which will occur immediately prior to the completion of the offering.

Investors participating in this offering will incur immediate, substantial dilution. Our pro forma net tangible book value was $913.2 million, computed as total stockholders' equity less goodwill and other intangible assets, or $3.55 per share of Class A and Class B common stock and preferred stock outstanding at June 30, 2004. Assuming the sale by us of shares of Class A common stock offered in this offering at our initial public offering price of $85.00 per share, and after deducting underwriting discounts and commissions and estimated offering expenses, our pro forma as adjusted net tangible book value at June 30, 2004, would have been $2,076.8 million, or $7.66 per share of common stock. This represents an immediate increase in pro forma net tangible book value of $4.11 per share of common stock to our existing stockholders and an immediate dilution of $77.34 per share to the new investors purchasing shares in this offering. The following table illustrates this per share dilution:

The following table sets forth on a pro forma as adjusted basis, at June 30, 2004, the number of

Assumed initial public offering price per share of Class A common stock		$85.00
Pro forma net tangible book value per share at June 30, 2004	$ 3.55	
Increase in pro forma net tangible book value per share attributable to this offering	$ 4.11	
Pro forma as adjusted net tangible book value per share after the offering		$ 7.66
Dilution per share to new investors		$77.34

shares of Class A common stock purchased or to be purchased from us, the total consideration paid or to be paid and the average price per share paid or to be paid by existing holders of common stock, by holders of options and warrants outstanding at June 30, 2004, and by the new investors, before deducting underwriting discounts and estimated offering expenses payable by us.

	Shares Purchased		Total Consideration		Average Price Per Share
	Number	Percent	Amount	Percent	
Existing stockholders	257,077,508	94.8%	$89,523	6.9%	$0.35
New investors	14,142,135	5.2%	$1,202,081	93.1%	$85.00
Total	271,219,643	100.0%	$1,291,604	100.0%	

dollars in thousands, except per share amounts

The discussion and tables above are based on the number of shares of common stock and preferred stock outstanding at June 30, 2004.

The discussion and tables above includes 62,187 shares of Class B common stock issuable upon exercise of a warrant that will be exercised in connection with the offering and 2,700,000 shares of Class A common stock issued to Yahoo in connection with a settlement arrangement. The pro forma and pro forma as adjusted net tangible book values do not assume any change that will result from this settlement arrangement. Note 14 of Notes to Consolidated Financial Statements included as part of this prospectus provides a preliminary pro forma stockholders' equity as if the settlement had occurred on December 31, 2003. The discussion and table below excludes the following shares:

- 1,933,953 shares of Class B common stock issuable upon the exercise of warrants outstanding, at June 30, 2004, at a weighted average exercise price of $0.62 per share.
- 6,276,573 shares of Class A common stock issuable upon the exercise of options outstanding at June 30, 2004, at a weighted average exercise price of $9.42 per share.
- 10,456,084 shares of Class B common stock issuable upon the exercise of options outstanding at June 30, 2004, at a weighted average exercise price of $2.68 per share.
- 3,891,192 shares of common stock available for future issuance under our stock option plans at June 30, 2004.

To the extent outstanding options and warrants are exercised, new investors will experience further dilution.

the company's success. The dilution information provided in the prospectus helps the potential investors gauge the extent of such intangible contributions to the company's value and decide whether the share price in the offering appropriately reflects these contributions.

Selling Security Holders (Item 7). If any of the securities to be registered are to be offered by existing stockholders, the prospectus must name each such stockholder holder and the seller's relationship with the company.

Understanding and Evaluating Prospectuses, Offering Documents, and Proxy Statements

This helps potential investors gauge how much of their money is simply changing hands rather than providing the company with funds. This is particularly important if the investor believes the funds being raised and kept within the company will not be sufficient to meet the company's long-term needs.

Google's prospectus discloses that directors and officers, as a group, are offering 2,044,651 shares. More than half of these are being offered by founders Larry Page and Sergey Brin and CEO Eric Schmidt. Although each of these three people will collect proceeds ranging from $30 to $40 million through the offering, they are giving up only a small fraction (1.25 percent–2.5 percent) of the total shares they own. In fact, since the shares sold convert from super-voting "B" shares to Class A common shares, their ownership percentage of the B shares and their total voting power are essentially unchanged subsequent to the offering.

In addition, selling stockholders Yahoo! and America Online (AOL) offered 1,610,758 and 927,952 shares, respectively. Subsequent to the offering, they will continue to own, respectively, 6,588,126 and 6,509,500 shares. Elsewhere in the prospectus, investors learn that these two companies were early affiliates of Google, who provided Google's search technology to their users under a revenue-sharing agreement. By virtue of the fact that the two companies delivered a large number of customers to the arrangement, they were able to negotiate an ownership stake in Google as part of the deal. Prior to Google's IPO, Yahoo! developed its own competitive search engine fearing that Google's expanding offerings, including e-mail services, were direct competitors to Yahoo! At the time of this writing, AOL continued to use Google for Internet search services.

In addition to directors, officers, Yahoo! and AOL, other existing shareholders offered 879,556 shares in Google's IPO. These consisted primarily of angel and venture capital investors.

Plan of Distribution (Item 8). The plan of distribution offers details about how the offering will be conducted and how investors receive their shares. It must disclose the names of the underwriters, the nature of their obligation (firm commitment or best efforts), the existence and nature of any over-allotment options, their compensation as underwriters, and any indemnification offered to the underwriters. Any material relationships between the company and the underwriters, such as representation on the board of directors, must be disclosed. Any shares being distributed other than through underwriters (through dividend reinvestment plans, employee options, in exchange for the assets or shares of another company, or otherwise) must be described as well. In addition, the company must indicate the exchange on which the securities will trade and whether the securities will be offered in conjunction with any exchange-traded call options.

Description of Securities to be Registered (Item 9). The prospectus must outline the rights conferred to shareholders of the security offered. These include, but are not limited to, dividend rights, voting rights, and liquidation rights. If the rights of the shareholder are limited by other classes of securities, this must be disclosed. For example, in Google's case, the fact that Class B shareholders are entitled to ten votes essentially negates the voting rights of Class A shares. Shareholders must also be aware of any other provisions that may be designed to delay or prevent an acquisition of the company by another (commonly known as poison pill provisions).

Interests of Named Experts and Counsel (Item 10). Due to the substantial regulations governing public securities, undertaking an IPO often requires considerable legal counsel. In addition, as discussed under "determination of offering price," the company may employ experts on valuation to obtain a fairness opinion. When such experts and counsel have an interest in the company or its underwriters, or when total compensation for such services exceeds $50,000, the details of the interests must be disclosed in the prospectus.

Information with Respect to the Registrant (Item 11). This item accounts for the bulk of the prospectus. It begins with a discussion of the general development of the business. This includes the year in which the company was organized and its form of organization; the nature and results of any bankruptcy, receivership or similar proceedings with respect to the registrant or any of its significant subsidiaries; the nature and results of any other material reclassification, merger, or consolidation of the registrant or any of its significant subsidiaries; the acquisition or disposition of any material amount of assets otherwise than in the ordinary course of business; and any material changes in the mode of conducting the business.

Exhibit 3.4: Business and Geographic Segment Information for Google

Revenues

The following table presents our revenues, by revenue source, for the periods presented:

	Year Ended December 31,			Three Months Ended		Six Months Ended	
	2001	2002	2003	March 31, 2004	June 30, 2004	June 30, 2003	June 30, 2004
				(unaudited)			
	(dolllars in thousands)						
Advertising revenues:							
Google Web sites	$66,932	$306,978	$792,063	$303,532	$343,442	$341,002	$646,974
Google Network Web sites	—	103,937	628,600	333,752	346,226	198,801	679,978
Total advertising revenues	66,932	410,915	1,420,663	637,284	689,668	539,803	1,326,952
Licensing and other revenues	19,494	28,593	45,271	14,339	10,544	20,014	24,883
Revenues	$86,426	$439,508	$1,465,934	$651,623	$700,212	$559,817	$1,351,835

The following table presents our revenues, by revenue source, as a percentage of total revenues for the periods presented:

	Year Ended December 31,			Three Months Ended		Six Months Ended	
	2001	2002	2003	March 31, 2004	June 30, 2004	June 30, 2003	June 30, 2004
				(unaudited)			
Advertising revenues:							
Google Web sites	77%	70%	54%	47%	49%	61%	48%
Google Network Web sites	—	24	43	51	49	35	50
Total advertising revenues	77	94	97	98	98	96	98
Google Web sites as % of advertising revenues	100	75	56	48	50	63	49
Google Network Web sites as % of advertising revenues	—	25	44	52	50	37	51
Licensing and other revenues	23%	6%	3%	2%	2%	4%	2%

Revenues by Geography

Domestic and international revenues as a percentage of consolidated revenues, determined based on the billing addresses of our advertisers, are set forth below.

	Year Ended December 31,			Three Months Ended		Six Months Ended	
	2001	2002	2003	March 31, 2004	June 30, 2004	June 30, 2003	June 30, 2004
				(unaudited)			
United States	82%	78%	71%	69%	69%	72%	69%
International	18%	22%	29%	31%	31%	28%	31%

Source: Google Prospectus, dated August 18, 2004.

Further, the company must provide all of the following, when applicable:

1. Financial information about its various business and geographic segments for each of the last three fiscal years, or for as long as the company has been in business, whichever is shorter.
2. A narrative description of the business.
3. The location and general character of its principal plants, mines, and other materially important physical properties and the segment(s) that use the properties described. If these assets are used to secure loans or are otherwise encumbered, this also needs to be disclosed.
4. Any lawsuits that are outside the ordinary course of business or which could result in damages in excess of 10 percent of the company's current assets.
5. Market information, including the principal United States market or markets in which each class of the registrant's common equity is being traded, major holders of the securities, dividend information, and securities authorized under equity compensation plans.
6. Financial statements.
7. Selected financial data.
8. Supplementary financial information, including selected quarterly financial data and information about oil- and gas- producing activities.

Understanding and Evaluating Prospectuses, Offering Documents, and Proxy Statements

9. Management's discussion and analysis of the financial condition and results of operations.
10. Any changes in or disagreements with the accountants on accounting and financial disclosure.
11. Quantitative and qualitative disclosures about market risk, and the sensitivity of risk-sensitive instruments to fluctuations in currency exchange or interest rates.
12. Directors and executive officers.
13. Executive compensation details.
14. Security ownership of certain beneficial owners and management.
15. Certain relationships and related transactions.

Obviously, given the sheer amount of information in this item, there are numerous implications investors should look out for. In this section, we will try to provide some of these indicators on a point-by-point basis.

Segment information. The business and geographic segment information must include disclosures relating to revenues from external customers, profit or loss, and total assets. These can give clues as to whether there have been significant changes in the business over the last few years, and signs as to whether these changes may continue. Google's information, provided in Exhibit 3.4, yields several insights. First, despite growing in absolute terms, the contribution provided by licensing revenues has been dwarfed by the contribution from advertising. Further, an increasing portion of advertising revenues are coming from Google Network Web sites. This illustrates some of the power of the Internet, and particularly of Google's business model. By providing independent content creators with a simple tool for generating advertising revenue, Google's network becomes more valuable to both advertisers and content providers. If each Web site needed its own advertising sales force, or if advertisers had to negotiate directly with each content provider, the logistics involved would be too cumbersome. Google provides an efficient intermediary that maximizes the benefit to both parties. Second, we learn that the contribution from non-U.S. geographies is increasing rapidly. This only makes sense since the Internet is by nature a global resource, but it is unusual for such a young company to experience such rapid growth outside its domestic market. Historically, companies have been able to penetrate their home market and then continue growing by expanding overseas. Although Google is enjoying a hypergrowth period now, its early penetration of foreign markets may leave it with no further sources of growth.

Narrative business description. The narrative business description allows investors to become familiar with the drivers of a company's revenues and profitability. In conjunction with the risk factors, this description should provide a true understanding of how the business works. Equity investors are literally owners of the business; this section should at least give the broad framework of knowledge that an owner must have. It must include each of the following:

1. The principal products produced and services rendered and the principal markets for, and methods of distribution of, the segment's principal products and services.
2. The sources and availability of raw materials.
3. The importance, effect, and duration of all patents, trademarks, licenses, franchises, and concessions held.
4. The extent to which the business of the segment is or may be seasonal.
5. The practices of the company and the industry relating to working capital items (for example, the need to carry significant amounts of inventory to meet rapid delivery requirements of customers or to ensure a continuous allotment of goods from suppliers; rights to return merchandise; or extended payment terms to customers).
6. The dependence upon a single customer, or a few customers, the loss of any one or more of whom would have a material adverse effect. The name of any customer shall be disclosed if sales to the customer by one or more segments are 10 percent or more of consolidated revenues.
7. The dollar amount of backlog orders believed to be firm, as of a recent date and as of a comparable date in the preceding fiscal year, along with any portion not reasonably expected to be filled within the current fiscal year, and any seasonal or other material aspects of the backlog.
8. A description of any material portion of the business subject to

Understanding and Evaluating Prospectuses, Offering Documents, and Proxy Statements

termination of contracts or renegotiation of profits at the election of the government.

9. Competitive conditions including, where material, the identity of the particular markets in which the registrant competes, an estimate of the number of competitors and the registrant's competitive position. When one or a small number of competitors is dominant in the industry, this must be identified. The principal methods of competition (for example, price, service, warranty, or product performance) must be disclosed, and positive and negative factors pertaining to the company's competitive position should be explained.
10. The estimated amount spent during each of the last three fiscal years on company-sponsored research and development activities. Separately, the estimated dollar amount spent during each year on customer-sponsored research activities relating to the development of new products, services, or techniques or the improvement of existing products, services, or techniques.
11. The material effects that compliance with federal, state, and local environmental provisions may have upon the capital expenditures, earnings, and competitive position.
12. The number of persons employed by the registrant.
13. The narrative section should also disclose the relevant SEC filings and regulations the company must file or adhere to, along with information as to how to receive such filings.

Financial statements and related disclosures. The financial statements, footnotes, and management discussion provide a wealth of information on the past performance and current standing of the company. These sections should be read and analyzed to evaluate the profitability, efficiency, liquidity (ability to meet short-term obligations), and solvency (ability to meet long-term obligations) of the company. This involves examining the company's income statement, balance sheet, statement of cash flows, and ratios developed from these statements. Methods for analysis of the financial statements, supplemental financial information, and selected financial data are discussed in Chapter 2.

Management is required to discuss their own performance in a section titled "Management's Discussion and Analysis." While not a substitute for an independent analysis, this is a critical section to review. In it, management discusses the factors that drove the financial results. It must specifically address liquidity, capital resources, results of operations, off-balance sheet arrangements, and provide a disclosure of contractual obligations. When reviewing this section, an investor often learns some of the details behind the numbers published in the financial statements. Below is a small sample of insights from Google's MD&A section:

1. Google's effective tax rate (56 percent in the first six months of 2004) exceeds statutory rates because the expense they recognize for stock option grants is not deductible for tax purposes.
2. To settle a legal dispute with Yahoo! over patents, Google issues 2.7 million shares of Class A Common Stock to Yahoo!
3. Google believes the strong sequential growth it has experienced is masking strong seasonality, with the fourth quarter being much stronger than summer months for Web-based transactions, much as it is for offline retail transactions. As the company matures, this seasonality could become much more apparent.
4. The company has contractual obligations totaling $644.5 million, almost 90 percent of which must be paid within the next five years. Only $7.4 million of these commitments (the portion related to capital lease obligations) is recorded on the balance sheet as a potential liability. The largest portion, $477 million, relates to minimum revenue guarantees it has made to various Google Network members. In the aggregate, Google has collected more in advertising revenues than it has paid to Network members, but in 2003 and the first half of 2004, respectively, on certain contracts it collected $22.5 million and $18.2 million less than the minimum.

Companies sometimes change accounting methods—how the financial statements are prepared. Companies are required to discuss the impact of any changes. These may result from management choosing one accounting treatment over another, or simply of a change in the accounting rules

Understanding and Evaluating Prospectuses, Offering Documents, and Proxy Statements

themselves for all companies. If the change in accounting will affect the reported financial statements, management must quantify and explain the effect. Discussion of disagreements with the accountants, if any, should be scrutinized and heighten the readers' awareness of potential risks.

Company results may be sensitive to market risks such as interest rates. The company must disclose how changes in interest rates or exchange rates could affect their income. For example, Google reports that "it (is) reasonably possible that adverse changes in exchange rates of 10 percent for all currencies could be experienced in the near term. These changes would have resulted in an adverse impact on income before taxes of approximately $18.7 million and $4.5 million at June 30, 2004, and December 31, 2003."[9]

Information on officers and directors. For officers and directors, a company must provide names, ages, positions, family relationships, experience, and any pending legal proceedings. Information must also be provided about management compensation.

In Google's prospectus, investors learn that founders Sergey Brin and Larry Page are 30 and 31 years old, respectively, and neither has any significant management experience. This is offset by a strong team of managers and directors that they have hired, but Brin, Page, and CEO Eric Schmidt control the voting shares and manage as a triumvirate. Further, of 15 listed managers and directors, ten have links to either Stanford University or Sun Microsystems. This suggests that their relationships may be cozier than their "independent" board status suggests. Finally, although board members do not receive cash compensation for their service on the board, they are awarded options to purchase 65,000 shares of stock upon election. Given that existing board members were awarded options at pre-IPO valuations, these grants are significant and may discourage board members from questioning the management that awarded them.

Google's prospectus discloses that its executives are rewarded primarily through stock options. Even the CEO collected just $250,000 in base salary and a $301,556 bonus in 2003, quite modest for a firm of Google's standing. However, when options are considered, he has been compensated to the tune of hundreds of millions of dollars. Such a structure makes sense for an early-stage technology company, but may not be sensible as the company matures. Shareholders can monitor this, but given the dual-class ownership structure, will be unable to do anything about it other than sell their shares if they lose comfort with the practice.

Finally, companies must disclose any relationships and related-party transactions. This includes any transactions, business relationships, or indebtedness between the company and any of its managers, directors, or entities affiliated with managers or directors. Google discloses that when Eric Schmidt was hired, he was required to purchase shares, but was allowed to do so by means of a promissory note rather than cash. In addition, Schmidt owns an interest in a business jet that he allows management to use on occasion. On these occasions, Schmidt is reimbursed by the company for any expenses he bears, but must reimburse the company for his share of any profits.

Disclosure of Commission Position on Indemnification for Securities Act Liabilities (Item 12). Companies may limit the liability of officers and directors. If so, the SEC requires that the company add SEC language that expresses the SEC opinion on such matters. Google's prospectus provides:[10]

> Our certificate of incorporation contains provisions that limit the liability of our directors for monetary damages to the fullest extent permitted by Delaware law. Consequently, our directors will not be personally liable to us or our stockholders for monetary damages for any breach of fiduciary duties as directors, except liability for the following:
> - Any breach of their duty of loyalty to our company or our stockholders.
> - Acts or omissions not in good faith or which involve intentional misconduct or a knowing violation of law.
> - Unlawful payments of dividends or unlawful stock repurchases or redemptions as provided in Section 174 of the Delaware General Corporation Law.
> - Any transaction from which the director derived an improper personal benefit.
>
> Shortly thereafter, Google includes the SEC required disclosure.[11]

Understanding and Evaluating Prospectuses, Offering Documents, and Proxy Statements

Insofar as the provisions of our certificate of incorporation or bylaws provide for indemnification of directors or officers for liabilities arising under the Securities Act of 1933, we have been informed that in the opinion of the Securities and Exchange Commission this indemnification is against public policy as expressed in the Securities Act of 1933 and is therefore unenforceable.

Information Not Required in the Prospectus. The company must include information in the SEC filing that is not required to be included in the prospectus. This can also provide useful information to prospective investors and can be found in the company's SEC filing related to the prospectus. For example, companies must furnish a reasonably itemized statement of all expenses in connection with the issuance and distribution of the securities to be registered, other than underwriting discounts and commissions. Further, if in the three years prior to going public the company issued securities that were not registered under the Securities Act, the company must include the following information in the prospectus:

1. The date of sale and the title and amount of securities sold.
2. The names of the principal underwriters, if any. For securities not publicly offered, the name of the persons or identification of the class of persons to whom the securities were sold.
3. The aggregate offering price and the underwriting discounts or commissions. For securities sold other than for cash, the nature of the transaction and the nature and aggregate amount of consideration received by the registrant.
4. The section of the Securities Act or the rule of the Commission under which exemption from registration was claimed and the facts relied upon to make the exemption available.
5. Terms of conversion or exercise.
6. Use of proceeds.

IPO RESEARCH

A great deal of academic finance research has focused on initial public offerings.

Some of the findings of this research are helpful in further evaluating the risks and rewards of investing in an equity IPO.

One aspect of IPO investing concerns the way that investors are allocated IPO shares. The investment banking firms will allocate shares to interested parties since there are often not enough shares for all. While this must be done in a fair manner, research has shown that shares are often allocated favorably to "regular" investors, both institutional and retail investors who regularly invest in IPOs.[12]

It has also been well documented that IPOs, on average, are underpriced throughout the world. In other words, the price paid by those allocated IPO shares is on average lower than the closing price on the first day of trading. Those who receive IPO shares at the offering price therefore have, on average, a first day positive return. This underpricing in the U.S. has been found to be about 15 percent.[13] Unfortunately, the long-term performance from the closing price of the first day of trading forward has been found to be lacking, with IPO firms underperforming similar non-IPO firms.[14] A variety of explanations have been proposed for the initial underpricing. Research has pointed out some interesting aspects. For example, the involvement of well-known audit firms has been found to be associated with less underpricing. On the other hand, negative relationships have been found between market share of law firms (particularly New York firms) representing investment banks and IPO price.[15] The researchers conclude that more experienced law firms representing investment bankers may require greater disclosure of negative issues in offering documents.

CONCLUSION

Investing in an equity IPO often involves a new venture, which can be risky. Even for existing public companies that are raising additional capital, risks can be higher than for other established companies that may not have a need for external financing. As a result, investors and their advisers should carefully study the prospectus for initial public offerings to assess the potential risks and rewards of the offering. Some of the key points to consider are:
- Why is the company raising capital/going public, and does the intended use of proceeds appear reasonable?
- How long has the company been in business, and what has its past

Understanding and Evaluating Prospectuses, Offering Documents, and Proxy Statements

performance been? What is the company's financial position before and after the IPO?
- What types of securities are being offered, and are they subordinate to other securities of the company?
- What are the risk factors of the company, and do they match the risk tolerance of the investor? Be particularly careful when there have been prior regulatory problems/investigations.
- What are the opportunities for the company's products/services/industry?
- Does the proposed offering price appear reasonable relative to other similar companies (for example, based on relative P/E ratios)? What is the expected dilution to new investors?
- What are the reputations of the investment banks, auditors, and law firms involved in performing due diligence?
- Is the investor able to obtain shares at the offering price, or must they purchase them in the open market (the former is preferred, given historic IPO pricing)?

ENDNOTES

[1] For an analysis of the relative importance of various reasons as perceived by chief financial officers (CFOs) for going public, see "Initial Public Offerings: An Analysis of Theory and Practice," by James C. Brau and Stanley E. Fawcett, *Journal of Finance* 26, no. 1, February 2006, pp. 399–436.

[2] For a comprehensive list of "good" due diligence steps, see *The Initial Public Offering: A Guidebook for Executives and Boards of Directors*, 2nd ed., Patrick J. Schultheis, Christian E. Montegut, Robert G. O'Conner, Shawn J. Lindquist and J. Randall Lewis, Wilson Sonsini Goodrich & Rosati, P.C., and Bowne & Co., Inc., 2004.

[3] Google Inc. FORM S-1/A (amended) filed with the Securities and Exchange Commission, August 18, 2004, p. 1.

[4] United States Securities and Exchange Commission, Regulation S-K, Subpart 229.503.

[5] Google Inc. FORM S-1/A (amended) filed with the Securities and Exchange Commission, August 18, 2004, pp. 6–11.

[6] Refco Inc. FORM S-1/A (amended) filed with the Securities and Exchange Commission, August 8, 2005, pp. 16–27.

[7] Michael J. Martinez, "Refco Struggles to Retain Cash, Customers" October 15, 2005 (Associated Press).

[8] Google Inc., Final Prospectus, August 18, 2004, p. 44.

[9] Google, Inc., Final Prospectus, August 18, 2004, p. 71.

[10] Google, Inc., Final Prospectus, August 18, 2004, p. 98.

[11] Google, Inc., Final Prospectus, August 18, 2004, p. 99.

[12] Ekkehart Boehmner and Raymond P.H. Fishe, "Who Receives IPO Allocations? An Analysis of 'Regular Investors,'" (March 14, 2004). AFA 2005 Philadelphia Meetings, http://ssrn.com/abstract=517302

[13] Jay R. Ritter, "Initial Public Offerings," in Warren Gorham & Lamont, *Handbook of Modern Finance*, edited by Dennis Logue and James Seward, reprinted in *Contemporary Finance Digest*, Vol 2, No. 1, Spring 1998, pp. 5–30.

[14] Ibid.

[15] Barondes, Royce de Rohan and Sanger, Gary C., "Lawyer Experience And IPO Pricing" (May 4, 2000). http://ssrn.com/abstract=227729.

DISCUSSION QUESTIONS:
1. Why do companies go public?
2. What is the difference between a firm commitment and a best efforts offering?
3. What is a "red herring"?
4. What factors should be considered when evaluating a company's prospectus summary and risk factors?
5. What is "dilution" as referred to in an IPO prospectus? Who might benefit from dilution?
6. You are reviewing the prospectus for Going Public Inc. (GPI). At present, the P/E ratio of GPI based on the offering price is 10, while the P/Es for similar peer companies cluster around 15. What might justify this lower P/E ratio for GPI? What factors might justify a higher deserved P/E for GPI? (You may also want to refer to Chapter 2 in answering this question.)
7. In the section of the prospectus requiring information on officers and directors, companies are required to provide information on family and business relationships among these parties. What are the implications of such relationships between officers and directors?

EXERCISE:
Google Inc. used an unusual auction process in pricing their IPO shares. Below is an extract from Google's prospectus describing their reasoning for using this process. Review this extract and consider the following questions:

- How does this process differ from traditional IPO pricing?
- What is the potential impact of this process on underpricing of an offering?

Now do some research on what happened to Google's price on the first day of IPO trading and subsequently. How have IPO investors fared in this instance?

> From Google prospectus, dated August 18, 2004, page 31
> IPO PRICING AND ALLOCATION

Understanding and Evaluating Prospectuses, Offering Documents, and Proxy Statements

It is important to us to have a fair process for our IPO that is inclusive of both small and large investors. It is also crucial that we achieve a good outcome for Google and its current shareholders. This has led us to pursue an auction-based IPO for our entire offering. Our goal is to have a share price that reflects an efficient market valuation of Google that moves rationally based on changes in our business and the stock market. (The auction process is discussed in more detail elsewhere in this prospectus.)

Many companies going public have suffered from unreasonable speculation, small initial share float, and stock price volatility that hurt them and their investors in the long run. We believe that our auction-based IPO will minimize these problems, though there is no guarantee that it will.

An auction is an unusual process for an IPO in the United States. Our experience with auction-based advertising systems has been helpful in the auction design process for the IPO. As in the stock market, if people bid for more shares than are available and bid at high prices, the IPO price will be higher. Of course, the IPO price will be lower if there are not enough bidders or if people bid lower prices. This is a simplification, but it captures the basic issues. Our goal is to have the price of our shares at the IPO and in the aftermarket reflect an efficient market price—in other words, a price set by rational and informed buyers and sellers. We seek to achieve a relatively stable price in the days following the IPO and that buyers and sellers receive an efficient market price at the IPO. We will try to achieve this outcome, but of course may not be successful. Our goal of achieving a relatively stable market price may result in Google determining with our underwriters to set the initial public offering price below the auction clearing price.

We are working to create a sufficient supply of shares to meet investor demand at IPO time and after. We are encouraging current shareholders to consider selling some of their shares as part of the offering. These shares will supplement the shares the company sells to provide more supply for investors and hopefully provide a more stable price. Sergey and I, among others, are currently planning to sell a fraction of our shares in the IPO. The more shares current shareholders sell, the more likely it is that they believe the price is not unfairly low. The supply of shares available will likely have an effect on the clearing price of the auction. Since the number of shares being sold is likely to be larger at a high price and smaller at a lower price, investors will likely want to consider the scope of current shareholder participation in the IPO. We may communicate from time to time that we are sellers rather than buyers at certain prices.

While we have designed our IPO to be inclusive for both small and large investors, for a variety of reasons described in "Auction Process" not all interested investors will be able to receive an allocation of shares in our IPO.

We would like you to invest for the long term, and you should not expect to sell Google shares for a profit shortly after Google's IPO. We encourage investors not to invest in Google at IPO or for some time after, if they believe the price is not sustainable over the long term. Even in the long term, the trading price of Google's stock may decline.

We intend to take steps to help ensure shareholders are well informed. We encourage you to read this prospectus, especially the Risk Factors section. We think that short term speculation without paying attention to price is likely to lose you money, especially with our auction structure. In particular, we caution you that investing in Google through our auction could be followed by a significant decline in the value of your investment after the IPO.

RECOMMENDED READING

The Initial Public Offering: A Guidebook for Executives and Boards of Directors, 2nd ed., Patrick J. Schultheis, Christian E. Montegut, Robert G. O'Conner, Shawn J. Lindquist and J. Randall Lewis, Wilson Sonsini Goodrich & Rosati, P.C., and Bowne & Co., Inc. 2004.

James C. Brau and Stanley E. Fawcett, "Initial Public Offerings: An Analysis of Theory and Practice," *Journal of Finance* 61, no. 1 (February 2006): 399–436.

Zohar Goshen and Gideon Parchomovsky, "The Essential Role of Securities Regulation," October 5, 2004, Columbia Law and Economics Working Paper No. 259, http://ssrn.com/abstract=600709.

Shin'ichi Hirota, and Shyam Sunder, "Stock Market as a 'Beauty Contest':

Investor Beliefs and Price Bubbles sans Dividend Anchors," November 2002, Yale ICF Working Paper No. 02-42; EFA 2003 Annual Conference Paper No. 119, http://ssrn.com/abstract=302393.

Jay R. Ritter, "Initial Public Offerings," in Warren Gorham & Lamont *Handbook of Modern Finance*, ed. by Dennis Logue and James Seward, reprinted in *Contemporary Finance Digest* 2, no. 1, Spring 1998: 5–30.

4 The Prospectus: Secondary Offerings and PIPEs

When public companies need to raise additional equity capital to fund growth, they can make a "secondary" offering of shares to investors. They can finance this growth with equity in the form of common shares or a more senior security with contractual terms that provide for conversion into common shares. The company may choose to conduct an offering of registered (and therefore freely tradable, or *public*) securities or unregistered (and therefore restricted, or *private*) securities. These "private investments in public equities," which have become very common in recent years, are referred to as PIPEs. These types of investments, while becoming more common, are not well known by individual investors. It is important for the adviser to understand these investments and assist the investor in evaluating the potential risks and rewards. In this chapter, we will focus on key considerations for public and private investments in equity secondary offerings.

PUBLIC DISCLOSURE PROTECTIONS

Investors buying newly issued public securities benefit from the standardized disclosure regime of the Securities Exchange Act of 1934 and requirements of the Securities Act of 1933. The rules of disclosure mandated under these acts are integrated. As a result, investors can make investment decisions with relatively higher confidence in the information they are provided; the diligence conducted on their behalf by underwriters, counsel, and

Understanding and Evaluating Prospectuses, Offering Documents, and Proxy Statements

accountants; and, therefore, in the liquidity of their shares after issuance. The shares are often interchangeable with previously issued shares after the offering.

Newly issued shares have the potential to change the risks and potential rewards for the existing investors as well as for the new investor in the securities. Therefore, the terms of the secondary offering must be disclosed to the public market, whether the offering was of public or private securities. In this way, the trading market can be made aware of the additional shares to be issued and the proposed use of the offering proceeds. The market signal of pricing for the traded common shares is the starting point for evaluating the benefits of the offering to the investor in new shares.

The prospectus for a secondary offering contains useful information alerting investors to the nature of the offering:

- The existence of a public security ticker symbol with a last trade price, indicating that the security is of a class that is publicly traded, and providing an external measure of value for the common shares
- Identification of any selling stockholders (this is more common in secondaries)
- Description of the nature of the security
- Description of private nature of the offering, if that is the case
- Use of proceeds of the offering
- Pro forma financial statements that give effect to the offering
- Risk factors related to the offering, the use of proceeds, or the company, if different from the last registration statement

PUBLIC OFFERINGS

If the offering is of public shares, the company normally enlists an investment banker to lead a firm commitment underwriting. The underwriter will advise the company on the steps necessary to market the offering to individual and institutional investors. The underwriter will also price the offering based upon the trading price for the public common shares and investor demand for the new shares to be issued.

Secondary public offerings are registered with the SEC with either the

Chapter 4 | The Prospectus: Secondary Offerings and PIPEs

filing of Form S-1 or Form S-3, each a registration statement under the Securities Act of 1933. The contents of the prospectus will be similar for the various forms, except that Form S-3 allows the company not to repeat disclosures, such as financial statements, already in public filings made in compliance with the Exchange Act of 1934. The information is instead incorporated by reference. In practice, the S-3 is a way to alert the investing market just to the new information related to the offering, expediting review by potential investors and by the trading market. However, for an investor who is not already familiar with the company, the process of reviewing previous filings and making a judgment about the offering is more cumbersome, due to the need to review documents outside the prospectus.

The offering process for S-3 issuers is relatively quick and easy. Most of the demand will come from investors familiar with the company. The valuation metrics are usually well established, and firm value is based upon observed trading prices for the common shares. Because the company has a trading history and a reporting history, the financial analyses referred to in Chapter 2 can be readily conducted. Therefore, the primary focus of the marketing process is on the use of proceeds and expected impact on balance sheet and earnings per share in future periods.

The underwriter must still perform a reasonable investigation of the information in the prospectus, or incorporated into the prospectus. This provides the investor with a measure of comfort that the documents at least disclose accurately whether there are any investment risks or terms that are material to the investment decision.

The underwriter will also participate in a "road show" with management where presentations are made to groups of retail brokers and institutional investors. As with an IPO, before securities are sold, the company must file a final prospectus with the SEC, which would now include the price and number of shares to be issued. The prospectus must contain certain disclosures as specified by the SEC or other relevant authorities, described in Chapter 3. One common disclosure on the cover of both public and private offerings is the following mandatory SEC disclosure:

Neither the Securities Exchange Commission nor any state securities commission has approved or disapproved of these securities or determined if this prospectus is truthful or complete. Any representation to the contrary is a criminal offense.

For a public offering, the SEC usually spends a great amount of time reviewing and ultimately permitting the use of the prospectus by the company. SEC examiners review the prospectus disclosures drafted by the company and their counsel and financial disclosures drafted by the company and audited by their accounting firm. It is not unusual for the SEC to require extensive changes before permitting the securities to be offered for sale. This review culminates when the SEC declares the registration statement, including the prospectus, "effective." If the SEC is not satisfied with the company's disclosure or supplemental support for claims made in the disclosure, it will simply fail to declare the registration statement effective. The point made by the italicized words above is to prevent companies from using the SEC approval as an assurance of quality of the company or of the terms of the offering.

When Google marketed its public secondary offering, its prospectus cover was very similar to its IPO prospectus, except for the reference to underlying common stock pricing. The prospectus also incorporated other Google disclosures by reference rather than by reproducing the information in those filings. Selected portions of the Google secondary offering preliminary prospectus are shown in Exhibit 4.1.

PRIVATE OFFERINGS

A company with public securities outstanding may prefer to use a private offering rather than a public offering of securities. The offering prospectus (called a private placement memorandum) will contain important information regarding the investment. There will usually be some reference on the cover page of the offering memorandum indicating that the securities are not being registered, and therefore, they are not tradable on an exchange after the offering. The same conditions that apply to private placements for private companies apply to private offerings for public companies. It is the period of restriction, the nature of the purchaser, and the nature of the marketing process that allow the company to conduct a lawful private placement.

Chapter 4 | The Prospectus: Secondary Offerings and PIPEs

> **Exhibit 4.1: Selected Provisions of Google Secondary Prospectus from a Registration Statement on Form S-3**
>
> **14,159,265 Shares: Google Class A Common Stock**
> *Google Inc. is offering 14,159,265 shares of Class A common stock.*
>
> Our Class A common stock is quoted on The Nasdaq National Market under the symbol "GOOG." The reported last sale price on September 7, 2005 was $294.87.
>
> **INFORMATION INCORPORATED BY REFERENCE**
> The following documents filed with the Commission are hereby incorporated by reference in this Prospectus:
>
> - Our Annual Report on Form 10-K for the fiscal year ended December 31, 2004, filed with the Commission on March 30, 2005.
> - Our Current Report on Form 8-K filed with the Commission on January 13, 2005.
> - Our Quarterly Report on Form 10-Q for the fiscal quarter ended March 31, 2005, filed with the Commission on May 16, 2005.
> - Our Quarterly Report on Form 10-Q for the fiscal quarter ended June 30, 2005, filed with the Commission on August 15, 2005.
> - The description of our common stock contained in Google's Registration Statement on Form 10 as filed with the Commission on April 29, 2004 pursuant to Section 12(g) of the Exchange Act and effective as of June 28, 2004.
>
> All reports and other documents subsequently filed by us pursuant to Sections 13(a), 13(c), 14 and 15(d) of the Exchange Act after the date of this Prospectus and prior to the termination of this offering shall be deemed to be incorporated by reference in this Prospectus and to be part hereof from the date of filing of such reports and other documents.

Source: Google Inc. FORM S-3/A (amended) filed with the Securities and Exchange Commission September 8, 2005, p. 35.

Private placements can be completed for lower cost and in less time than a public offering for the company. The securities are usually sold at a relatively lower valuation than the potential public offering price, however, to compensate the investor for bearing the risk of not owning a publicly tradable security. The attractive relative pricing of a private deal creates investor interest, and the ability to complete the offering quickly creates issuer interest in this type of offering.

Although not able to trade the securities, investors in private offerings

Understanding and Evaluating Prospectuses, Offering Documents, and Proxy Statements

are able to review information in public filings, which follow mandated disclosures under the rules of the Exchange Act and from public market valuation of the tradable common stock of the company. Often there is other useful market information about the company and its prospects, such as research reports from independent brokerage firms, news articles, and industry research mentioning the company.

EVALUATING THE PROSPECTUS OR PRIVATE PLACEMENT MEMORANDUM

Offering Price of the Securities. The price of the securities, the underwriter's discounts and commissions, the net proceeds to the company, and any selling shareholder's net proceeds must be disclosed on both a per share or unit basis and for the total amount of the offering. For the preliminary prospectus (red herring), the last reported sales price of the common stock must be disclosed. Google's red herring states the last reported sales price and the market on which it is traded. The offering price is usually related to that trade price and is either the same or some slight discount based upon investor demand, before underwriting discount and expenses.

It is common for the market price of securities to react adversely to the news of the offering after the red herring prospectus is delivered in a registered offering. There are many studies of this phenomenon related to signaling, optimal capital structure, pricing of risk, and even reverse signaling of the market to management about expected outcome of the use of proceeds. Regardless of the expected (that is, speculative future) benefits to the company from deploying the offering proceeds, there will definitely be more shares outstanding over which to spread the historical and prospective net income. This certainty provides an event of economic dilution to existing shareholders due to spreading the same earnings over more shares, at least in the short run, which must be overcome by the earnings power of the growth initiative.

This is a conundrum, since management and the board of directors are typically issuing new shares in order to increase the potential return to all shareholders, as part of their fiduciary duties and usually pecuniary interests if they have options to buy common stock. Nonetheless, it is the market's way of building in a reward for the buyers of the new issue, akin to an IPO discount for the risk that the market will not trade well after the deal for some time.

Chapter 4 | The Prospectus: Secondary Offerings and PIPEs

If the offering is conducted privately, then public market participants may not be aware of the pending offering until it is completed. In this case, the offering price can be based on the market trade with adjustments based on the nature of the security being sold, usually in a negotiated transaction. There is not a trading effect of additional shares being issued because there is no new supply of shares to come onto the market until some future date, which all market participants can anticipate.

Selling Stockholders. If any of the securities to be registered are to be offered by existing stockholders, the prospectus must name each such stockholder and the seller's relationship with the company. The occurrence of a secondary offering provides insiders and founders with an organized marketing effort that accommodates their shares. This is beneficial to market traders, because it helps keep an orderly and predictable level of volume. For an investor, the sellers' relationships to the company (whether the sellers are key managers or uninvolved passive investors) are indicators of insider sentiment, which should always be questioned when making an investment.

Many investors prefer that insiders are buying in the offering rather than selling, using this action as a proxy for management's perception of the chances of success in growing the earnings of the company.

Description of the Security Being Offered. If the company is selling common stock, either in a public or private offering, then the description of its terms is identical to the stock trading in the public market. If the securities are of a different class or priority than the publicly traded stock, then the description of its terms is much more detailed. PIPE transactions and structured public securities require additional thought as the structure influences price of the securities and relative risk and opportunity versus the common stock.

Structured public offerings may also be used where convertible preferred stock or convertible debt is issued. The terms are relatively standardized so that comparisons can be made and market efficiency is enhanced. These structures usually include a current coupon or dividend, preference in return of principal, and upside participation through conversion to common stock at some premium to the last traded price before closing. These structures are widely used when the issuer has a high confidence in the

Understanding and Evaluating Prospectuses, Offering Documents, and Proxy Statements

use of proceeds, but market participants want to be paid to wait and see whether the proceeds in fact add value to the common stock. Investors are willing to accept less upside (through the higher conversion price) in exchange for downside protection of a current coupon and preference.

The rapidly growing use by issuers of PIPEs is a direct result of limitations of capital markets to fund growth of small and midsize public companies. The transactions are negotiated to bridge the same expectations gap as the structured deals in the public market. However, as a negotiated structure, each company and structure needs to be assessed independently to determine where the tension between investor skepticism and company optimism should cross. This tension has been referred to as "fear versus greed." Essentially, the structure must tip the scale in favor of greed or investors will, and should, allocate capital elsewhere. Investors in PIPEs are rarely making strategic investments but are evaluating PIPEs alongside other potential investments as part of a portfolio's assets.

Description of Private Nature of the Offering, If That Is the Case. A registered offering will not contain the disclaimers on the cover page of the prospectus regarding the lack of a trading market for the securities. It is the lack of a trading market for the securities that is the essence of a private placement. The right of the investor to require the company to provide for liquid shares at some point in the future is a fundamental term of any private placement.

Since future liquidity is a premise of the investment, investors should question why the company elected not to undertake a public offering. The pricing should provide some additional return expectation for the illiquid nature of the securities, which might be avoided by the company if it sold new securities directly to the public market.

There are several legitimate reasons why a company may prefer a private placement, but the use of proceeds or market conditions should usually be consistent with the private nature of the offering. There is always some risk that the company could not find an underwriter to take the risk of selling the security in a firm commitment basis, so it's important for the investor to understand the reasons for the private offering.

Chapter 4 | The Prospectus: Secondary Offerings and PIPEs

- The size of the equity need is too small to attract underwriters for the effort involved in a public offering. This generally means the private placement is $5 to $50 million.
- The time to get to the public market exceeds the issuer's requirements. This could be the case, for instance, when the company has a time constraint on the investment of the proceeds in order to take full advantage of the opportunity. The use of proceeds would describe this constraint.
- The company has a small market capitalization relative to the size of the offering. This should cause investors to question how the trading market will accommodate the eventual liquidity event for the securities being purchased.
- There is little interest in the sector among institutional investors in public securities. This makes the investor story more difficult to tell, so a more limited investor base may be required to raise any capital.
- The company desires confidentiality during the offering process. This is very common when the use of proceeds is to complete an acquisition. The company may not have the luxury of time to prepare pro forma financial statements and audits of the acquired business, await SEC review, and attendant uncertainty of financial wherewithal to complete the deal. Sellers of companies are rarely willing to take market risk with the buyer for a long time.

PIPEs are usually offered pursuant to an exemption from registration with the SEC based upon Section 4(2) of the Securities Act. The conditions to this exemption include a requirement to provide a disclosure similar to that available in a public offering, so the offering memorandum should be reasonably complete. Typically, these offerings are made to a limited number of wealthy "qualified institutional buyers," and to "accredited investors."

Regulation D, under the Securities Act, limits a lawful private placement to only investors who, alone or together with a "purchaser representative," are sophisticated, and who can accept the lack of liquidity. The investors will fill out a subscription agreement indicating the basis for their qualifications to purchase the securities and agree to trading restrictions. Exhibit 4.2 provides an example of a PIPE offering disclosure.

Structures in Secondaries. Exhibit 4.3 summarizes typical structures of

Understanding and Evaluating Prospectuses, Offering Documents, and Proxy Statements

> **Exhibit 4.2: Cascade Closes $3.5 Million Financing**
>
> TUCSON, AX–(MARKET WIRE)–12/12/2005 Cascade Energy, Inc. (OTC BB: CSCE) is pleased to announce that the Company has closed the initial $1.75 million tranche of a $3.5 million financing.
>
> On November 30, 2005, the Company entered into a securities purchase agreement with an institutional investor for an aggregate purchase price of $3,500,000, of which the Company has issued (i) a $1,750,000 secured convertible debenture, convertible into shares of our common stock, par value $0.001, and (ii) a warrant to purchase an aggregate of 12,000,000 additional shares of our common stock at an exercise price of $0.2902 per share exercisable until November 30, 2010. An additional $1,750,000 secured convertible debenture will be issued on similar terms at the time the Company files a registration statement with the United States Securities and Exchange Commission. Pursuant to the registration rights agreement entered into between the Company and the investor, the Company agreed to file a registration statement registering the shares of our common stock issuable upon conversion of the convertible debentures, accrued interest and liquidated damages, and the shares of our common stock issuable upon the exercise of the warrants. The proceeds of the private placement will be used for general corporate purposes.
>
> The secured convertible debenture is convertible into shares of our common stock at any time by dividing the dollar amount being converted by the lower of $0.2902 or 80% of the volume the weighted average trading price per share of our common stock for five trading days immediately preceding the conversion date. The interest on the convertible debenture shall accrue on the outstanding principal balance at a rate of 5% per annum.
>
> Yorkville Advisors Management LLC will receive a fee of $350,000, which will be paid pro rata from the gross proceeds of each closing.
>
> The Company issued the securities to an accredited investor pursuant to exemptions from registration as set out in Rule 506 of Regulation D and/or Section 4(2) of the Securities Act of 1933, as amended. No advertising or general solicitation was employed in offering the securities.
>
> The securities offered in the private placement to the institutional investor the were not registered under the Securities Act of 1933 as amended (the "Act"), and may not be offered or sold in the United States absent registration, or an applicable exemption from registration, under the Act.
>
> **ABOUT CASCADE ENERGY**
>
> Cascade is an explorer for natural gas and oil. The primary objective of Cascade is to acquire, discover, upgrade and expand North American onshore oil and gas reserves towards near-term production and cash flow, together with identifying and participating in exploration opportunities. By maintaining a balanced debt and equity mix, Cascade's operating strategy is to become cash flow positive in the short term to allow the Company a re-investment of production dollars to enhance and grow company assets. By searching and identifying exploration and producing properties that fit the company's investment and production criteria, Cascade has formulated a strategy to prioritize assets that provide low risk, short payback period and long life reserves.

> **Notice Regarding Forward-Looking Statements**
>
> This news release contains "forward-looking statements," as that term is defined in Section 27A of the United States Securities Act of 1933 and Section 21E of the Securities Exchange Act of 1934. Statements in this press release which are not purely historical are forward-looking statements and include any statements regarding beliefs, plans, expectations or intentions regarding the future. Such forward-looking statements include, among other things, the acquisition of oil and gas reserves, any near-term production or cash flow and our ability to become cash flow positive in the short term to allow us to re-invest production dollars to enhance and grow company assets.
>
> Actual results could differ from those projected in any forward-looking statements due to numerous factors. Such factors include, among others, the numerous inherent uncertainties associated with oil and gas exploration. These forward-looking statements are made as of the date of this news release, and we assume no obligation to update the forward-looking statements, or to update the reasons why actual results could differ from those projected in the forward-looking statements. Although we believe that the beliefs, plans, expectations and intentions contained in this press release are reasonable, there can be no assurance that such beliefs, plans, expectations or intentions will prove to be accurate. Investors should consult all of the information set forth herein and should also refer to the risk factors disclosure outlined in our annual report on Form 10-KSB, our quarterly reports on Form 10-QSB and other periodic reports filed from time-to-time with the Securities and Exchange Commission.
>
> **ON BEHALF OF THE BOARD**
> *Cascade Energy, Inc.*
> *William Marshall — President*
> **Investor Relations**
> *Tel: 1-888-359-9565*

PIPE offerings. The most common form of PIPE today is straight common stock issued at a discount to current market price, possibly accompanied by warrants to acquire additional shares.[1] Prior to 2004, convertible preferred stock and convertible debt structures were more common. Typically, the terms of the private placement provide investors with conversion rights to participate in the upside of common stock appreciation. This opportunity is usually based upon the passage of time or an event in the future.

Use of Proceeds of the Offering. Issuers must tell potential investors how they intend to use the money raised through the offering. If the investor executed a confidentiality agreement, the company may provide detailed financial projections. These can form the basis for discussion with management regarding assumptions used to prepare the financial

Understanding and Evaluating Prospectuses, Offering Documents, and Proxy Statements

Exhibit 4.3: Summary of Structural Alternatives

Security	Benefits	Considerations
Common Stock	• Straight equity PIPE • Broad target investor base • May be executed with limited marketing	• May require (modest warrant coverage and/or short-lived options) • Dilution consideration given discounts
Convertible Preferred Stock	• Can result in less expensive cost of capital than common stock—depending on terms • Convertible at market price or at a premium to market price into a fixed or variable number of shares • May be executed with limited marketing	• May require (modest) warrant coverage and/or short-lived options • Dividend payment • Redemption/nonredemption features
Convertible Debt	• Can result in less expensive cost of capital than common stock—depending on terms • Convertible at market price or at a premium to market price into a fixed or variable number of shares • May be executed with limited marketing	• May require (modest) warrant coverage and/or short-lived options • Interest payment • Leverage and repayment profile • Antidilution features • May require financial covenants • Senior or subordinated ranking

Source: SG Cowan & Co., LLC.

projections and may allow the investor to consider other scenarios for sensitivity on earnings. The projections usually will impact pricing as well as structure or covenants in securities such that investor expectations are protected. The riskier the use of proceeds, the more likely it is for investors to demand a highly structured security prior to investing.

Pro Forma Financial Statements that Give Effect to the Offering. Offering documents provide pro forma financial information presenting the information as it would appear if the offering occurred at the beginning of a prior financial period. These pro forma financials help an investor evaluate the profitability, efficiency, liquidity (ability to meet short-term obligations), and solvency (ability to meet long-term obligations) of the company. These financial statements also establish a new baseline for comparative analysis in future periods, since the historical financial statements will no longer be comparable to the post-offering capital structure. Chapter 2 presents techniques for analyzing financial statements.

Chapter 4 | The Prospectus: Secondary Offerings and PIPEs

Risk Factors Related to the Securities Offered, the Use of Proceeds, or the Company, If Different From the Last Registration Statement. This section provides a discussion of the most significant factors that make the offering speculative or risky and should be read carefully by the investor and his or her representatives. It is the starting point for investment risk management by providing a checklist of factors to be considered. However, there could be other risks and mitigating factors that can be flushed out by investors. Investors in PIPEs have a greater burden of diligence than public investors. Exhibit 4.4 presents a list of common PIPE terminology found in offerings.

This checklist is only a partial list of considerations for PIPE investors:

- Do you understand how the company makes gross profit, and will it continue?
- Have management background checks been completed?
- What is the priority of the security being offered?

Exhibit 4.4: Sample PIPE Terms

Issue	Unregistered Common Stock
Market Price	Based on recent trailing average trading price
Purchase Price	Discount to market price
Warrants	May be included; negotiable
Investor Option	May be included; negotiable
Registration	Subsequent to closing
Expense	Issuer pays all reasonable transaction expenses

Issue	Unregistered Convertible Preferred Stock/Convertible Debt
Market Price	Based on recent trailing average trading price
Redemption/Term	Negotiable
Conversion Price	Convertible at market price or at a premium to closing price (into a fixed/variable number of shares)
Dividend/Interest	Negotiable
Additional Features	Forced conversion provisions, antidilution provisions
Warrants	May be included; negotiable
Investor Option	May be included; negotiable
Expenses	Issuer pays all reasonable transaction expenses

Source: SG Cowen & Co., LLC.

Understanding and Evaluating Prospectuses, Offering Documents, and Proxy Statements

- What other dilutive equity could be issued that could reduce the investor's return?
- What is the use of funds in the offering, and what are management's qualifications to engage in that business?
- Does management or others accountable for success have significant capital at risk?

If the investor cannot answer these questions based on the prospectus alone, he or she should seek the information from trusted sources or avoid the investment altogether.

IMPORTANCE OF SECONDARY PRICING

A great deal of academic finance research has focused on pricing of securities, and a discussion of valuation is core to the Chartered Financial Analyst curriculum. For public companies raising additional capital, Chapter 2 of this book, the valuation methods discussed in Chapter 3, and other literature provide useful guidance regarding the valuation of the common stock of a public company. Market signals based upon price are critical to the allocation of fresh capital to any company, and the efficiency of the signaling should be the greatest for public companies raising additional equity capital to fund growth.

Investors in public and private secondaries are critical to the ongoing creation of real wealth in the economy. The flow of capital from investors to companies is aided by the disclosure and market regulations under the Securities Act and the Exchange Act, even if the offering is a private placement. The growing importance of the PIPEs market helps smaller companies attract capital on terms that are cost effective for the company, with returns that are attractive to investors.

CONCLUSION

Investing in a new issue for a public company can be more rewarding than merely buying stock in the after-market. Management teams should try to enhance the prospects of the company, either by growth or risk reduction initiatives, which are achievable with the proceeds of the new issue. The terms of the secondary offering should be compelling enough to invite new capital to participate. The pricing mechanisms and trading characteristics of the company will help determine whether it seeks a public or private offering, and whether it issues common stock or a structured security. If the proceeds will fund a new growth initiative, the character of the company will be different after the offering. Even for existing public companies, which are raising additional capital, risks can be higher than for other established companies that may not have a need for external financing.

As a result, investors and their advisers should carefully study existing public disclosures and the prospectus for the new securities to assess the potential risks and rewards of the offering. Some of the key points to consider are:

- Why is the company raising capital, and does the intended use of proceeds appear reasonable?
- How long has the company been in business, and what has its past performance been? What is the company's financial position before and after the IPO?
- What types of securities are being offered, and are they senior to other securities of the company?
- What are the risk factors of the company, and do they match the risk tolerance of the investor? Be particularly careful when there is a limited trading float for existing stockholders, as liquidity may be difficult to achieve.
- Does the proposed offering price appear reasonable relative to other similar companies (for example, based on relative P/E ratios)? What is the expected dilution to existing investors? Is the company protecting their interests?
- What are the reputations of the investment banks, auditors, and law firms involved in performing due diligence?
- Is there a lead investor in a PIPE transaction, which has experience in successfully completing investments and eventually obtaining liquidity for the investment? What can be done to confirm their diligence?

Understanding and Evaluating Prospectuses, Offering Documents, and Proxy Statements

ENDNOTES
[1] PlacementTracker.com. Excluding issuers with a market capitalization of less than $25 million.

DISCUSSION QUESTIONS:
1. Why do companies issue new equity following an IPO?
2. What is the difference between a PIPE and a registered secondary offering?
3. What is the nature of the investor in a PIPE?
4. What factors should be considered when evaluating the reasons for a PIPE?
5. What is "dilution" in the context of a secondary offering? How is it different from an IPO dilution concept?
6. You are reviewing the prospectus for Wait Till Next Year Inc. (WTNY). At present, the P/E ratio of WTNY based on the offering price is 25 while the P/Es for similar peer companies cluster around 15. What else would you need to know to evaluate the reasonableness of the P/E ratio? Would you expect a structured offering or a straight common stock offering at this P/E ratio, and why?

EXERCISE:
Investors should have had the following concerns about Google's secondary, and been sufficiently comfortable with the implications, before investing:

1. The stock price has appreciated significantly in the short time since the IPO. Are you comfortable investing in the company at this price?
2. The company does not appear to need the money. They are generating cash and have no plans for the proceeds. The company still has proceeds of its IPO available. Why should the cash sit on Google's balance sheet rather than stay in the investor's account until a specific use of proceeds is established?
3. Is there any justification for certain share dilution that will result from the sale? This is a concern to existing owners of Google as well as new investors.
4. Is the company preparing for a battle for customers with Yahoo! and Microsoft?

Chapter 4 | The Prospectus: Secondary Offerings and PIPEs

RECOMMENDED READING

PIPEs: A Guide to Private Investing in Public Equity, Revised and updated edition, Steven Dresner, ed. with E. Kurt Kim, Bloomberg, 2005.

Convertible Securities: The Latest Instruments, Portfolio Strategies, and Valuation Analysis, Rev. edition, John P. Calamos, McGraw-Hill, 1998.

Analysis of Equity Investments: Valuation, John D. Stowe, Thomas R. Robinson, Jerald E. Pinto, Dennis W. McLeavey, CFA Institute, 2002.

5 The Prospectus: Mutual Funds

One of the most common types of prospectuses that you will encounter is that of a mutual fund. Regulations generally require that a prospectus be delivered to investors at the time of, or before, the purchase of a mutual fund. This requirement exists for a good reason. There are potential risks and conflicts of interests involved in the investments and operation of a mutual fund, and it is important that an investor understand these factors. You as the adviser should encourage the investor to review the prospectus. You can assist in this process by pointing out key points regarding risks and opportunities that the investor should consider. This chapter discusses the regulations that govern mutual fund prospectuses and how to evaluate them to uncover the risks and opportunities.

MUTUAL FUND STRUCTURE AND REGULATION

While the term *mutual funds* is often used to describe a wide variety of fund types (as we have done in the title of this chapter), the U.S. SEC uses more precise language. The Investment Company Act of 1940 regulates the organization of investment companies, including mutual funds, and the disclosure of relevant information about the investment objectives, structure, and operations of investment companies. The SEC categorizes investment companies into three main types:[1]
- Open-end companies, also known as mutual funds

Understanding and Evaluating Prospectuses, Offering Documents, and Proxy Statements

- Closed-end companies, also known as closed-end funds
- Unit investment trusts or UITs

Note that the SEC uses the term mutual funds specifically for open-end investment companies. Other fund types, such as exchange-traded funds, are legally classified into one of the above fund types, but may have unique characteristics that are discussed further in this section.

Open-End Companies or Mutual Funds. In an open-end investment company, shares in the fund are purchased at net asset value from the fund or through a broker. Sales loads or transaction fees may also apply. Net asset value is the value of fund investments minus liabilities, and is normally expressed on a per share basis. When an investor desires to sell shares in an open-end investment company, they are redeemed by the fund (less any transaction or redemption fees that may apply).

Open-end investment companies do not have a fixed number of shares and sell new shares on a continuous basis. Sometimes a fund's trustees may decide to close the fund to new investors. In this case, existing fund holders may be permitted to purchase new shares and usually can reinvest dividends.

There are a number of parties involved in the oversight and management of an open-end investment company, as depicted in Figure 5.1. The fund holders are represented by a board of directors or trustees. The board oversees the fund and hires an investment adviser or management company to manage the fund's portfolio and a distributor to sell fund shares. Other parties include the custodian who holds the fund's assets, a transfer agent who processes trades, and independent accountants who audit the fund's financial statements. Ideally, these parties are all truly independent; however, often the management company sponsored the fund at inception and has representatives on the board. In the past, many boards have been reluctant to replace the management company. This has changed after a number of recent fund scandals. Boards now have more independent directors who have more direct responsibility over the fund, such as in the hiring and oversight of the auditors. There have even been instances of boards replacing fund managers, such as:

Chapter 5 | The Prospectus: Mutual Funds

The board of directors of the $7 billion Clipper Fund shocked the mutual fund industry by deciding Nov. 30 to hire new managers. In the 65-year history of funds, boards have tossed out incumbent managers only a handful of times. But boards find themselves under increased scrutiny following the fund-trading and sales scandals uncovered by New York Attorney General Elliot Spitzer and the Securities & Exchange Commission. The move by Clipper's board, which also included a big cut in management fees, is a sign of things to come, say analysts and fund attorneys.[2]

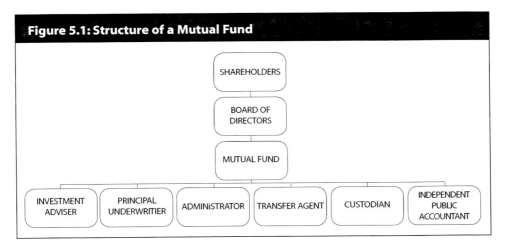

Figure 5.1: Structure of a Mutual Fund

Since new shares are purchased from the fund itself, each investor must be furnished with a prospectus containing information about the fund's fees, expenses, objectives, strategies, and risks, as described further below. In response to requests for fund information, some open-end funds provide a "fund profile" to prospective investors. This profile is a summary of key points found in the prospectus. In such cases, the prospectus is delivered later when an investment is made. Fund companies will, however, recommend that the prospectus be read carefully *before* making an investment, and this advice should always be followed. Open-end funds must also have a statement of additional information (SAI) that is available to investors upon request. (It is not automatically provided.) The SAI provides additional useful information for fund investors. The contents of the prospectus and SAI are discussed in detail below.

In addition to these documents, periodic reports on fund holdings and performance are required. An annual report must be provided to fund holders within 60 days of the end of the fund's fiscal year. A semiannual report is due 60 days after the middle of the fund's fiscal year.

Closed-End Companies. Unlike open-end investment companies, closed-end investment companies normally sell a fixed number of shares in an initial public offering (IPO). After the IPO, these shares trade on a secondary market and are usually not redeemable. The price paid by subsequent investors therefore depends on market conditions such as supply and demand. The fund may trade at a discount or premium to net asset value.

The structure of a closed-end company is similar to that depicted for an open-end company, but the requirements regarding the provision of a prospectus differ. Since closed-end funds do not continuously sell new shares, the prospectus is delivered to the original investors only at the time of the IPO. Subsequent investors who purchase shares from another fund holder do not automatically receive a prospectus. Subsequent investors would be well-advised, however, to obtain and evaluate the IPO prospectus (generally available online). Closed-end funds do not use a fund profile; however, they are required to make available a statement of additional information and file the semiannual and annual reports as with open-end funds.

Unit Investment Trusts. Unit investment trusts (UIT) have some characteristics of closed-end investment companies and others of open-end investment companies. Typically, a UIT makes an initial offering of a fixed number of shares. The proceeds are used to buy a portfolio of securities that is typically not traded but, instead, held until maturity. A UIT will terminate at some particular date with proceeds paid to any remaining investors. Shares in a UIT may be redeemable by the UIT, and there may be provisions for new investors to purchase these shares. Shares may also be purchased in a secondary market from other investors. Since a fixed portfolio is purchased, there is typically no need for an investment management company or board.

The trust will have provisions as to how the investments are to be monitored and sold.

The UIT must provide purchasers of shares from the fund with a prospectus. A UIT prospectus may also contain a list of securities held, or intended to be held, in the portfolio. UITs do not use a profile and are not required to provide an SAI.

Exchange-Traded Funds (ETFs). While not a separate category under the SEC's classification system, the proliferation of new ETFs and the popularity of using ETFs in asset allocation warrant a separate discussion. For Investment Company Act of 1940 purposes, an ETF is classified as either an open-end company or an UIT. An ETF is typically designed to mimic some index or asset class and is similar to an open-end index fund. Recent additions to ETFs include those that invest in commodities. ETFs are initially issued in large blocks called "creation units." These are typically issued to large institutional investors in exchange for a basket of the underlying securities. The blocks are then split up and the individual shares are traded on a secondary market. Only creation units can be redeemed by the fund, and this is done in exchange for the underlying basket of securities. Individual investors therefore sell their shares in the secondary market rather than redeeming them.

ETFs provide a prospectus to purchasers of creation units. For secondary market purchasers, they can either provide a prospectus or a "product description." The product description is similar to a profile in that it provides key prospectus information and details about how to obtain a prospectus, which must be available upon request. Some ETFs will also have an SAI and provide periodic reports (if they are classified as an open-end fund).

EVALUATING THE FUND PROSPECTUS

Regardless of the type of investment company under consideration, you should obtain and read all available information including the prospectus and statement of additional information. In this section, we discuss how to evaluate the most commonly encountered mutual fund prospectus—that of an open-end investment company. We also highlight key points that apply to other investment company prospectuses.

Open-end investment companies must file a registration statement with

Understanding and Evaluating Prospectuses, Offering Documents, and Proxy Statements

the SEC on Form N-1A. This form contains the requirements for what must be provided to investors in the prospectus as well as in the statement of additional information. It also requires additional information that is not required to be made available to investors. You can view Form N-1A on the SEC's Web site. This document contains the prospectus in Part A, the Statement of Additional Information in Part B, and other information in Part C (Part C is not required to be provided to investors but available for viewing in the Form N-1A). Within each section, the SEC designates the numbering and order of each item. In most cases, investors will be evaluating a prospectus in hard copy form obtained from the mutual fund company. In this case, the material will not have item numbers, but should appear in a similar order to the SEC filing. The discussion below includes the SEC's item number in parentheses for each piece of required information in case you are evaluating an electronic version of the firm's N-1A as filed with the SEC.

Front and Back Cover Pages (Item 1). The front cover page of a mutual fund prospectus must include the fund's name, the date of the prospectus, and a statement that the SEC has neither approved nor disapproved the fund shares. A fund may also include a statement of its investment objectives, a brief description of its operations, or other additional information. For example, a recent prospectus for the Janus Twenty Fund stated that the fund is closed to new investors but that current investors may continue to invest.

The back cover page must reference the SAI that contains additional information about the fund, and a statement to the following effect:

> Additional information about the fund's investments is available in the fund's annual and semiannual reports to shareholders. In the fund's annual report, you will find a discussion of the market conditions and investment strategies that significantly affected the fund's performance during its last fiscal year.

The fund must disclose that the SAI and the fund's annual and semiannual reports are available without charge, and explain how shareholders in the fund may make inquiries to the fund. They must also provide a toll-free or collect telephone number for investors to call. If the reports are available through the fund's Web site, the Internet address can be given. You should order or download the periodic reports and SAI so that they can be evaluated at the same time as the prospectus.

Risk/Return Summary: Investments, Risks, and Performance (Item 2). In this section, the fund discloses its investment objectives or goals. It may also identify its type or category (for example, that it is a money market fund or a balanced fund). Janus Twenty Fund describes its objective as long-term growth of capital and notes that the fund is designed for "long-term investors who... can tolerate the greater risks associated with common stock investments."

The fund must also discuss its principal investment strategies. This includes the types of securities in which the fund invests and any policy to concentrate in securities of issuers in a particular industry or group of industries. Janus Twenty Fund describes its investment strategy as follows:

> The Fund pursues its objective by investing primarily in a core group of 20–30 common stocks selected for their growth potential. The portfolio manager applies a "bottom up" approach in choosing investments.
>
> In other words, the Fund's portfolio manager looks at companies one at a time to determine if a company is an attractive investment opportunity and if it is consistent with the Fund's investment policies. If the portfolio manager is unable to find such investments, the Fund's uninvested assets may be held in cash or similar investments, subject to the Fund's specific investment policies.
>
> Within the parameters of its specific investment policies, the Fund may invest without limit in foreign equity and debt securities. The Fund will limit its investment in high-yield/high-risk bonds to less than 35 percent of its net assets.

The prospectus will then discuss the principal risks of investing in the fund. This begins with a narrative risk disclosure. For funds other than money market funds, this disclosure must include a statement that a potential loss of money is a risk of investing in the fund. Money market funds

Understanding and Evaluating Prospectuses, Offering Documents, and Proxy Statements

must disclose that they are not insured by the Federal Deposit Insurance Corporation or any other government agency and that losses are possible. Janus Twenty notes that its main risks are that returns may vary, that investors may lose money, that the value of the fund may decrease due to a decline in one of the fund's holdings or in the stock market as a whole, and that the fund is nondiversified. Since the fund holds only 20–30 names, a loss in any one name can have a significant impact on the fund's overall returns.

The prospectus must display a risk/return bar chart and table. The chart and table from the Janus Twenty Fund is presented in Exhibit 5.1. It begins with a bar chart showing the annual returns in each of the last ten years. This shows graphically that while there were strong returns in most of the years, a string of three very poor years lasted from 2000–2002. Further, the chart shows that the fund lost 25.42 percent in its worst *quarter*, and that its best quarter was a 38.35 percent gain.

The table shows average returns over one-, five-, and ten-year holding periods and compares these returns to those of its benchmark. In this case, the firm has changed its benchmark and therefore lists both the Russell 1000 Growth Index and the S&P 500 Index. The notes and disclosures beneath the chart are required. For any mutual fund, it is important to compare the performance to a benchmark. For any changes in benchmarks, the investor should consider whether the change was appropriate or done to make the manager look better. A change in benchmark may also signal a change in management style.

Risk/Return Summary: Fee Table (Item 3). This table describes the fees and expenses that the investor may pay if they buy and hold shares of the fund. Janus Twenty Fund's fee table is included in Exhibit 5.2. It discloses that 0.88 percent of the fund's assets are taken as fees each year, and that there are no shareholder fees. Shareholder fees or loads are charged by some funds when investors purchase or sell shares. The sales load is used to pay sales commissions and to discourage investors from turning over funds frequently.

Since fees reduce the investors' return, this information should be examined closely in comparison with other similar funds to see if the fees

Chapter 5 | The Prospectus: Mutual Funds

Exhibit 5.1: Risk/Return Bar Chart and Table Included in Janus Twenty Prospectus

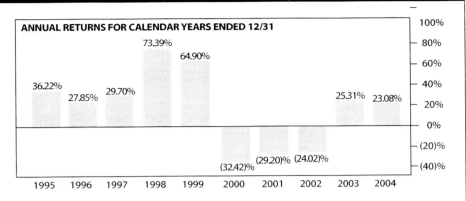

ANNUAL RETURNS FOR CALENDAR YEARS ENDED 12/31

Year	Return
1995	36.22%
1996	27.85%
1997	29.70%
1998	73.39%
1999	64.90%
2000	(32.42)%
2001	(29.20)%
2002	(24.02)%
2003	25.31%
2004	23.08%

Best Quarter: 4th-1999 38.35%   Worst Quarter: 4th-2000 (25.42)%

	Average Annual Total Return for Periods Ended 12/31/04			
	1 year	5 years	10 years	Since Inception (4/30/85)
Janus Twenty Fund				
Return Before Taxes	23.89%	(10.81)%	13.81%	13.68%
Return After Taxes on Distributions	23.89%	(11.04)%	11.79%	11.68%
Return After Taxes on Distributions and Sale of Fund Shares[1]	15.54%	(8.91)%	11.13%	11.20%
Russell 1000® Growth Index[2] (reflects no deduction for expenses, fees, or taxes)	6.30%	(9.29)%	9.59%	11.68%
S&P 500® Index[3] (reflects no deduction for expenses, fees, or taxes)	10.88%	(2.30)%	12.07%	12.96%

(1) If the Fund incurs a loss, which generates a tax benefit, the Return After Taxes on Distributions and Sale of Fund Shares may exceed the Fund's other return figures.

(2) Effective February 25, 2005, the Fund changed its primary benchmark from the S&P 500® Index to the Russell 1000® Growth Index. The new primary benchmark will provide a more appropriate comparison to the Fund's investment style. The Russell 1000® Growth Index measures the performance of those Russell 1000 companies with higher price-to-book ratios and higher forecasted growth values. The Fund will retain the S&P 500® Index as a secondary index.

(3) The S&P 500® Index is the Standard & Poor's Composite Index of 500 stocks, a widely recognized, unmanaged index of common stock prices.

Understanding and Evaluating Prospectuses, Offering Documents, and Proxy Statements

> After-tax returns are calculated using the historical highest individual federal marginal income tax rates and do not reflect the impact of state and local taxes. Actual after-tax returns depend on your individual tax situation and may differ from those shown in the preceding table. The after-tax return information shown above does not apply to Fund shares held through a tax-deferred account, such as a 401(k) plan or IRA.
>
> The Fund's past performance (before and after taxes) does not necessarily indicate how it will perform in the future.

Source: *Investment Company Institute* 2005 Investment Company Fact Book, *45th Edition*

Exhibit 5.2: Janus Twenty Fund Fee Table

The following table describes the shareholder fees and annual fund operating expenses that you may pay if you buy and hold shares of the Fund. All of the fees and expenses shown were determined based on net assets as of the fiscal year ended October 31, 2004, restated to reflect a reduction in the Fund's management fee effective July 1, 2004. All expenses are shown without the effect of expense offset arrangements.

Shareholder fees are those paid directly from your investment and may include sales loads, redemption fees or exchange fees. The Fund is a no-load investment, so you will generally not pay any shareholder fees when you buy or sell shares of the Fund.

Annual fund operating expenses are paid out of the Fund's assets and include fees for portfolio management, maintenance of shareholder accounts, shareholder servicing, accounting and other services. You do not pay these fees directly but, as the example shows, these costs are borne indirectly by all shareholders.

Annual Fund Operating Expenses (deducted from fund assets)			
	Management Fee	Other Expenses	Total Annual Fund Operating Expenses
Janus Twenty Fund	0.64%	0.24%	0.88%

EXAMPLE: This example is intended to help you compare the cost of investing in the Fund with the cost of investing in other mutual funds. The example assumes that you invest $10,000 in the Fund for the time periods indicated and then redeem all of your shares at the end of those periods. The example also assumes that your investment has a 5% return each year and that the Fund's operating expenses remain the same. Although your actual costs may be higher or lower, based on these assumptions your costs would be:

1 year	3 years	5 years	10 years
$90	$281	$488	$1,084

Source: *Investment Company Institute* 2005 Investment Company Fact Book, *45th Edition*

are appropriate for the level of management involved in the fund.

Investment Objectives, Principal Investment Strategies, Related Risks, and Disclosure of Portfolio Holdings (Item 4). This section takes a closer look at the fund's principal investment strategies and risks, with a more detailed discussion of the information in the risk/return summary.

For example, Janus Twenty describes general portfolio policies for stepping outside its general strategy of selecting 20–30 U.S. stocks. Funds inflows, for example, could result in a large cash position. In addition, other securities that may be used in the portfolio include foreign equities, debt securities, indexed or structured securities, high-yield/high-risk bonds (up to 35 percent of fund assets), options, futures, swaps and other derivative securities, short sales (up to 8 percent of fund assets), and securities purchased on a when-issued or delayed-delivery commitment. Up to 15 percent of fund assets can be invested in illiquid investments that cannot be disposed of quickly.

Janus Twenty also offers a more detailed discussion of specific risk factors. These include their lack of diversification, risks related to holding foreign securities and high-yield instruments, and risks related to holding smaller or newer companies. One interesting segment is their description for "How does the fund try to reduce risk?" In this section, they describe how options and other derivative instruments may be used to "hedge" the portfolio against certain risks the managers anticipate. The prospectus notes that if the risks fail to materialize, the performance could be worse than it would have been if the risk had not been hedged.

Management, Organization, and Capital Structure (Item 5). This section contains the name and address of each investment adviser of the fund and describes the investment adviser's experience and the services that it provides. It will also describe the compensation of each investment adviser. The prospectus for Buffalo Funds, which includes several funds in one prospectus, provides the following:

> Kornitzer Capital Management, Inc. ("KCM" or the "Adviser") is the manager and investment adviser for each of the Buffalo Funds. KCM was founded in 1989. In addition to managing and advising the Buffalo Funds, it provides investment advisory services to a broad variety of

Understanding and Evaluating Prospectuses, Offering Documents, and Proxy Statements

individual, corporate, and other institutional clients. As manager, KCM provides or pays the cost of all management, supervisory, and administrative services required in the normal operation of the Funds. This includes investment management and supervision; fees of the custodian, independent auditors and legal counsel; fees and expenses of officers, directors and other personnel; rent; shareholder services; and other items incidental to corporate administration. KCM is located at 5420 West 61st Place, Shawnee Mission, KS 66205. As compensation for KCM's services, each Fund (except the Buffalo Micro Cap Fund) pays KCM a fee each month at the annual rate of 1.00 percent of each Fund's average daily net assets (1.45 percent for the Buffalo Micro Cap Fund).

Operating expenses not required in the normal operation of the Funds are payable by the Funds. These expenses include taxes, interest, governmental charges, and fees, including registration of the Funds with the Securities and Exchange Commission and the various states, brokerage costs, dues, and all extraordinary costs including expenses arising out of anticipated or actual litigation or administrative proceedings. A discussion regarding the Board of Trustees' basis for approving the Funds' investment advisory agreements is included in the Funds' annual report to shareholders for the fiscal year ended March 31, 2005.

Next, the prospectus will provide a brief description of the portfolio manager. It will also include a statement that the SAI provides additional information about the portfolio manager's compensation, other accounts managed by the portfolio manager(s), and the portfolio manager's(s') ownership of securities in the fund. Two of the Buffalo Funds manager profiles are provided below, along with their accompanying statement.

John Kornitzer. Mr. Kornitzer is the president and chief investment officer of KCM, and has over 35 years of investment experience. He served as investment manager at several Fortune 500 companies prior to founding KCM in 1989. Mr. Kornitzer received his degree in Business Administration from St. Francis College in Pennsylvania. Mr. Kornitzer is the lead portfolio manager of the Buffalo Balanced Fund.

Kent Gasaway, CFA, Portfolio Manager. Mr. Gasaway joined KCM in 1991 and has more than 22 years of research and management experience. Previously, Mr. Gasaway spent 10 years as an investment professional with Waddell & Reed Mutual Funds Group. He holds a B.S. in Business Administration from Kansas State University. Mr. Gasaway serves as lead portfolio manager of the Buffalo High Yield Fund. He also serves as co-portfolio manager of the Buffalo Large Cap, Buffalo Micro Cap, Buffalo Mid Cap, Buffalo Small Cap, Buffalo Science & Technology, and Buffalo USA Global Funds.

The Statement of Additional Information provides additional information about the Portfolio Managers' compensation, other accounts managed by the Portfolio Managers and their ownership of securities in the Buffalo Funds.

In this section, the fund is also required to describe any material pending legal proceedings, other than ordinary routine litigation incidental to the business, to which the fund or the fund's investment adviser or principal underwriter is a party.

Finally, with regard to the capital structure, the fund must disclose any unique or unusual restrictions on the right freely to retain or dispose of the fund's shares or material obligations or potential liabilities associated with holding the fund's shares that may expose investors to significant risks.

In evaluating this section, the investor should examine the experience of the portfolio manager and their advisory firm. If they are new to this fund, their performance at other funds should be examined. Any pending legal proceedings or significant restrictions noted in this section should also be scrutinized and consideration should be given to seeking out similar funds in the same asset class without such items.

Shareholder Information (Item 6). This section begins with a description of how the fund's shares are priced. Since mutual funds have many investments that fluctuate in price throughout the day, buyers on a particular day usually do not know in advance what they will pay for the shares. Instead, the price is based on the fund's overall value at the time the market closes. The fund prospectus must disclose the specific details, including the

Understanding and Evaluating Prospectuses, Offering Documents, and Proxy Statements

method used to value fund shares, when calculations of net asset value are made, and that the price at which a purchase or redemption is effected will be determined after the order is placed.

In its prospectus, Buffalo Funds discusses the fact that there are no sales commissions or Rule 12b-1 distribution fees charged on investments in the fund. They also provide information as to how to purchase shares (phone, Internet, automatic investments, cashier's checks, etc.) and the minimum amount required for initial investments, additional investments, and account size. They also include the following discussion related to share pricing:

> Shares of each Fund are purchased or redeemed at their net asset value per share next calculated after your purchase order and payment or redemption order is received in "good order" by the Funds. In the case of certain authorized financial intermediaries, such as broker-dealers, fund supermarkets, retirement plan record-keepers, or other financial institutions that have made satisfactory payment or redemption arrangements with the Funds, orders will be processed at the net asset value per share next effective after receipt by such intermediary, consistent with applicable laws and regulations. Other intermediaries may set cut-off times for the receipt of orders that are earlier than the Funds'.
>
> A Fund's net asset value is calculated by subtracting from the Fund's total assets any liabilities and then dividing this amount by the total outstanding shares as of the date of the calculation. The net asset value per share is computed once daily, Monday through Friday, at 4:00 p.m. (Eastern Time), on days when the Funds are open for business. The Funds are generally closed on weekends, days when the New York Stock Exchange is not open for unrestricted trading, and certain national holidays as disclosed in the SAI.
>
> .... When market quotations are not readily available, any security or other asset is valued at its fair value as determined under procedures approved by the applicable Buffalo Funds Board. Under these fair value procedures, the authority to determine estimates of fair value has been delegated to a valuation committee consisting of members of the Funds' Adviser and administrator. These fair value procedures are used by the

valuation committee to price a security when corporate events, events in the securities market, or world events cause the Funds' management to believe that a security's last sale price may not reflect its actual market value. In addition, the fair value procedures are used by the valuation committee to price thinly traded securities (such as junk bonds and small- or micro-cap securities) when Funds' management believes that the last sale price may not accurately reflect the securities' market value. By using fair value pricing procedures, the goal is to ensure that the Funds are accurately priced. The effects of using fair value pricing are that the value derived may only best reflect the value as determined, and the real value may vary higher or lower. To the extent that the valuation committee determines the fair market value of a security, it is possible that the fair market value determined by the committee will not exactly match the market price of the security when the security is sold by a Fund.

The procedures for redeeming shares must also be discussed, including any restrictions on redemptions, redemption charges, whether the fund has reserved the right to redeem in kind, any procedure that a shareholder can use to sell the fund's shares to the fund or its underwriter through a broker-dealer, any charges that may be imposed for such service, any circumstances under which the fund may redeem shares automatically without action by the shareholder or under which the fund may delay honoring a request for redemption for a certain time after a shareholder's investment, and any restrictions on, or costs associated with, transferring shares held in street name accounts. For example, Buffalo Funds notes that a guaranteed signature is required for any redemptions exceeding $25,000, and that redemptions from IRAs or other retirement plans must indicate whether taxes should be withheld.

The prospectus must also describe the fund's policy with respect to dividends and distributions, including any options that shareholders may have as to the receipt of dividends and distributions (for example, reinvestment). Further, there must be a discussion of the risks, policies, restrictions, and fees, if any, surrounding frequent purchases and redemptions of fund shares.

Understanding and Evaluating Prospectuses, Offering Documents, and Proxy Statements

The tax consequences of investing in mutual funds can be complicated, and the fund is required to discuss them in the prospectus. This discussion must include:

1. That fund distributions may be taxed as ordinary income and capital gains (which may be taxable at different rates depending on the length of time the fund holds its assets) and whether the fund expects that its distributions will consist primarily of ordinary income or capital gains.
2. That distributions, whether received in cash or reinvested in additional shares of the Fund, may be subject to federal income tax.
3. That an exchange of the fund's shares for shares of another fund will be treated as a sale of the fund's shares, and any gain on the transaction may be subject to federal income tax.

For this section, the main focus of evaluation should be on any restrictions on fund redemptions and any redemption charges. The valuation of the fund's investments and taxation will be similar from fund to fund. However, you may want to watch out for any disclosure that highlights a particular tax impact. For example, a fund selling covered calls may be more inclined to generate short-term gains, which are taxed at ordinary tax rates.

Distribution Arrangements (Item 7). Many funds are distributed (sold) via brokers, who are paid a commission for bringing new investors to the funds. In addition, many funds try to discourage investors from short-term holding periods. Many funds thus include "loads," which are used to pay commissions and which create a hurdle to selling the shares quickly. In its prospectus, a fund must describe any sales loads, including deferred sales loads, applied to purchases of the fund's shares. They must also include in a table any front-end sales load (and each breakpoint in the sales load, if any) as a percentage of both the offering price and the net amount invested.

Buffalo Funds provides the following disclosure related to its redemption load:[3]

Redemption Fee—If shares of the Buffalo High Yield, Buffalo Micro Cap, or Buffalo Small Cap Funds are sold or exchanged within six months of their purchase, or if shares of the Buffalo Balanced, Buffalo Large Cap, Buffalo Mid Cap, Buffalo Science & Technology, or Buffalo USA Global Funds are sold or exchanged within two months of their purchase, a redemption fee of 2.00 percent of the value of the shares sold or exchanged will be assessed. The Fund will employ the "first in, first out" method to calculate the two month or six month holding period. The redemption fee does not apply to shares purchased through reinvested distributions (dividends and capital gains). The redemption fee is retained by the Fund to help pay transaction and tax costs that long-term investors may bear when the Fund incurs brokerage or other transaction expenses and/or realizes capital gains as a result of selling securities to meet investor redemptions.

In addition, SEC Rule 12b-1 allows funds to pass through to investors certain marketing-related expenses. If the Fund has adopted a plan under Rule 12b-1, the fund must state the amount of the distribution fee payable under the plan and explain that because these fees are paid out of the Fund's assets on an ongoing basis, over time these fees will increase the cost of the investment and may cost more than paying other types of sales charges.

As with the disclosures related to management fees, any loads or 12b-1 fees should be examined in comparison to other available funds in this asset class. If similar performing funds can be found with lower distribution fees, they should be considered as an alternative.

Financial Highlights Information (Item 8). Exhibit 5.3 contains the page from the Janus Twenty Fund prospectus that provides the information required in Item 8.

Net asset value is the per share value of the fund's investments. Net investment income/loss represents dividends or interest payments generated by the fund's holdings. The net gain/loss on securities is the change in the value of the fund's holdings due to price movement. Combined, the income and gain/loss constitute the investment performance of the fund. For example, in 2003, Janus Twenty collected $0.17 per share in dividends or interest from its holdings while the value of its holdings increased by $3.63 per share. Combined, these resulted in a total return of $3.80, which represented a return of 12.6 percent. By contrast, in 2001, the fund collected $0.32 of dividends and interest but the value of its holdings declined by $33.33 per fund share. This resulted in a total net loss of $30.01 or a (47.43) percent return.

Distributions represent money that is paid out to shareholders. Since the assets are no longer held in the fund, distributions reduce the per share value of the fund. As is apparent in the table, distributions may bear no relationship to the actual fund performance for a given year since distributions are based on realized gains and losses while fund performance includes unrealized gains and losses. Also, distributions may be made as a return of capital.

Finally, the table provides investors with information regarding the expenses of the fund as a percentage of total assets, as well as the portfolio turnover. Turnover refers to the percentage of net assets that is transferred from one investment to another during the course of the year. Whenever one security is sold and another is purchased, turnover is created. Since taxes are levied when securities are sold, turnover has a direct impact on many investors. Thus, generally, taxable investors should prefer funds with low turnover of investments, all else being equal. For funds in tax-deferred accounts such as IRAs, this may not be a concern. High levels of turnover, however, should also be evaluated in relation to the objectives of the firm. If the firm has an objective of making long-term strategic investments but has a high turnover rate, this inconsistency should be questioned.

Key Points in the Prospectus of Other Investment Companies. The items discussed above for an open-end investment company will also be found in a prospectus for a closed-end company or unit investment trust, and the key points to evaluate remain the same (investment objective, risks, fees, management, legal proceedings, and redemption restrictions). There are additional considerations, however, for the prospectus of a closed-end fund or unit investment trust.

Since a closed-end fund involves an IPO such as those discussed in Chapter 3, the offering price is only important to the initial purchaser. This

Chapter 5 | The Prospectus: Mutual Funds

Exhibit 5.3: Financial Highlights from Janus Twenty Prospectus

The financial highlights table is intended to help you understand the Fund's financial performance for the past 5 years through October 31st of each fiscal year shown. Items "Net asset value, beginning of period" through "Net asset value, end of period" reflect financial results for a single Fund share.

The total returns in the table represent the rate that an investor would have earned (or lost) on an investment in the Fund (assuming reinvestment of all dividends and distributions). This information has been audited by PricewaterhouseCoopers LLP, whose report, along with the Fund's financial statements, is included in the Annual Report, which is available upon request and incorporated by reference into the SAI.

Janus Twenty Fund					
	\multicolumn{5}{c}{Years ended October 31}				
	2004	2003	2002	2001	2000
Net asset value, beginning of period	$34.06	$30.47	$36.31	$71.07	$69.72
Income from investment operations:					
Net investment income/(loss)	0.03	0.17	0.21	0.32	—[1]
Net gain/(loss) on securities (both realized and unrealized)	5.68	3.63	(5.71)	(33.33)	5.62
Total from investment operations	5.71	3.80	(5.50)	(33.01)	5.62
Less distributions:					
Dividends (from net investment income)	(0.17)	(0.21)	(0.34)	—	(0.19)
Distributions (from capital gains)	—	—	—	(1.75)	(4.08)
Total distributions	(0.17)	(0.21)	(0.34)	(1.75)	(4.27)
Net asset value, end of period	$39.60	$34.06	$30.47	$36.31	$71.07
Total return	16.85%[2]	12.60%	(15.35)%	(47.43)%	7.40%
Net assets, end of period (in millions)	$9,023	$9,821	$10,107	$14,378	$31,008
Average net assets for the period (in millions)	$9,320	$9,749	$12,573	$20,321	$34,529
Ratio of gross expenses to average net assets[3]	0.89%	0.88%	0.84%	0.84%	0.86%
Ratio of net expenses to average net assets	0.89%	0.88%	0.83%	0.84%	0.85%
Ratio of net investment income/(loss) to average net assets	0.06%	0.52%	0.56%	0.63%	(0.13)%
Portfolio turnover rate	14%	44%	53%	50%	27%

(1) Net investment income/(loss) aggregated less than $0.01 on a per share basis for the fiscal year end.
(2) In 2004, Janus Capital and/or Janus Services LLC fully reimbursed the Fund for a loss on a transaction resulting from certain trading, pricing, and/or shareholder activity errors, which otherwise would have reduced total return by less than 0.01%.
(3) The effect of non-recurring costs assumed by Janus Capital is included in the ratio of gross expenses to average net assets and was less than 0.01%.

Source: Janus Twenty Fund prospectus, page 42.

purchaser should be concerned about how much of the proceeds are going into fund investment versus fund sponsors. The outside front cover of a closed-end fund must disclose the price to the public, any sales loads, and the proceeds to be received by the fund or others involved in the process. The prospectus will also disclose how the proceeds are to be used (investment, debt repayment, acquisition of noninvestment assets, commissions, and other organizational expenses). This information should be evaluated to determine how much of the offering price is actually accruing to fund investors in terms of investments. Any amounts paid for sales loads or fees result in an immediate loss to investors and would need to be made up from future performance. For a closed-end fund, disclosure must also be made of the secondary market on which the shares will trade. Investors should consider the liquidity of the market in which the fund's shares will trade. Ideally, they will be traded on a national securities exchange or NASDAQ. Some closed-end funds use leverage. If so, the fund must disclose the effect of leverage on the returns to shareholders versus the return from the investment portfolio alone. Any use of leverage should be scrutinized carefully, since this adds risk to the fund.

In the case of a unit-investment trust, detailed disclosures are required about how the trust is organized, how the investments are managed, and the procedures for withdrawal or redemption. Since there may not be a management company, the investor should evaluate who the trustees of the trust assets ares, their experience in such matters, and solvency. There may also be officers and directors of the trust and the compensation of these persons must be disclosed. Investors should consider if this compensation is reasonable for a nonactively traded investment company and in relation to similar UITs. The trust should also provide a schedule showing the component securities that make up the offering price. The investor can therefore determine what they are buying. Most importantly, the investor should evaluate how easily the UIT can be redeemed or sold in a secondary market.

EVALUATING THE STATEMENT OF ADDITIONAL INFORMATION

The statement of additional information should be obtained and evaluated at the same time as the prospectus. Open-end and closed-end investment companies must make the SAI available upon request. The SEC specifies the contents of the SAI, as they do for the prospectus. Since the SAI is part of the fund's registration statement SEC filing, the SEC's item numbers continue consecutively from the prospectus section.

Cover Page and Table of Contents (Item 9). The front cover page of the SAI must include the fund's name. Note that some funds are issued as a series, where multiple funds are found in a single SAI and prospectus. For example the Tweedy, Browne Global Value Fund and Tweedy, Browne American Value Fund are each actually a series of Tweedy, Browne Fund, Inc. In these cases, the name of the registrant must also be included on the cover of the SAI (that is, Tweedy, Browne Fund, Inc.). The cover must also include a statement that the SAI is not a prospectus and how the prospectus may be obtained. Finally, it must include the date of the SAI and of the prospectus to which it relates. Pilgrim Baxter Funds use the following statement:[4]

> This Statement of Additional Information (SAI) is not a prospectus. It is intended to provide additional information regarding the activities and operations of PBHG Funds (the "Trust" or "Registrant") and the PBHG Class and Adviser Class shares of the Funds named above. It should be read in conjunction with the current Prospectuses for the PBHG Class and Adviser Class shares of the Funds. The Prospectuses dated January 14, 2005, may be obtained without charge by calling 1-800-433-0051.
>
> The Annual Report, except for page 1, is incorporated herein by reference for each Fund. The financial statements included in the Trust's 2004 Semi-Annual Report are also incorporated herein by reference for each Fund. The Annual and Semi-Annual Report may each be obtained without charge by calling 1-800-433-0051.

Fund History (Item 10). In this section, the fund must provide the date and form of organization of the fund and the name of the state or other jurisdiction in which the fund is organized. If the fund has engaged in a business other than that of an investment company during the past five years or its name was changed during that period, such items must be discussed. In particular, funds must describe the nature and results of any

Understanding and Evaluating Prospectuses, Offering Documents, and Proxy Statements

change in the fund's business or name that occurred in connection with any bankruptcy, receivership, or similar proceeding, or any other material reorganization, readjustment, or succession.

Description of the Fund and Its Investments and Risks (Item 11). The fund description must include all of the following:

1. The classification of the fund (open-end investment management company)
2. Investment strategies and risks, including risks related to investments outside principal strategies
3. Fund policies with respect to issuing senior securities, borrowing money, underwriting securities of other issuers, concentrating investments in a particular industry or industries, purchasing or selling real estate or commodities, making loans, and any other policy the fund deems fundamental or that may not be changed without shareholder approval
4. The types of investments a fund may make while assuming a temporary defensive position
5. An explanation of any significant variation in the fund's portfolio turnover rates over the two most recently completed fiscal years or any anticipated variation in the portfolio turnover rate from that reported for the last fiscal year
6. Policies regarding disclosure of portfolio holdings to others

PBHG includes the following discussion, which satisfies some of the disclosures under both Item 10 and Item 11:[5]

> The Trust is an open-end management investment company which was originally incorporated in Delaware on August 2, 1985, under the name PBHG Growth Fund, Inc. and commenced business shortly thereafter as an open-end management investment company under the Investment Company Act of 1940, as amended (the "1940 Act"). On July 21, 1992, shareholders of the Trust approved an Agreement and Articles of Merger pursuant to which the Fund was reorganized and merged into a new Maryland corporation, also named PBHG Growth Fund, Inc. On September 8, 1993, the shareholders of the Trust voted to

change the name of the Trust to The Advisors' Inner Circle Fund II, Inc. On May 2, 1994, the shareholders voted to change the Trust's name to The PBHG Funds, Inc. On July 16, 2001, The PBHG Funds, Inc. was reorganized as a Delaware business trust and the Trust's name changed to PBHG Funds.

PBHG also discloses specific obligations to which it must comply in settlement of lawsuits related to market timing and selective disclosure. When such disclosures are observed, the investor should consider what was done, to what extent other fund holders were harmed, whether the individuals involved are still with the fund or management company and what steps have been taken to ensure that these activities do not recur.

Management of the Fund (Item 12). This section of the prospectus must include detailed information regarding the management and board of directors, including compensation, treatment regarding fund loads, codes of ethics, and proxy voting policies.

Management. The prospectus must provide a table listing each director, officer, and any advisory board member. A footnote to the table should explain any family relationships that exist among these individuals. A sample of this table from the PBHG Funds Statement of Additional Information is presented in Exhibit 5.4. PBHG satisfies this requirement through the following statement in the SAI:[6]

> The management and affairs of the Trust are supervised by the Board of Trustees under the laws of the State of Delaware. The Trustees have approved agreements under which, as described below, certain companies provide essential management services to the Trust. The Trustees and executive officers of the Trust and their principal occupations for the last five years are set forth below. Each may have held other positions with the named companies during that period. Each Trustee serves as a Trustee and each officer serves as an officer in a similar capacity for PBHG Insurance Series Fund, another registered investment company managed by the Adviser. Unless otherwise noted, all Trustees and officers can be contacted c/o Liberty Ridge Capital, Inc., 1400 Liberty Ridge Drive, Wayne, PA 19087.

Understanding and Evaluating Prospectuses, Offering Documents, and Proxy Statements

Board of Directors. In addition to the information provided in the table in Exhibit 5.4, the fund must describe the responsibilities of the board of directors with respect to the fund's management. In addition, it must identify any committees of the fund's board of directors; and for each committee provide a statement of its functions, the members of the committee, the number of committee meetings held during the last fiscal year; and, if the committee is a nominating or similar committee, state whether the committee will consider nominees recommended by security holders and the procedures to be followed by security holders in submitting recommendations. For example, PBHG provides the following paragraphs:[7]

> The Trustees of PBHG Funds are responsible for major decisions relating to the Fund's investment goal, policies, strategies, and techniques. The Trustees also supervise the operation of PBHG Funds by its officers and service various service providers, but they do not actively participate in the day-to-day operation of, or decision making process related to, PBHG Funds. The Board of Trustees has two standing committees: Governance and Nominating Committee (formerly the Nominating and Compensation Committee) and an Audit Committee. Currently, the members of each Committee are Jettie Edwards, John Bartholdson, Leigh Wilson, and Albert Miller, comprising all the disinterested Trustees of PBHG Funds. The Governance and Nominating Committee selects and nominates those persons for membership on the PBHG Funds' Board of Trustees who are disinterested trustees, reviews and determines compensation for the disinterested Trustees of PBHG Funds, and selects independent legal counsel, as set forth in Rule 0-1(6), to provide the disinterested Trustees of PBHG Funds with legal advice as needed. During PBHG Funds' fiscal year ended March 31, 2004, the Nominating and Compensation Committee held three meetings.
>
> The Governance and Nominating Committee shall consider nominees recommended in writing by a shareholder (other than shareholder recommendations of himself or herself) to serve as trustees, provided: (i) that such person is a shareholder of one or more series of the Trust at the time he or she submits such names and is entitled to vote at the

Exhibit 5.4: Sample of Table Entry Requirements for Fund Managers and Directors

TRUSTEES AND OFFICERS OF THE TRUST

The management and affairs of the Trust are supervised by the Board of Trustees under the laws of the State of Delaware. The Trustees have approved agreements under which, as described below, certain companies provide essential management services to the Trust. The Trustees and executive officers of the Trust and their principal occupations for the last five years are set forth below. Each may have held other positions with the named companies during that period. Each Trustee serves as a Trustee and each officer serves as an officer in a similar capacity for PBHG Insurance Series Fund, another registered investment company managed by the Adviser. Unless otherwise noted, all Trustees and officers can be contacted c/o Liberty Ridge Capital, Inc., 1400 Liberty Ridge Drive, Wayne, PA 19087.

Independent Trustees*

Name, Address, and Age	Position Held with the Trust	Term of office* and length of time served	Principal Occupation(s) during the Last Five Years	Number of Portfolios in the PBHG Fund Family Complex Overseen by Trustee	Other Directorships Held by Trustee
Leigh A. Wilson (60)	Chairman of the Board	Trustee since 2005	Chief executive officer, New Century Living, Inc. (older adult housing) since 1992; Director, Chimney Rock Winery LLC, 2000 to 2004, and Chimney Rock Winery Corp (winery), 1985 to 2004.	26	Trustee, the Victory Portfolios (since 1992), The Victory Institutional Funds (since 2003), and the Victory Variable Insurance Funds (since 1998) (investment companies — 22 total portfolios). Trustee, PBHG Insurance Series Fund, since 2005.
John R. Barthpldson (60)	Trustee	Trustee since 1995	Chief Financial Officer, The Triumph Group, Inc. (manufacturing) since 1992.	26	Director, The Triumph Group, Inc. since 1992. Trustee, PBHG Insurance Series Fund, since 1995. Trustee, Old Mutual Advisor Funds since 2004.
Jettie M. Edwards (58)	Trustee	Trustee since 1995	Consultant, Syrus Associates (business and marketing consulting firm) since 1986–2002.	26	Trustee, EQ Advisor Trust (investment company — 37 portfolios) since 1995. Trustee, PBHG Insurance Series Fund, since 1997.
Albert A. Miller (70)	Trustee	Trustee since 1995	Senior Vice President, Cherry & Webb, CWT Specialty Stores 1995–2000, Advisor and Secretary, the Underwoman Shoppes, Inc. (retail clothing stores), 1980–2002. Merchandising Group Vice President, R.H. Macy & Co. (retail department stores), 1958–1995. Retired.	26	Trustee, PBHG Insurance Series Fund, since 1997.

Understanding and Evaluating Prospectuses, Offering Documents, and Proxy Statements

Officers

Name, Address, and Age	Position Held with the Trust	Term of Office* and Length of Time Served	Principal Occupation(s) During the Last Five Years
David J Bullock (48)	President	President since 2003*	President and Chief Executive Officer; Old Mutual Capital, Inc. and Trustee Old Mutual Advisor Funds since May 2004. President and Director, Liberty Ridge, Capital, Inc. since July 2003; Chief Executive Officer, Liberty Ridge Capital, Inc.; Trustee, Old Mutual Investment Partners; Old Mutual Shareholder Services, and Old Mutual Fund Services, Inc. since November 2003; President, PBHG Insurance Series Fund since November 2003; Chief Operating Officer, Liberty Ridge Capital, Inc., July 2003 to March 2004; President and Chief Executive Officer, Transamerica Capital, Inc. 1998–2003.
Lee T. Cummings (41)	Treasurer, Chief Financial Officer	Treasurer, Chief Financial Officer, Controller since 1997*	Vice President since January 2001 and Sales and Marketing Director since April 2004, Liberty Ridge Capital, Inc.; Vice President, Old Mutual Fund Services since November 2004 and President from December 1998 to November 2004. Treasurer, Chief Financial Officer and Controller, PBHG Insurance Series Fund since March 1997 and Old Mutual Advisor Funds since May 2004. President, Old Mutual Shareholders Services, Inc. since June 2001. President, Old Mutual Investment Partners, 1999–2003. Vice President, Old Mutual Investment Partners since March 2003. Treasurer Old Mutual Investment Partners, 1996–1999. Director of Mutual Fund Operations, Liberty Ridge Capital, Inc., 1996–2001. Vice President, Old Mutual Shareholder Services, Inc. since November 2004. President of Old Mutual Shareholder Services, Inc. from 2001 to November 2004.
Edward J. Veilleux (61)	Senior Vice President	Since January, 2005. Employed for an initial term of three years and thereafter successive one year terms unless terminated prior to the end of the then current term.	President, EJV Financial Services, LLC since May 2002; Director Deutsche Bank (and predecessor companies) and Administrative Officer Investement Company Capital Corp. (registered investment advisoor and registered transfer agent, August 1987 to May 2002.)

*Trustee of the Trust until such time as his or her successor is duly elected and appointed.

Source: PBHG Funds Statement of Additional Information, January 14, 2005.

meeting of shareholders at which trustees will be elected; and (ii) that the Governance and Nominating Committee or the Board, as applicable, shall make the final determination of persons to be nominated. The Governance and Nominating Committee shall evaluate nominees recommended by a shareholder to serve as trustees in the same manner as they evaluate nominees identified by the Committee. A shareholder who desires to recommend a nominee shall submit a request in writing by regular mail or delivery service to the following address: Liberty Ridge Capital, Inc., 1400 Liberty Ridge Drive, Wayne, PA 19087, Attention: SECRETARY OF PBHG FUNDS. Such request shall contain (i) the name, address, and telephone number of, and number of Trust shares owned by, the person or entity or group of persons or entities on whose behalf the recommendation is being made, and the related account name, number, and broker or account provider name, and (ii) if any of such persons were not record owners of the Trust at the time the recommendation was submitted, verification acceptable in form and substance to the Trust of such person's ownership of the Trust at the time the recommendation was made.

The Audit Committee oversees the financial reporting process for PBHG Funds, monitoring the PBHG Funds' audit process and results. As part of this process, the Audit Committee recommends the selection of an independent audit firm for the approval of the entire PBHG Funds Board of Trustees and evaluates the independent audit firm's performance, costs, and financial stability. During PBHG Funds' fiscal year ended March 31, 2004, the Audit Committee held two meetings.

In addition, for each director, the fund must state the dollar range of equity securities owned directly or indirectly, both in the fund and in any related investment companies. Exhibit 5.5 illustrates PBHG's presentation of this information.

Similarly, the SAI should disclose director, or family ownership in the shares of the adviser itself, in a principal underwriter, or a controlling party. Any transactions of $60,000 or greater between directors and the fund or related parties must also be disclosed. Related party transactions are areas of concern. They should be examined carefully to determine if they result in a conflict of interest, could potentially harm fund holders, or if any transactions could just as easily been performed with independent parties.

Compensation. The SAI will also provide a table detailing director compensation. This includes any pension, retirement, or other plans provided. Exhibit 5.6 presents the PBHG table of director compensation.

Sales Loads. The SAI must disclose any arrangements that result in breakpoints in, or elimination of, sales loads for directors and other affiliated persons of the fund. It must also explain the reasons for the difference in the price at which securities are offered generally to the public and the prices at which securities are offered to directors and other affiliated persons of the fund.

Exhibit 5.5: Independent Director Ownership of PBHG and Related Funds

The table below provides the dollar range of shares of the Fund and the aggregate dollar range of shares of all funds advised by Liberty Ridge Capital, owned by each Trustee as of December 31, 2004.

*Independent Trustees**

Name of Trustee	Dollar Range of Equity Securities in the Funds	Aggregate Dollar Range of Equity Securities in all Registered Investement Companies in the PBHG Family Complex Overseen by Trustees
Leigh A. Wilson	Not applicable*	Not applicable*
John R. Batholdson	PBHG Emerging Growth Fund 0–$10,000, PBHG Select Growth Fund $10,000–$50,000	$10,000–$50,000
Jettie M. Edwards	PBHG Emerging Growth Fund $10,000–$50,000, Clipper Focus Fund $10,000–$50,000	$50,000–$100,000
Albert A. Miller	PBHG Emerging Growth Fund $50,000–$100,000; PBHG Growth Fund $10,000–$50,000; PBHG Select Growth Fund $10,000–$50,000; PBHG Technology & Communications Fund $10,000–$50,000; PBHG Strategic Small Company Fund $10,000–$50,000	Over $100,000

*Mr. Wilson was not appointed a trustee until January 6, 2005. The information in this table is as of December 31, 2004.

Source: PBHG Funds Statement of Additional Information, January 14, 2005.

Codes of Ethics. The fund must provide a brief statement disclosing whether the fund and its investment adviser and principal underwriter have adopted codes of ethics under the Investment Company Act and whether these codes of ethics permit personnel subject to the codes to invest in securities, including securities that may be purchased or held by the fund. Investors would generally prefer that fund personnel invest in the fund itself along with other fund holders rather than purchasing the individual securities directly. This eliminates potential conflicts and trading ahead of fund holders.

Proxy Voting Policies. Unless the fund invests exclusively in nonvoting securities, it must describe the policies and procedures used to determine how to vote proxies relating to portfolio securities. If the voting could present a conflict between the interests of fund shareholders and those of the fund's investment adviser or related parties, this too must be disclosed.

Finally, information must be provided to allow shareholders to request records of how proxies have been voted. Any conflicts noted should be evaluated to determine how they are resolved and whether this process favors fund holders or others.

Control Persons and Principal Holders of Securities (Item 13). Control persons are people who control the fund. The SAI must provide the name and address of each such person, explain the effect of that control on the voting rights of other security holders, and state the percentage of the fund's voting securities owned or any other basis of control. If the control person is a company, it will give the jurisdiction under the laws of which it is organized.

Principal holders are shareholders who own at least 5 percent of any class of the fund's outstanding equity securities. The SAI must provide the name, address, and percentage of ownership of each principal holder.

The SAI must also state the percentage of the fund's equity securities

Exhibit 5.6: Director Compensation at PBHG Funds

Each current Trustee of the Trust received the following compensation during PBHG Funds' fiscal year ended March 31, 2004:

Name of Person, Position	Aggregate Compensation from Trust	Pension or Retirement Benefits Accrued as Part of Trust Expenses	Estimated Annual Benefits Upon Retirement	Total Compensation from Trust and Trust Complex Paid to Trustees*
Leigh A. Wilson	Not applicable**	Not applicable**	Not applicable**	Not applicable**
John R. Bartholdson, Trustee	$63,455	N/A	N/A	$97,750 for services on two boards
Jettie M. Edwards, Trustee	$63,455	N/A	N/A	$97,750 for services on two boards
Albert A. Miller, Trustee	$63,455	N/A	N/A	$97,750 for services on two boards

* Mr. Wilson was not appointed a trustee until January 6, 2005. The information in this table is as of March 31, 2004.
**Compensation expenses are allocated pro rata based on the relative net assets of each Fund included in the Trust Complex.

Source: PBHG Funds Statement of Additional Information, January 14, 2005.

owned by all officers, directors, and members of any advisory board of the fund as a group. If the amount owned by directors and officers as a group is less than 1 percent, that too must be disclosed.

A sample of the PBHG Funds table in compliance with Item 13 is presented in Exhibit 5.7.

Investment Advisory and Other Services (Item 14). Funds must disclose the following information with respect to each investment adviser:

1. The name of any person who controls the adviser, the basis of the person's control, and the general nature of the person's business as well as the business history of any organization that controls the adviser
2. The name of any affiliated person of the fund who also is an affiliated person of the adviser, and a list of all capacities in which the person is affiliated with the fund and with the adviser
3. The method of calculating the advisory fee payable by the fund.
PBHG Funds provides the following discussion:[8]

THE ADVISER

The Trust and Liberty Ridge Capital have entered into an advisory agreement with respect to each Fund (the "Advisory Agreement"). The Advisory Agreement provides certain limitations on the Adviser's liability, but also provides that the Adviser shall not be protected against any liability to the Trust or each of its Funds or its shareholders by reason of willful misfeasance, bad faith or gross negligence on its part in the performance of its duties or from reckless disregard of its obligations or duties thereunder.

Liberty Ridge Capital (formerly Pilgrim Baxter & Associates, Ltd.) is an indirect wholly owned subsidiary of Old Mutual plc ("Old Mutual"). Old Mutual is an international financial services group based in London, with operations in life assurance, asset management, banking, and general insurance. Old Mutual's principal offices are located at Old Mutual Place, 2 Lambeth Hill, London, EC4V 4GG, United Kingdom.

Old Mutual Fund Services, the Trust's Administrator, is an affiliate of the Adviser and an indirect wholly-owned subsidiary of the Adviser's

> **Exhibit 5.7: Section of PBHG Funds Disclosure of Principal Holders 5% and 25% Shareholders**
>
> As of December 31, 2004, the following persons were the only persons who were record owners (or to the knowledge of the Trust, beneficial owners) of 5 percent or more of the shares of each Fund of the Trust. The Trust believes that most of the shares referred to below were held by the persons indicated in accounts for their fiduciary, agency, or custodial clients. Persons owning of record or beneficially 25 percent or more of the outstanding share class of a Fund may be deemed to be a controlling person of that Fund for purposes of the 1940 Act.
>
> **PBHG EMERGING GROWTH FUND PBHG CLASS**
>
> | | |
> |---|---|
> | National Financial Services
For the Exclusive Benefit of our Customer
200 Liberty St., One World Financial Center
Attn: Mutual Funds, Dept. 5th Floor
New York, NY 10281-1003 | 16.24% |
> | Charles Schwab & Co. Inc.
Reinvest Account
Attn: Mutual Fund Department
101 Montgomery Street
San Francisco, CA 94104-4122 | 13.16% |
> | American United Life Insurance Company
Group Retirement Annuity Separate Account II
One American Square
P.O. Box 1995
Indianapolis, IN 46206-9202 | 5.27% |
>
> **PBHG EMERGING GROWTH FUND PBHG CLASS**
>
> | | |
> |---|---|
> | PBHG EMERGING GROWTH FUND ADVISOR CLASS | N/A |
> | PBHG EMERGING GROWTH FUND CLASS A | |
> | Liberty Ridge Capital, Inc.
Attn: Terri Simonetti
1400 Liberty Ridge Drive
Wayne, PA 19087-5525 | 100.00% |
>
> Source: PBHG Funds Statement of Additional Information, January 14, 2005.

parent, Old Mutual (US) Holdings Inc. (see "The Administrator" for more detail on Old Mutual Fund Services). Old Mutual Fund Services also serves as administrator to PBHG Insurance Series Fund, a management investment company also managed by the Adviser. Old Mutual Investment Partners (which also does business as PBHG Fund

Understanding and Evaluating Prospectuses, Offering Documents, and Proxy Statements

Distributors), the Trust's Distributor, is also an affiliate of the Adviser and an indirect wholly owned subsidiary of the Adviser's parent, Old Mutual (U.S.) Holdings Inc. (see "The Distributor" for more detail on Old Mutual Investment Partners). Old Mutual Investment Partners also serves as distributor to PBHG Insurance Series Fund. The Adviser has discretionary management authority with respect [to] over $7.0 billion in assets as of June 30, 2004. In addition to advising the Funds, the Adviser provides advisory services to other mutual funds and to pension and profit-sharing plans, charitable institutions, corporations, trusts and estates, and other investment companies. The principal business address of the Adviser is 1400 Liberty Ridge Drive, Wayne, Pennsylvania 19087-5593.

The Advisory Agreement obligates the Adviser to: (i) provide a program of continuous investment management for the Trust in accordance with the Trust's investment objectives, policies, and limitations; (ii) make investment decisions for the Trust; and (iii) place orders to purchase and sell securities for the Trust, subject to the supervision of the Board of Trustees. The Advisory Agreement also requires the Adviser to pay its overhead and employee costs and the compensation and expenses of all its partners, officers, and employees who serve as officers and executive employees of the Trust. The Advisory Agreement provides that the Adviser is not responsible for other expenses of operating the Trust.

The continuance of the Advisory Agreement after the first two years must be specifically approved at least annually (i) by the Trust's Board of Trustees or by vote of a majority of the Trust's outstanding voting securities and (ii) by the affirmative vote of a majority of the Trustees who are not parties to the agreement or interested persons of any such party by votes cast in person at a meeting called for such purpose. The Advisory Agreement may be terminated (i) at any time without penalty by the Trust upon the vote of a majority of the Trustees or by vote of the majority of the Trust's outstanding voting securities upon 60 days' written notice to the Adviser or (ii) by the Adviser at any time without penalty upon 60 days' written notice to the Trust. The Advisory Agreement will also terminate automatically in the event of its assignment (as defined in the 1940 Act).

For its services, the Adviser is entitled to a fee, which is calculated daily and paid monthly, at an annual rate of each Fund's average daily net assets as set forth in the table below. In addition, in the interest of limiting the expenses of the Funds during the current fiscal year, the Adviser has signed expense limitation contracts with the Trust on behalf of certain Funds ("Expense Limitation Agreements") pursuant to which, with respect to the PBHG Class and Adviser Class shares, the Adviser has agreed to waive or limit a portion of its fee and to assume other expenses in an amount necessary to limit total annual operating expenses (but excluding fees and expenses incurred under the Trust's Adviser Class Service Plan ("12b-1 fees"), if any, interest, taxes, brokerage commissions, and any expenditures that are capitalized in accordance with generally accepted accounting principles, and any extraordinary expenses not incurred in the ordinary course of the Fund's business)....

PBHG accompanies this discussion with two tables, one outlining the fee schedule for its various funds and the other showing the actual fees either paid or waived. It also notes that its fee schedules are higher than the average investment fund, but that management believes they are in line with funds that have similar objectives.

In addition to the investment adviser, the fund must provide the name and business address of any principal underwriter for the fund. If an affiliated person of the fund is an affiliated person of the principal underwriter, that person must be identified. Furthermore, disclosure must be made of any of the following that are applicable:

- Services performed for the fund supplied or paid for by each investment adviser.
- Anyone other than a fund adviser paying fees, expenses, and costs of the fund, and the amount paid.
- Any other management-related service contract under which services are provided to the fund, indicating the parties to the contract, the total dollars paid, and by whom for the past three years.
- The name, nature, and remuneration involved in any arrangement in

which someone other than a director, officer, member of an advisory board, employee, or investment adviser of the fund regularly advises the fund or the fund's adviser with respect to investing in, purchasing, or selling securities or other property.
- Any front-end sales load re-allowed to dealers as a percentage of the offering price of the fund's shares.
- If the fund has adopted a plan under Rule 12b-1, it must describe the material aspects of the plan, and any agreements relating to the implementation of the plan. Disclosures must include the types of activities (advertising, printing, etc.) for which payments were made, the relationship between amounts paid to the distributor and expenses it incurs, the amount of any unreimbursed expenses, whether the fund participates in joint distribution activities, whether fund directors or interested persons had a direct financial interest in the operation of the plan, and the anticipated benefits to the fund that may result from the plan.
- Any person who provides significant administrative or business affairs management services for the fund (for example, an "administrator"), the services provided, and the compensation paid for the services.
- The name and principal business address of the fund's transfer agent and the dividend-paying agent.
- The name and address of the fund's custodian and independent public accountant and the services performed by each.
- The outside services that any person related to the fund performs and the basis for remuneration.

In this section, the investor should consider whether the compensation, fees, and loads are reasonable compared to other similar funds. If any fund expenses are being subsidized, the investor should consider the impact on returns should these subsidies end.

Portfolio Managers (Part 15). The fund must disclose whether its portfolio manager is primarily responsible for the day-to-day management of the portfolio of any other account, and if so, must provide the portfolio manager's name; the number of other accounts managed, the total assets in the accounts managed, whether fees for such assets are performance-based, and any resulting conflicts of interest with accounts within each of the following categories:

   A. Registered investment companies
   B. Other pooled investment vehicles
   C. Other accounts

The fund must also describe the structure of, and the method used to determine, the compensation of each portfolio. For each type of compensation (for example, salary, bonus, deferred compensation, retirement plans, and arrangements), it must describe the criteria on which that type of compensation is based. For example, if compensation is based solely or in part on performance, the fund should identify any benchmark used to measure performance and the length of the period over which performance is measured. The fund must also disclose, within the ranges prescribed for directors and other officers, the number of equity securities in the fund owned by each manager.

This information supplements the prospectus disclosure. In addition to evaluating the managers' performance history, the investor should consider whether the compensation paid is justified by the performance.

Brokerage Allocation and Other Practices (Item 16). The fund must describe how transactions in portfolio securities are effected, including a general statement about brokerage commissions, markups, and markdowns on principal transactions and the aggregate amount of any brokerage commissions paid by the fund during its three most recent fiscal years. Any large fluctuations in commissions should be explained.

Any commissions paid to affiliated parties must be disclosed. For each such broker, the fund should provide the percentage of the fund's aggregate brokerage commissions paid to the broker during the most recent fiscal year, and the percentage of the fund's aggregate dollar amount of commission transactions effected through the broker during the most recent fiscal year.

The fund should describe how it will select brokers to effect securities transactions and how the fund will evaluate the overall reasonableness of brokerage commissions paid. If the fund or its investment adviser directed the fund's brokerage transactions to a broker because of research services provided, it should state the amount of the transactions and related commissions. If the fund has recently acquired securities of its regular brokers or dealers or of their parents, it should identify those brokers or dealers and state the value of the fund's aggregate holdings of the securities of each issuer as of the close of the fund's most recent fiscal year.

Capital Stock and Other Securities (Item 17). For each class of capital stock of the fund, the SAI should disclose the title of each class and provide a full discussion of the following provisions or characteristics of each class, if applicable:

1. Restrictions on the right freely to retain or dispose of the fund's shares
2. Material obligations or potential liabilities associated with owning the fund's shares (not including investment risks)
3. Dividend rights
4. Voting rights (including whether the rights of shareholders can be modified by other than a majority vote)
5. Liquidation rights
6. Preemptive rights
7. Conversion rights
8. Redemption provisions
9. Sinking fund provisions
10. Liability to further calls or to assessment by the fund

Purchase, Redemption, and Pricing of Shares (Item 18). To the extent that the prospectus does not do so, the SAI must describe how the fund's shares are offered to the public. This includes any special purchase plans or methods not described in the prospectus or elsewhere in the SAI, including letters of intent, accumulation plans, dividend reinvestment plans, withdrawal plans, exchange privileges, employee benefit plans, redemption reinvestment plans, and waivers for particular classes of shareholders.

Fund Reorganizations. The fund must disclose any arrangements that result in breakpoints in, or elimination of, sales loads in connection with the terms of a merger, acquisition, or exchange offer made under a plan of reorganization. It must also identify each class of individuals to which the arrangements apply and state each different sales load available as a percentage of both the offering price and the net amount invested.

Offering Price. The fund must describe the method followed or to be followed by the fund in determining the total offering price at which its shares may be offered to the public and the method(s) used to value the fund's assets.

Arrangements Permitting Frequent Purchases and Redemptions of Fund Shares. The fund must describe any arrangements with any person to permit frequent purchases and redemptions of fund shares, including the identity of the persons permitted to engage in frequent purchases and redemptions pursuant to such arrangements, and any compensation or other consideration received by the fund, its investment adviser, or any other party pursuant to such arrangements.

Investors must evaluate the extent to which any such arrangements may benefit some individual fund holders at the expense of others.

Taxation of the Fund (Item 19). If applicable, the fund must state that it is qualified or intends to qualify under Subchapter M of the Internal Revenue Code. The consequences to the fund if it does not qualify under Subchapter M must also be disclosed. Failure to qualify will result in taxes at the fund level, as well as, to individual fund holders. Any special or unusual tax aspects of the fund, such as taxation resulting from foreign investment or from status as a personal holding company, or any tax loss carry-forward to which the fund may be entitled, must be discussed.

Underwriters (Item 20). For each principal underwriter distributing securities of the fund, the fund must state the nature of the obligation to distribute the fund's securities; whether the offering is continuous; and the aggregate dollar amount of underwriting commissions and the amount retained by the principal underwriter for each of the fund's last three fiscal years. A table should be provided, detailing commissions and other compensation received by each principal underwriter who is an affiliated person of the fund or an affiliated person of that affiliated person, directly or indirectly, from

Understanding and Evaluating Prospectuses, Offering Documents, and Proxy Statements

the fund during the most recent fiscal year. Any payments made by the fund to an underwriter or dealer in the fund's shares during the last fiscal year must be disclosed along with the name and address of the underwriter or dealer, the amount paid and basis for determining that amount, the circumstances surrounding the payments, and the consideration received by the fund.

Calculation of Performance Data (Item 21). The procedures for calculating performance are very specific. This helps ensure comparability across various funds of a given type. Some of the required disclosures are discussed below.

Money market funds must provide a yield quotation, effective yield quotation, tax equivalent current yield quotation, and tax equivalent effective yield quotation.

Other funds must provide an average annual total return quotation, an average annual total return (after taxes on distributions) quotation, an average annual total return (after taxes on distributions and redemption) quotation, a yield quotation, a tax equivalent yield quotation, and a nonstandardized performance quotation. The last quotation refers to any calculation based on other historical measures of performance.

Performance data should be compared with other similar funds.

Financial Statements (Item 22). The primary statements are a balance sheet, income statement, and statement of changes in shareholder equity for the fund itself, although others are required in certain circumstances. Typically, these are not included within the SAI but are incorporated by reference from the fund's most recent annual report. This means a statement in the SAI refers the reader to the annual report. The investor should obtain the annual report, any recent semiannual report, and examine the fund's performance, which is likely on a fiscal year different than the calendar year financial data typically found for mutual funds. Chapter 2 provides a discussion of financial statements and their evaluation. Financial statements of mutual funds differ from those of other companies in that most assets are investments and are reported at fair market value (rather than their cost). The annual report will contain a listing of portfolio investments and management's analysis of fund performance. These two items will yield better information for most investors than the financial statements themselves. The investor should carefully evaluate management's discussion of the performance and whether management is frank and honest or tries to put itself in the best light by blaming poor performance on outside factors. The financial statements should not be ignored. The investor should examine whether the portfolio holdings are consistent with the fund's objectives. The financial statements will also detail the computation of net asset value for the fund (the balance sheet) and fund expenses (the income statement). The investor should confirm that the auditors have provided a clean (unqualified) opinion and ascertain whether there were any disclosures regarding disagreements with auditors. If so, the investor should be wary.

EVALUATING OTHER INFORMATION

The registration statement filed with the SEC will contain additional information that investors may find useful, but which is not required to be provided by the fund. This information can be viewed by obtaining the SEC filing from the SEC or fund manager's Web sites. For example, the following exhibits are filed as part of the registration statement (among others):

- Articles of incorporation
- Bylaws
- Instruments defining rights of security holders
- Investment advisory contracts
- Underwriting contracts
- Bonus or profit sharing contracts
- Custodian agreements
- Other material contracts

If investors have questions regarding investment advisory fees or other arrangements, the contracts can be reviewed. A number of other disclosures found in the registration statement may prove informative.

Business and Other Connections of the Investment Adviser. The fund should describe any other business, profession, vocation, or employment of a substantial nature that each investment adviser, and each director, officer, or partner of the adviser, is or has been engaged inwithin the last two fiscal years for his or her own account or in the capacity of director, officer, employee, partner, or trustee.

Principal Underwriters. The fund should state the name of each investment company (other than the fund) for which each principal underwriter currently distributing the fund's securities also acts as a principal underwriter, depositor, or investment adviser. It should also provide the name each of director, officer, or partner of each principal underwriter for which there are potential conflicts of interest. In addition, commissions paid to potentially conflicted parties should be discussed.

CONCLUSION

When investors provide funds to an investment company, they are entrusting their wealth to others. Investors need to be comfortable that the investment company's managers are being good stewards of the investors' assets. The prospectus, SAI, and periodic reports provide important information to judge that stewardship. Some key points for you to consider in evaluating these documents are:

- What are the investment objectives of the fund, and are they aligned with the portion of the investor's asset allocation under consideration?
- Are the fund's investments consistent with the fund's objectives?
- What risks are involved in the fund?
- Are the returns commensurate with the risks?
- Are the fund's fees, sales loads, and other expenses reasonable relative to comparable funds?
- Do any conflicts exist that could benefit a few parties at the expense of other fund holders?
- How liquid are fund shares? Can they be sold easily in a secondary market or redeemed?
- What is the experience and past performance of the investment advisory firm and individual fund managers?
- Are there sufficient outside directors or trustees to adequately monitor the fund for fund holders?

ENDNOTES

1. www.sec.gov/answers/mfinvco.htm.
2. Aaron Pressman, "New Captains for the Clipper Fund," Business Week Online, December 1, 2005, www.businessweek.com.
3. Buffalo Funds prospectus, July 31, 2005, p. 23.
4. PBHG Funds Statement of Additional Information, January 14, 2005, front cover.
5. PBHG Funds Statement of Additional Information, January 14, 2005, page 3.
6. PBHG Funds Statement of Additional Information, January 14, 2005, p. 36.
7. PBHG Funds Statement of Additional Information, January 14, 2005, pp. 39–40.
8. PBHG Funds Statement of Additional Information, January 14, 2005, pp. 57–58.

DISCUSSION QUESTIONS:

1. What are the types of investment companies as classified by the SEC?
2. What documents must be provided to investors in registered investment companies?
3. Why are the tax status and characteristics of the mutual fund important?
4. In which document would the fund's financial statements and management's discussion of performance be found?
5. What key factors should investors consider in the financial statements?
6. What useful information may be found in SEC filings but is not provided to fund investors?
7. Recently, some mutual funds have resisted attempts to increase the number of outside trustees. Some view this as necessary to reduce potential conflicts and oversight. In the extreme, trustees may replace the investment adviser. An alternative view is that the investment adviser often started the fund and should continue to manage it. Shareholders could "vote with their feet" (take their investments elsewhere). What are some other pros and cons to outside oversight of mutual funds?

EXERCISE:

The Investment Company Institute (ICI) is the national association of U.S. investment companies. The ICI compiles a great deal of information and statistics on the investment company industry that are available free of charge on their Web site at www.ici.org.

From the ICI's Web site, obtain the most recent version of their *Investment Company Fact Book* (2005 or later). Consider the following questions:

Understanding and Evaluating Prospectuses, Offering Documents, and Proxy Statements

- What has been the trend in total investment company assets over the last ten years? What is the breakdown of assets by type of investment company?
- What factors explain these trends and why are some types of investment companies' assets more predominant than others?
- What has been the trend in fund costs over time?

RECOMMENDED READING

2005 Investment Company Fact Book, 45th ed., *Investment Company Institute*. See in particular the appendices about the types of investment companies and taxation of fund earnings, www.ici.org.

Invest Wisely: An Introduction to Mutual Funds. U. S. Securities and Exchange Commission, www.sec.gov/investor/pubs/inwsmg.htm.

The SEC Mutual Fund Cost Calculator: A Tool for Comparing Mutual Funds, www.sec.gov/investor/tools/mfcc/mfcc-int.htm.

Understanding Mutual Funds, Investment Company Institute, www.ici.org.

6 The Prospectus: Principal Protected Securities

What are principal protected securities (PPSs)? In what important respects do these hybrid securities differ from conventional mutual funds, closed-end mutual funds, and other investments, and how are these distinctions manifested in the prospectus for this category of initial public offerings? While offerings of principal protected notes, certificates, funds, or securities (hereafter collectively known as PPSs) are still less prevalent than other types of investments, an understanding of PPSs is important by virtue of both their allure to conservative investors and their recent, rapid proliferation. This chapter is designed to address these questions and enable advisers and investors to identify the critical issues that determine whether a given PPS is suitable, given their financial objectives. As is true for the other types of offerings that are discussed in this text, the prospectus is the primary document from which the investor can learn fundamental aspects of the potential risks and rewards of the investment, and must be evaluated carefully.

The first major section of the chapter provides additional background information on the PPS. The generic concept of a PPS is explained along with a brief historical perspective on PPSs, which may explain their sudden popularity. PPSs are structured products that have some unusual investment characteristics; consequently, it is not surprising to find that the contents of a prospectus for a PPS are likewise distinctive.

Understanding and Evaluating Prospectuses, Offering Documents, and Proxy Statements

Therefore, the second section of the chapter focuses on the noteworthy aspects of this type of prospectus and their implications. Particular emphasis is devoted to the risk factors that one finds in the prospectuses for various PPSs. In the final section, four specific examples of PPSs, illustrative of each of the major PPS categories, are described in detail to provide the reader with a sense of the myriad varieties of PPS that they may encounter. In each case, we discuss one or more nuances of the investment that could result in an actual market return that is significantly less than the unsophisticated investor might have anticipated. In view of the accumulating body of empirical evidence on the performance of existing PPSs, we conclude by offering a recommendation for analysis that goes beyond the information provided in the prospectus for most PPSs.

BACKGROUND

PPSs are structured products that have been offered in the U.S. for over a decade by leading financial service firms. These hybrid instruments are sometimes called "safer mutual funds," because they purport to offer equity-like return potential without the corresponding downside risk. While the return on an investment in a PPS is based upon the performance of a basket of equities, such as a mutual fund or market index, these instruments typically have a fixed term of five to seven years. At that point, they "mature" and the investor receives the principal and any accrued gains. Thus, PPSs have attributes of fixed-income instruments as well as equities. Also, like a bond, the term of each PPS is defined prior to issuance.[1]

Following three consecutive years of significant market declines in the U.S. from 2000 through 2002, investors' interest in initial public offerings for equities waned, and inflows to existing mutual funds slowed markedly. Investment firms responded by developing and marketing an array of PPSs; in fact, investors purchased over $7 billion of PPSs between August 2001 and May 2003.[2] With PPSs, the potential return to investors often appears high while the downside risk seems low, explaining the allure of this emerging category of investment. Since the exact structure of each PPS is tailored by the offering firm, these instruments vary dramatically, making it very difficult to generalize further about this type of investment. Therefore, in the next section of the chapter, we delineate the most important dimensions on which PPSs differ and examine the implications for investors.

DISTINCTIVE CHARACTERISTICS OF THE PPS

PPSs are endowed with several attributes that are attractive to investors. Following our description and explanation of these characteristics, we focus our attention on a number of the potentially negative, and perhaps less obvious, features of some PPSs.

Advantageous Attributes of Many PPSs.

- *Low minimum required investment.* Many PPSs allow the investor to participate in the category with a total investment of $1,000 without any loss of efficiency or effectiveness.
- *Low credit risk.* While PPSs are not insured by the federal government or agency thereof, nearly all PPSs are issued and/or insured by a firm with a triple-A credit Rating.
- *Principal protection.* Similar to bondholders, investors in PPSs are promised that they will receive their principal if they hold the instrument to maturity.
- *High upside return potential.* Similar to stockholders, investors in many PPSs have the possibility of receiving double-digit, compounded annual returns.
- *Diversification.* Most PPSs are invested by the issuing firm in a number of stocks (for example, S&P 500 or NASDAQ 100). As a result, weak performance or even bankruptcy of a single firm will not necessarily cause the investor to incur losses or even achieve a poor return on the PPS.
- *Professional investment management.* In some cases, the PPS is invested in a combination of stocks and bonds in an active fashion by the fund's manager. For investors who believe that this is likely to improve their return relative to a passively managed fund, this is a potential advantage.
- *Investment time horizon.* While a typical PPS has a term of five to seven years, some may mature in as little as three years while others require the investor to hold them for as long as ten years to maintain the guarantee; there is no inherent reason why a PPS could not be even shorter or longer. Thus, investors should be able to identify a PPS that is matched to their own investment time horizon.

Understanding and Evaluating Prospectuses, Offering Documents, and Proxy Statements

Potentially Disadvantageous Attributes of Many PPSs.

- *Low liquidity.* Unlike an open-ended (that is, conventional) mutual fund, PPSs are not a continuous offering (in which the fund redeems shares on a daily basis at the closing net asset value). Moreover, the issuer of a PPS will generally indicate that it intends to make a secondary market in the security but is under no obligation to do so. Thus, investors in PPSs often lose the benefit of the existence of an efficient secondary market, which is an essential characteristic of closed-end mutual funds. At any time prior to the scheduled maturity, there is no assurance that the investor could obtain the net asset value of the PPS, or even a roughly equivalent amount. For example, the prospectus often states: "… the investor selling the certificates prior to maturity could thus receive substantially less than the amount of their original investment."
- *Complex return cap.* In exchange for the protection of principal, the investor must sacrifice a part of the upside return potential—there is a cap on returns (return cap). Therefore, all PPSs stipulate the approach or formula that will be used to compute the investor's periodic (for example, quarterly) and total return. Additionally, the prospectus often provides examples that illustrate what the return would be for a given pattern of behavior of the underlying stocks or index; nonetheless, the expected return from a PPS is rarely estimated by the issuer or intuitively apparent to the investor. Furthermore, there is no assurance that the examples chosen for purposes of illustration by the issuer are either comprehensive or representative of the returns that investors will receive.

Further complicating the investor's task of deciphering the return cap provision are the facts that the approaches that will be used by the issuers of PPSs to guarantee the return of principal vary widely, may not be disclosed in a transparent fashion, and can impact the investor's return directly and substantially. Among the approaches that issuers use are put and call options, stock futures, and/or zero-coupon bonds that mature concurrently with the PPS in the amount of the guaranteed principal. In many other cases, as noted below, the prospectus discloses that the issuer reserves the right to increase the proportion of the investment that is allocated to fixed income instruments to ensure the return of principal in the event of declines in its equity holdings. Since investors' desired exposure to equities is reduced commensurately, the rate of return on the PPS is then highly contingent upon the pattern of its stocks' behavior during the term of the PPS.

A Main Street PPS prospectus lists the aforementioned issue among its risk factors to investors and labels it as a "Risk Associated with Asset Allocation." To its credit for the thoroughness and candor of its disclosure, it states the following:

> At times, the Fund's assets may be largely invested in the debt portfolio in order to increase the likelihood of preserving the original principal of the Fund. If Fund assets are largely invested in the debt portfolio, the Fund's exposure to equity markets will be reduced and the Fund will be more highly correlated with bonds. In addition, if during the warranty period the equity markets experience a major decline, the Fund's assets may become largely or entirely invested in the debt portfolio. In fact, if the value of the shares of the underlying Fund decline significantly, a complete and irreversible reallocation to the debt portfolio may occur. In this circumstance, the Fund would not participate in any subsequent recovery of the equity market.... The terms of the Warranty Agreement could require the Fund to liquidate an equity position when it otherwise would not be in the shareholders' best interest or at a time when the manager would not recommend that the securities be sold.

The foregoing risk to investors also spills over into its description of potential expenses that investors may bear.

> The asset allocation process may result in additional transaction costs. This process can have an adverse effect on the performance of the Fund during periods of increased equity market volatility. In addition, a high portfolio turnover rate may increase the Fund's transaction costs, which could adversely affect performance. Also, you may receive taxable gains

from portfolio transactions of the Fund, whether you take payment in cash or reinvest them to purchase additional Fund shares.

Thus, hidden expenses as well as potential for unfavorable tax treatment must also be considered among the disadvantageous attributes of some PPSs.

Issuer in Position of Conflict of Interest vis-à-vis the Investors in the PPS. While it is somewhat reasonable for an investor to assume that an investment bank or mutual fund that is offering a PPS has a vested interest in maintaining long-term relationships with its clients and will, therefore, act in the best interest of the client, history has shown that this may not always be the case. In the context of offerings of PPSs, the return to the issuer may be negatively related to the outcomes of the investors. When this may be the case, then the issuer should disclose this fact to the investor. For example, a number of PPSs state: "We or our affiliates may have adverse economic interests to the holders of the notes." Additionally, the issuer may serve as the "calculation agent." This entity is entrusted to determine if an extraordinary event has occurred and, if so, the relevant price of a security or index that affects the return received by the PPS holder. Since the return to the investor may reduce the yield to the issuer, it is possible that the calculation agent may not be unbiased in its role as calculation agent.

CATEGORIES OF PPS

This section describes and illustrates four common types or categories of PPS.

Category A: High Total Return Potential, Subject to Periodic Caps. The first category is exemplified by way of a PPS that was issued by a major investment firm in late 2000 and matured November 2005. The distinguishing characteristic of this category is that the investor can participate fully in the upside return from the underlying stocks, subject to a periodic (for example, quarterly) cap; consequently, with this category of PPS, the investor generally has very high apparent return potential.

As with all of the PPSs that we examine, investors of this particular PPS were assured that, at minimum, their principal was to be returned. The potential return to be received by the investor was based upon the performance of the AMEX Semiconductor Index (ASI), which is comprised of the stocks of 18 of the largest companies in this industry. With this PPS, the maximum quarterly return that is used to compute the investor's total return is 15 percent. As a result, the maximum total return that could have been received after the five-year term was 1536.65 percent. That is, for every $10 that was invested, one could receive over $163. The investor's total return was, in fact, computed as:

Total Return = [Product of (1 + the quarterly capped returns)] − 1.00.

So, for example, if the Index rose by exactly 10 percent each quarter for the five-year horizon of this PPS, the return would be $(1.10)^{20} -1$, or about 573 percent. In fact, the issuer chose this possible outcome as the first of seven examples in its prospectus to articulate the mechanics of the return formula for investors considering this PPS.

Five additional examples were included in this prospectus to highlight the ways that other patterns of return on the ASI would translate into actual returns to investors. Without delving into all of the details for each of these examples, it is worth noting the following about the issuer's choices of possible outcomes for presentation (and omission). In addition to the two aforementioned examples of superlative returns to investors, one example showed that if the ASI went down every quarter, investors still received their entire principal at maturity. A somewhat less flattering example showed that it was possible for the capped quarterly index to show a negative return over five years while the ASI manifested a small (3.5 percent annual) gain over the same horizon. This would have occurred if some of the quarterly returns exceeded 15 percent so that the PPS investor would have missed out on some or all of the underlying appreciation in the Index. Interestingly, none of the examples illustrated a five-year scenario whereby the PPS investor received little or no appreciation while the ASI achieved a solid return (for example, 10–15 percent compounded annually). While the issuer may not have presented such a scenario because it was deemed unlikely to occur, the rationale for this omission is not entirely clear.

What does it all mean and how could the prospective investor have assessed the expected return given this plethora of examples? Two alternative approaches for assessing the expected return are feasible. First, the investor could examine how this instrument would have performed if it existed in the past (or how a very similar instrument would have performed, if necessary, due to a lack of history on this exact group of stocks). One limitation of this approach is that a back-test of even ten years of history would provide only a very preliminary indication of the expected return in a "normal" market period. Therefore, a second approach would entail use of a simulation to mimic market behavior. One begins by making assumptions about the long-run expected mean and variance of returns for the underlying basket of stocks (that is, the ASI in this case) and simulates a large number of periods of market behavior in order to estimate the resulting distribution of returns on the PPS (including the quarterly cap). Using either of the two aforementioned approaches, one might then compare the returns from the PPS to a fixed-income instrument of the same duration. In fact, as noted below, the prospectus for some PPSs provides information of this nature to facilitate investors' analysis.

In sum, numerous other PPSs have a structure similar to the preceding example and category. Clearly, considerable research is required before determining the expected return or suitability of this category of PPS for any investor.

Category B: Percentage of Index Return. Fortunately, among the other common types of PPS are some that are structured in a much simpler, more straightforward fashion than those that we just examined. In this category of PPS, the investor sacrifices the potential for a 100 percent "participation rate" but is not plagued by any periodic cap. As an example, consider another major firm offering where at maturity the notes offered to pay the principal amount plus 70 percent of the upside five-year price return on the S&P 500 Index.

Consistent with this uncomplicated structure, the prospectus then presents the simple (hypothetical) payment table, Exhibit 6.1, that shows the relationship between the performance of the underlying securities (that is, S&P 500 Index) and the return that investors will receive.

In addition to the table, this prospectus also purports to provide

Chapter 6 | The Prospectus: Principal Protected Securities

Exhibit 6.1: Hypothetical Payment at Maturity for Each Note

Hypothetical Initial Index Level	1,160.00		Participation Rate	70%		Principal Protection at Maturity	100%
Hypothetical Final Index Level	Index Return	Index Return Participation Rate (70%)	Index Return Payment	PLUS	Principal	Equals	Payment at Maturity
2,088.00	80%	56%	$560.00	+	$1,000	=	$1,560
1,972.00	70%	49%	$490.00	+	$1,000	=	$1,490
1,856.00	60%	42%	$420.00	+	$1,000	=	$1,420
1,740.00	50%	35%	$350.00	+	$1,000	=	$1,350
1,624.00	40%	28%	$280.00	+	$1,000	=	$1,280
1,508.00	30%	21%	$210.00	+	$1,000	=	$1,210
1,392.00	20%	14%	$140.00	+	$1,000	=	$1,140
1,276.00	10%	7%	$70.00	+	$1,000	=	$1,070
1,160.00	0%	0%	$ -	+	$1,000	=	$1,000
1,044.00	-10%	0%	$ -	+	$1,000	=	$1,000
928.00	-20%	0%	$ -	+	$1,000	=	$1,000
812.00	-30%	0%	$ -	+	$1,000	=	$1,000
696.00	-40%	0%	$ -	+	$1,000	=	$1,000
580.00	-50%	0%	$ -	+	$1,000	=	$1,000

information on the expected return to investors in both numerical and graphical formats. Specifically, the data that are presented show the average return to investors would have been 8.678 percent per year if they had held an identical investment over the past 20 years. From the graphic display, one learns that the return would have exceeded 12 percent per year for almost one-quarter of the five-year rolling periods that were examined. Likewise, the investor is informed that the downside guarantee would have applied on about 13 percent of all periods, in which case, the investor would have received only their principal back at the end of the five-year term. Certainly, the issuer has provided a great deal of assistance in interpreting this PPS offering.

Note, however, that even with this commendable degree of disclosure, there are two additional nuances of which the investor should have been aware prior to undertaking this investment. First, the issuer elected to use

Understanding and Evaluating Prospectuses, Offering Documents, and Proxy Statements

the period from 1985 to 2005 to calibrate the distribution of historical returns. While this is certainly a reasonable, lengthy period of time by almost any investment standard, in fact, this specific 20-year period was among the strongest stretches for stocks in U.S. history. Had either a prior 20-year period been used or a longer period (for example, 40 years) that encompassed those years as well as others, the expected returns would not have appeared to be quite as favorable.

Second, the investor does not own the S&P 500 Index and therefore does not receive dividends in these underlying stocks. While the diligent investor would have noted that the structure of this PPS explicitly excludes dividends, this fact could easily have been missed. Why does this matter? Suppose an investor expected the S&P 500 to generate a total return to investors of about 8 percent per year for the next five years. That investor might then expect a return on this PPS of 5.6 percent per year (that is, .70 x .08). Unfortunately, about 2 percent per year of the total appreciation on the S&P 500 now comes from dividends. So, if the investor's expectation is exactly right, then the PPS holder will actually obtain a return of 4.2 percent per year (that is, .07 x .06). While the difference from the earlier estimate of 5.6 percent is not enormous, the dividend portion of the total return is much safer and of higher probability of occurring. The difference in return estimate together with the nature of the dividend component that was not being distributed might have been enough to persuade the investor to choose an alternative investment vehicle that had a higher expected return, or a higher confidence at the same expected return, for the forthcoming five-year period.

Category C: Actively Managed with Varying Proportions of Stocks and Bonds. Often offered by investment companies that manage mutual funds, this category of PPS seeks to provide a "safer mutual fund." Like the other categories, the return of principal is ensured. Among the distinguishing features of this type of PPS is the explicit disclosure that a bond portfolio of varying magnitude will be used to ensure that the full amount of their principal can be returned to investors at maturity. As a result, as stocks decline, the PPS manager must increase the weight of fixed-income instruments that are held and reduce the proportion of assets that are held in equities.

The astute investor may recognize a parallel to the concept and use of a

Chapter 6 | The Prospectus: Principal Protected Securities

stop-loss order, which many investors believe is a sound, conservative investment practice. Unfortunately, there is no assurance in this context that the PPS will subsequently attempt to re-invest in equities later at a lower price. In fact, the evidence on how this category of PPSs performed during the uptrending equity markets in the U.S. in 2003 and 2004 suggests that the structure of these PPSs is suboptimal for many investors. Consider the following information that was obtained by an independent firm that tracks fund performance. At one specific point in time "…the average principal protected fund had less than 20 percent of its money in stocks… ."[3] Likewise the largest seller of PPSs in the U.S. revealed that it had between 1 percent and 39 percent equities in its PPSs as of early 2005.[4]

The upshot of this investing approach was that PPSs returned an average of 2 percent and 5 percent, respectively in 2003 and 2004 in the U.S. while the average diversified equity fund gained 12 percent and 33 percent during these same periods.[5] While not definitive, these data suggest that this category of PPSs many not capture 70 percent or 80 percent of upside potential from equities that many investors probably expected. The good news is that in 2002, the average fund lost over 20 percent while the average PPS gained 3.3 percent.[6]

The prospective investor in this category of PPS might be well advised to recall our earlier extract from the prospectus for a Main Street PPS that stated: "In fact, if the value of the shares of the underlying Fund decline significantly, a complete and irreversible reallocation to the debt portfolio may occur. In this circumstance, the Fund would not participate in any subsequent recovery of the equity market."

To lend some (positive) balance to our coverage of these PPSs, we should point out that Merrill Lynch's PPSs are reported to have had between 50 and 85 percent of their funds invested in equities at this same time.[7] This divergence highlights the need for investors to have a deeper understanding of the formulae and mechanics that are used to manage these funds and calculate investors' returns before making an investment in this type of PPS.

Category D: Idiosyncratic PPSs. Some PPSs defy any attempt at categorization. The structures of these PPSs are idiosyncratic and their diversity

Understanding and Evaluating Prospectuses, Offering Documents, and Proxy Statements

is only bound by the creativity of their issuers. To illustrate this category and facilitate a discussion of the associated issues, we examine an offering from another major investment firm.

As always, the investor is guaranteed to receive the return of principal. The annual return hinges upon the performance of a group of reference stocks during each year of this five-year investment. The reference stocks, which are chosen by the issuer and could be almost any conceivable set of stocks, include 29 companies in this case: the 30 Dow Jones Industrial companies excluding the issuing firm. The annual return to investors is computed each year.

In tabular form, the performance of the reference stocks is translated into returns on the PPS as follows:

Number of reference stocks with closing prices lower than 25 percent below their initial price

0	1	2	3	4+

That year's payment (in percent)

10	7.5	5	2.5	0

The table shows that if none of the reference stocks close 25 percent below their initial price, then the investor receives a return of 10 percent for that year. If exactly one reference stock dips by 25 percent (or more), then the investor receives a return of 7.5 percent for that year, etc.... As indicated, if four or more reference stocks fall below their respective threshold levels, then investors earn a zero return for that year.

Having described the structure of this PPS, some additional observations are warranted. First, unlike an earlier PPS that we commended for its forthright disclosure, this prospectus makes no attempt to describe what the historical performance would have been over any past period of time. Instead, it simply presents three specific years from the recent past to illustrate that in some years the investor receives a 10 percent return, some years no return (that is, 0 percent), and some years the return is somewhere in between. Thus, the investor must either collect a great deal of data or subjectively estimate the likelihood of the scenarios that will determine their actual return on investment. Second, there are nuances to this PPS that only the most diligent reader would discover. Specifically, if a reference stock declines by a large amount in the first year and stays below its threshold level for the full five-year term (for example, due to bankruptcy), then that one stock could effectively limit the annual return to 7.5 percent annually, all by itself. That is, the stock does not need to fall by 25 percent more than once to reduce the return in subsequent years. Additionally, the return each year is reduced when a stock falls 25 percent below its initial price at any point during the year. Thus, it is possible for an investor to receive no return (that is, 0 percent) for the first or any given year despite the fact that all of the 29 reference stocks rise substantially by the end of that year. Again, we do not intend to suggest that this PPS is inherently flawed in any absolute sense or that it might not be a perfect addition to an investor's portfolio; rather, we seek to highlight some of the nuances that could result in an actual return to investors that departs significantly from their expectations.

CONCLUSION

This chapter provides a conceptual analysis of the characteristics of PPSs that investors must scrutinize carefully in the prospectus prior to investing. Potential advantages of each of the categories of PPS were identified and important risk factors were highlighted. Two approaches for the investor to use to estimate the expected return from any given PPS were also suggested. While, on average, the actual returns to PPS holders in the past few years have not been stellar, we noted at least one PPS that was straightforward to interpret and had "historical returns" that compared favorably with fixed-income investments of the same term. It seems likely that both the structure of these instruments and the disclosures for investors will improve over time, rendering some PPSs suitable for specific investors with well-defined financial objectives.

ENDNOTES

[1] In a few instances, the prospectus will indicate that the issuer retains a "call provision" on the PPS whereby the issuer has the right to re-purchase the securities from the investor at a given point in time at a specific price.

Understanding and Evaluating Prospectuses, Offering Documents, and Proxy Statements

[2] Ian McDonald, "'Safer' Mutual Funds Look Sorry," *Wall Street Journal* (Eastern Edition), New York, NY, January 28, 2005, P. C. 1.
[3] Ibid.
[4] Ibid.
[5] Ibid.
[6] Ibid.
[7] Ibid.

DISCUSSION QUESTIONS:

1. For what reasons are PPSs classified as hybrid securities?
2. Why is "liquidity" considered an important issue for investors in PPSs?
3. Identify and explain at least three alternative approaches that issuers of PPSs commonly use to ensure that they will be able to return the principal to investors at maturity.
4. In the text, we noted that some PPSs were reported to have as little as 20 percent of their funds invested in equities. What could have caused this situation and how is it likely to affect returns to investors in these PPSs?
5. Discuss two possible approaches that an investor might use to estimate the expected return on a given PPS.

EXERCISE:

Based on the evidence provided in the text on returns earned by PPS holders in the past five years, how satisfied do you believe these investors are with this portion of their portfolios?

Explain how holders of some PPSs could achieve a near-zero annualized return on their investment despite double-digit annual returns on the underlying stock or index on which investors' return is based.

RECOMMENDED READING

National Association of Securities Dealers, "Principal-Protected Funds—Security Has a Price," March 27, 2003, www.nasd.com.

7 The Proxy Statement

Investors in companies and mutual funds are part owners of the entities and are entitled to vote on important matters. The SEC requires that a proxy statement or similar report be issued whenever there is a vote required by shareholders on matters related to a company or mutual fund. A proxy statement provides information on those issues that will be voted on at the annual (or interim) shareholder meeting. Examples are voting on nominees for the board of directors or approving the audit firm. As the adviser, you should recommend that the shareholder examine the proxy statement to obtain the information necessary to make an informed decision on how to cast his or her vote. You should also examine it yourself so that you can point out key issues to the shareholder. A shareholder may vote his or her shares using the proxy card accompanying the statement or may attend the meeting and vote in person. Alternatively, a shareholder may elect to allow management or another party to vote the shares (hence the term "proxy"—allowing someone else to act for you). In fact, management normally makes a recommendation in the proxy statement regarding how they would like the voting to go. It is important to review these recommendations and determine whether they are in the shareholders' best interest. This is particularly important for mutual fund proxy statements, which may involve a significant change in the strategy or expenses of the fund. The next section discusses evaluating a standard proxy statement for a company or mutual fund. The

Understanding and Evaluating Prospectuses, Offering Documents, and Proxy Statements

following section highlights additional points of interest particular to an investment company.

EVALUATING A PROXY STATEMENT

The proxy will disclose the date, time, and place of the meeting of security holders. Security holders are not required to attend the meeting, but if important issues are to be discussed, this may be advisable. Generally, the board of directors or trustees determine the issues that will be presented to security holders for a vote. In addition to items submitted by the board for shareholder votes, shareholders themselves can propose issues for a vote for the next annual meeting. The proxy must provide shareholders with the deadline for submitting shareholder proposals for the registrant's next annual meeting, and the date after which notice of a shareholder proposal is considered untimely. Exhibit 7.1 presents the front cover of TDS Telecom's 2004 Proxy Statement as an example.

In some cases, a shareholder may send in his or her vote on the proxy card accompanying the proxy statement and later decide to attend the annual meeting and vote in person. The company must state whether or not the person giving the proxy has the power to revoke it. TDS Telecom notes that:

> proxies given pursuant to this solicitation may be revoked at any time prior to the closing of polls at the annual meeting, by written notice to the Secretary of TDS which is received by the Secretary prior to the closing of the polls or by attendance at the annual meeting of shareholders and notice to the Secretary of such revocation at the meeting. Proxies may not be revoked after the polls are closed for voting.[1]

Typically, the company itself solicits proxies for management to vote the shares. Proxies may also be solicited by parties other than the company—for example, to oppose a company proxy or slate of directors. An investor should carefully evaluate proxies from both the company and outside parties, but should also make an independent assessment of what is in the investor's best interest, not management's or the opposing party.

Conflicts of Interest. When deciding how to vote shares or to whom to

Exhibit 7.1: Front Cover of TDS Telecom 2004 Proxy Statement

TELEPHONE AND DATA SYSTEMS, INC.
30 North LaSalle Street
Suite 4000
Chicago, Illinois 60602
Phone: (312) 630-1900
Fax: (312) 630-1908

May 28, 2004

Dear Shareholders:

You are cordially invited to attend our 2004 annual meeting of shareholders on Tuesday, June 29, 2004, at 10:00 a.m., Chicago time, at the LaSalle Bank building, 135 South LaSalle Street, Chicago, Illinois, on the 43rd floor. At the meeting, we will report on the plans and accomplishments of Telephone and Data Systems, Inc. ("TDS").

The formal notice of the meeting, our board of directors' proxy statement and our 2003 annual report are enclosed. At our 2004 annual meeting, shareholders are being asked to take the following actions:

1. consider and approve an amendment to TDS's Restated Certificate of Incorporation to declassify the board of directors so that all directors are elected annually;
2. elect members of the board of directors;
3. consider and approve TDS's 2004 Long-Term Incentive Plan; and
4. ratify the selection of independent auditors for the current fiscal year.

The board of directors recommends a vote "FOR" its nominees for election as directors and each of the proposals.

Our board of directors and members of our management team will be at the annual meeting to meet with shareholders and discuss our record of achievement and plans for the future. We would like to have as many shareholders as possible represented at the meeting. Therefore, please sign and return the enclosed proxy card(s), whether or not you plan to attend the meeting or vote on the Internet in accordance with the instructions set forth on the proxy card.

We look forward to visiting with you at the annual meeting.

Very truly yours,

Walter C.D. Carlson
Chairman of the Board

LeRoy T. Carlson, Jr.
President and Chief Executive Officer

Please help us avoid the expense of follow-up
proxy mailings to shareholders by
signing and returning the enclosed proxy card(s) promptly or
vote on the Internet in accordance with the instructions
set forth on the proxy card.

Understanding and Evaluating Prospectuses, Offering Documents, and Proxy Statements

give a proxy to vote shares, the investor should consider the interests of the parties involved and whether they are aligned with shareholders or are in conflict with shareholders. Those soliciting proxies who are also significant shareholders are more likely to have interests aligned with the investor. The company should describe any substantial interest, like investment in the company, held by any person who has been a director or executive officer since the beginning of the last fiscal year, each nominee for election as a director, and each associate of any of the directors or nominees. For proxies filed by parties other than the company, the proxy should describe any substantial interest of the proxy filers and their representatives. This disclosure should include the participant's:

1. Name and business address
2. Present principal occupation and the name, business, and address of any corporation or other organization in which such employment is carried on
3. Conviction, during the past ten years, in a criminal proceeding (excluding traffic violations or similar misdemeanors) and the dates, nature of conviction, name and location of court, and penalty imposed or other disposition of the case
4. Beneficial ownership of each class of securities of the registrant
5. Record, but not beneficial, ownership of each class of securities of the registrant
6. Purchases and sales of all securities of the registrant within the past two years, including the dates on which they were purchased or sold and the amount purchased or sold on each date
7. Use of borrowed funds for such purchases and sales
8. Participation in any contract, arrangements, or understandings with respect to any securities of the registrant, the parties to such contracts, arrangements or understandings and the details thereof
9. Associates' beneficial ownership of securities of the registrant
10. Beneficial ownership of any parent or subsidiary of the registrant
11. Transactions since the beginning of the company's last fiscal year, in which the amount involved exceeds $60,000
12. Arrangement or understanding with any person with respect to any

future employment by the registrant or its affiliates or any future transactions to which the registrant or any of its affiliates will or may be a party

The investor should carefully review these disclosures, particularly any transactions between the company and the person soliciting the proxy. The investor should also evaluate the solicitor's current shareholdings and any significant sales or purchases to determine how serious this solicitor is in acting in the best interest of all shareholders as opposed to their own personal interest or short-term profit motive.

Voting Securities. So that investors can determine which shareholders, if any, have more or less control in issues subject to a vote, the company must provide the number of shares outstanding and the number of votes to which each class is entitled. TDS Telecom's presentation of this information is presented in Exhibit 7.2. Note that in this case, the Series A common shareholders have much more voting power than the preferred shareholders or even the other common shareholders.

The company must also state the record date or other means of determining which shareholders are qualified to vote. Since the shareholder base of public firms changes daily as shares are bought and sold, the record date establishes who owned the shares at the time of the vote.

The company must also present a table listing the share ownership of managers and anyone owning more than 5 percent of the shares in any class of securities. In addition, any arrangements that could result in a change in control should be discussed. This disclosure should be formatted similar to the way in which TDS Telecom provides the disclosure in Exhibit 7.3. Note that management controls the majority of the Series A common shares and has more than 50 percent of the voting power.

Election of Directors. When directors are being elected, the proxy must include certain information in a table. This information includes:

1. Details of any material pending legal proceedings
2. The names and ages of all directors and nominees, company positions and offices held, the tenure and term of office as director

Understanding and Evaluating Prospectuses, Offering Documents, and Proxy Statements

Exhibit 7.2: TDS Telecom Voting Securities

What is the voting power of the outstanding shares in the election of directors?
The following shows certain information relating to the outstanding shares and voting power of such shares in the election of directors as of the record date:

Class of Common Stock	Outstanding Shares	Votes Per Share	Voting Power	Numbers of Class II Directors Standing for Election in Regular Election	Total Number of Directors Elected by Voting Group and Standing for Election in Alternate Election
Series A Common shares	6,433,654	10	64,336,540		
Preferred shares	38,645	1	38,645		
Subtotal			64,375,185	2	8
Common shares	50,878,054	1	50,878,054	2	4
Total directors				4	12

What is the voting power of the outstanding shares in matters other than the election of directors?
The following shows certain information relating to the outstanding shares and voting power of such shares as of the record date:

Class of Common Stock	Outstanding Shares	Votes Per Share	Total Voting Power	Percent
Series A common shares	6,433,654	10	64,336,540	55.8%
Common shares	50,878,054	1	50,878,054	44.2%
Preferred shares	38,645	1	38,645	* %
			115,253,239	100.0%

Source: TDS Telecom 2004 Proxy Statement, dated May 28, 2004, page 3.

3. Disclosure of any material transactions between the director or nominee and parties related to the company
4. Any business relationships between the company and the director or nominee
5. Details of major committees and committee members, including the audit, nominating, and compensation committees
6. The total number of meetings of the board of directors (including regularly scheduled and special meetings) held during the last full fiscal year;

Chapter 7 | The Proxy Statement

Exhibit 7.3: TDS Telecom Security Ownership by Management

Security Ownership of Management

The following table sets forth as of March 31, 2004, or the latest practicable date, the number of common shares and Series A Common Shares beneficially owned, and the percentage of the outstanding shares of each such class so owned by each director and nominee for director of TDS, by each of the executive officers named in the Summary Compensation Table and by all directors and executive officers as a group.

Name of Individual or Number of Persons in Group	Title of Class or Series	Amount and Nature of Beneficial Ownership (1)	Percent of Class or Series	Percent of Shares of Common Stock	Percent of Voting Power (2)
LeRoy T. Carlson, Jr., Walter C.D. Carlson, Letitia G.C. Carlson and Prudence E. Carlson (3)	Series A Common Shares	6,062,302	94.3%	10.6%	52.6%
LeRoy T. Carlson (4)(10)	Common Shares	224,339	*	*	*
	Series A Common Shares	52,325	*	*	*
LeRoy T. Carlson, Jr. (5)(10)	Common Shares	406,366	*	*	*
	Series A Common Shares	17,620	*	*	*
Walter C.D. Carlson (6)	Common Shares	3,134	*	*	*
	Series A Common Shares	864	*	*	*
Letitia G.C. Carlson (7)	Common Shares	1,262	*	*	*
	Series A Common Shares	934	*	*	*
Sandra L. Helton (10)	Common Shares	149,724	*	*	*
James Barr III (10)	Common Shares	48,560	*	*	*
Donald C. Nebergall (9)	Common Shares	2,332	*	*	*
	Series A Common Shares	1,032	*	*	*
Herbert S. Wander	Common Shares	2,152	*	*	*
George W. Off	Common Shares	3,235	*	*	*
Martin L. Solomon	Common Shares	12,259	*	*	*
Kevin A. Mundt	Common Shares	1,970	*	*	*
Mitchell H. Saranow	Common Shares	1,000	*	*	*
John E. Rooney	Common Shares	932	*	*	*
All directors, director nominees and executive officers as a group (26 persons) (8) (10)	Common Shares	1,346,068	2.6%	2.4%	1.2%
	Series A Common Shares	6,142,193	95.5%	10.7%	53.3%

*Less than 1%

(1) The nature of beneficial ownership for shares in this column is sole voting and investment power, except as otherwise set forth in these footnotes

(2) Represents the percent of voting power in matters other than the election of directors.

(3) The shares listed are held by the persons named as trustees under a voting trust which expires June 30, 2035, created to facilitate long standing relationships amoung the trust certificate holders.

Under the terms of the voting trusts, the trustees hold and vote the TDS Series A Common Shares held in the trusts. If the voting trusts were terminated, the following individuals; directly or indirectly, would each be deemed to own beneficially more than 5% of the outstanding TDS Series A. Common Shares: LeRoy T. Carlson, Jr..

Source: TDS Telecom 2004 Proxy Statement, May 28, 2004, pages 42–45.

any incumbent director attending fewer than 75 percent of the meetings must be named

7. Any director resignations due to a disagreement on any matter relating to the company's operations, policies, or practices

When reviewing the proxy, investors should look for any relationships among the directors that could indicate a lack of independence. In particular, the makeup of committees should be evaluated to determine whether the committee members appear qualified and independent. Two important committees are the compensation committee, which determines management's compensation, and the audit committee, which oversees the external audit. In reviewing these disclosures, it is wise to obtain proxy statements for companies employing the directors. For example, if the CEOs of two companies serve as directors and members of the other company's compensation committee, they are in a position to provide a quid pro quo pay package at the expense of stockholders. The directors are supposed to be looking out for the interests of shareholders, and shareholders should use their voting rights to elect directors who will do so.

Compensation of Directors. The proxy statement must provide clear, concise, and understandable disclosure of all compensation awarded to directors as well as executive officers. TDS Telecom's presentation of this information is excerpted below.[2]

> **Compensation of Directors.**
> The board of directors amended the compensation plan (the "Non-Employee Directors' Plan") for non-employee directors in 2002. A non-employee director is a director of TDS who is not an employee of TDS or its affiliates, U.S. Cellular or TDS Telecom. The purpose of the Non-Employee Directors' Plan is to provide reasonable compensation to non-employee directors for their services to TDS, and to induce qualified persons to serve as non-employee members of the board of directors.
>
> The Non-Employee Directors' Plan provides that each non-employee director will receive an annual director's fee of $34,000 payable

quarterly, and the chairperson will receive an additional $34,000 fee. The plan also provides that each non-employee director serving on the audit committee will receive an annual director's fee of $8,000 payable quarterly, except for the chairperson, who will receive a fee of $18,000. The plan also provides that each non-employee director will receive an annual fee of $2,000 payable quarterly, for serving on the long-term compensation committee, except for the chairperson, who will receive a fee of $4,000. It also provides that each non-employee director will receive a fee of $1,500 for board of directors and committee meetings, plus reimbursement of reasonable out-of-pocket expenses incurred in connection with travel to, and attendance at, each regularly scheduled or special meeting.

The Non-Employee Directors' Plan further provides that each non-employee director will receive 50 percent, and may elect to receive on an annual basis up to 100 percent, of their retainers and meeting fees for regularly scheduled meetings of the board (five per year), by the delivery of Common Shares of TDS having a fair market value as of the date of payment equal to the cash amount of the retainer or fee foregone.

Under the Non-Employee Directors' Plan, for purposes of determining the number of Common Shares deliverable in connection with any of the foregoing elections, the fair market value of a Common Share will be the average closing price of our Common Shares as reported in the American Stock Exchange Composite Transactions section of *The Wall Street Journal* for the twenty trading days before the end of the quarter or the date of the board meeting, as applicable. Our board of directors has reserved 65,000 Common Shares of TDS for issuance pursuant to the Non-Employee Directors' Plan.

In addition, TDS pays life insurance premiums to provide life insurance of $100,000 for each of its directors. Except for such life insurance premiums, directors who are also employees of TDS or any affiliate do not receive any additional compensation for services rendered as directors.

When evaluating director compensation, shareholders should question whether the package is appropriate. It should be compared with that of other companies in similar industries and of similar size. While there is significant work and liability involved these days in performing duties as a director and investors would like directors to be compensated accordingly, it is not desirable for the directors to be overpaid at the expense of other shareholders.

Independent Public Accountants. The annual proxy must furnish the following information describing the company's relationship with its independent public accountant:

1. The name of the principal accountant selected or being recommended
2. Whether a change has been made regarding the principal accountant
3. Whether or not representatives of the principal accountant are expected to be present at the security holders' meeting, whether or not they will have the opportunity to make a statement if they desire to do so, and whether or not such representatives are expected to be available to respond to appropriate questions
4. Details of any disagreements with current or former accountants
5. The amounts paid to the principal accountants for audit fees, audit-related fees, tax fees, and any other fees, and any policies related to fee approval by the audit committee

The investor should be wary of any changes in or disagreements with auditors. These are sometimes signs of more problems to come. It is desirable that the fees received by the auditors relate primarily to audit and audit-related fees. After Sarbanes-Oxley, many consulting arrangements with auditors are now prohibited, but some services are still permitted, and it is not desirable for the auditor to receive a large portion of their fees for non-audit work. This may impair their independent frame of mind. TDS Telecom's disclosures regarding their independent public accountants are presented in Exhibit 7.4. Note that, in accordance with Sarbanes-Oxley, non-audit-related fees have been substantially reduced.

Compensation Plans. For new or amended compensation plans subject to security holder action, the company must describe the material features of the plan, and identify each class of persons eligible to participate, the approxi-

Chapter 7 | The Proxy Statement

Exhibit 7.4: TDS Disclosure of Fees Paid to Principal Accountants

Fees Paid to Principal Accountants

The following sets forth the aggregate fees (including expenses) billed by TDS's principal auditors PricewaterhouseCoopers LLP for 2003 and 2002:

	2003	2002
Audit fees (1)	$2,082,246	$1,892,575
Audit-related fees (2)	132,156	560,000
Tax fees (3)	—	439,409
All other fees (4)	21,000	297,925
Total fees	$2,235,402	$3,189,909

(1) Represents the aggregate fees billed by PricewaterhouseCoopers LLP for professional services rendered for the audit of the annual financial statements for the years 2003 and 2002 included in TDS's and U.S. Cellular's Form 10-Ks for those years and the reviews of the financial statements included in TDS's and U.S. Cellular's Form 10-Qs for each of these years, as well as accounting research, review of financial information included in other SEC filings, and the issuance of consents and comfort letters. Does not include fees of $53,500 paid to Arthur Andersen in 2002.

(2) Represents the aggregate fees billed by PricewaterhouseCoopers LLP for assurance and related services for TDS and U.S. Cellular in the years 2003 and 2002 that are reasonably related to the performance of the audit or review of financial statements other than the fees disclosed in the foregoing paragraph. These services include acquisition and divestiture-related services, accounting consultation and (for 2003 only) Sarbanes-Oxley planning. There were no fees paid to Arthur Andersen for audit-related services in 2002.

(3) Represents the aggregate fees billed by PricewaterhouseCoopers LLP for professional services rendered to TDS and U.S. Cellular in 2003 and 2002 for tax compliance, tax advice, and tax planning. These services represented tax consulting services. Does not include fees of $179,125 paid to Arthur Andersen in 2002.

(4) Represents the aggregate fees billed by PricewaterhouseCoopers LLP for services, other than services covered in (1), (2) or (3) above, for the years 2003 and 2002. These services include consulting on internal audit leadership for 2002 and licensing of a best practice database for 2003. Does not include fees of $27,360 paid to Arthur Andersen in 2002.

The audit committee determined that the payment of fees for non-audit related services does not conflict.

Source: TDS Telecom 2004 Proxy Statement, May 28, 2004, page 25.

mate number of persons in each class, and the basis of participation. Further, the company must provide a table disclosing, if possible, the benefits or amounts that will be received by or allocated to officers and directors. Exhibit 7.5 presents TDS Telecom's tabular disclosure.

Typically, retirement plans are based on the employee's tenure with the firm, and new plans must take into account the time employees worked prior to the plan's implementation. If the plan submitted to shareholders is a pension or retirement plan, the company should state the approximate amount necessary to fund the plan with respect to past services, the period over which the plan will be funded, and the estimated annual payments. Then the company should disclose the estimated annual payment to be made with respect to *current* services.

For compensation plans involving grants of options, warrants, or rights, the company should state the title and amount of securities underlying the options, the prices, expiration dates, and other material conditions of exercise, the consideration received or to be received by the company for granting or extending of the options, the market value of the underlying securities, and any federal income tax consequences to the recipient and the registrant. Further, the company should provide details regarding the amount of such awards to be received by officers and directors. A separate disclosure should be presented delineating between plans that require shareholder approval and those that do not. The existence of plans that award ownership interests to employees is useful in aligning the interests of employees with those of investors. The investor should be wary, however, when these plans transfer significant wealth to management at the expense of shareholders (and other employees).

Authorization, Issuance, or Modification of Securities. If the company plans to authorize, issue, or modify any securities, the proxy statement must state the title and amount of securities to be authorized or issued. It must also describe the security, providing the same information regarding the issue as is required in a prospectus. (See Chapter 3.) It must then describe how the securities are to be issued, including the nature and amount of consideration to be received and the likely uses of the funds. If the securities will not be issued in a public offering for cash, the company

Exhibit 7.5: TDS Telecom Compensation Plan Disclosures

The following table discloses the benefits or amounts that will be received by or allocated to each of the following under the plan being acted upon, if such benefits or amounts are determinable, as of December 31, 2003.

New Plan Benefits
2004 Long-Term Incentive Plan

Name	Number of Common Shares Subject to Opinions(1)	Company Match Award for 2003 (2)	
		Dollar Value	Numbers of Shares
LeRoy T. Carlson, Jr.	361,681	$—	—
Sandra L. Helton	152,825	$—	—
James Barr III	66,204	$—	—
John E. Rooney (3)	—	$—	—
LeRoy T. Carlson	188,745	$—	1,018
Other Executives	467,561	$67,570	264
Executive Group	1,237,016	$17,478	1,282
Non-Executive Board of Director Group	—	$85,048	—
Non-Executive Employee Group	931,984	$—	—
Total	2,169,000	$85,048	1,282

(1) Since the option exercise price for all awards is equal to the fair market value of the Common Shares on the grant date, no value was assigned to the options for purposes of the above table.

(2) Represents the dollar value and the number of shares of the company Match Awards for 2003, which is represented by phantom Common Shares of TDS.

(3) John E. Rooney does not participate in the 2004 Long-Term Incentive Plan but is listed above pursuant to the rules of the SEC. Mr. Rooney participates in U.S. Cellular's long-term incentive plan.

Source: *TDS Telecom 2004 Proxy Statement, May 28, 2004, page 24.*

must state the reasons for the authorization and the general effect upon the rights of existing security holders. Investors should assess whether the resulting dilution to their ownership interest is worth the consideration to be received.

When a company is issuing or modifying securities, the company must also provide appropriate financial statements, supplementary financial information, management's discussion, and analysis of financial condition and results of operations, changes in and disagreements with accountants on accounting and financial disclosure, quantitative and qualitative disclosures about market risk, and a statement as to the availability of the principal accountants at the security holders' meeting. These disclosures should be provided in the manner described for prospectuses in Chapter 3. This required information may be incorporated by reference into the proxy statement, provided that the information is contained in an annual report to security holders or a previously filed statement or report.

Mergers, Consolidations, Acquisitions, and Similar Matters. Certain information needs to be provided when a company is proposing a merger or consolidation, an acquisition of securities, an acquisition of any other going business or its assets, a sale or transfer of any substantial part of assets, or a liquidation or dissolution. This includes (among other items) the following information for each of the parties to the transaction:

1. Terms of the transaction.
2. Information relating to any report, opinion, or appraisal materially relating to the transaction from an outside party.
3. Past contacts, transactions, or negotiations.
4. Selected financial data.
5. Pro forma selected financial data showing the effect of the transaction.
6. A table comparing historical and pro forma per share data of the acquiring company and historical and equivalent pro forma per share data of the target company. This table should include book value per share as of the date financial data is presented, cash dividends declared per share, and income (loss) per share from continuing operations.

Chapter 2 provides techniques for analyzing this financial data in order to assess whether the transaction makes sense to shareholders.

Acquisition or Disposition of Property. If action is to be taken with respect to the acquisition or disposition of any property, the company must provide the general character and location of the property. It must also state the nature and amount of consideration to be paid or received. To the extent practicable, the company should outline the facts pertaining to the fairness of the consideration. It must also disclose the name and address of the transferor or transferee, and the nature of any material relationship of such person to the company or its affiliates. Finally, any other material features of the contract or transaction should be outlined. The investor should be wary of any purchases or sales of property between the company and related persons. If they exist, the investor should ascertain whether the purchase price appears to be determined at arm's length.

Restatement of Accounts. If the company must restate the value of any asset, capital, or surplus account, it must state the nature of the restatement and the date as of which it is to be effective. It must also outline the reasons for the restatement and for the selection of the effective date. It must state the name and amount of each account (including any reserve accounts) affected by the restatement and the effect of the restatement on those accounts. Finally, the extent of any effect on the amount available for distribution to equity holders should be disclosed. Restatements should be rare, and if any are reported, the investor should examine what factor lead to the restatement and whether the company has taken corrective action.

Matters Not Required to Be Submitted. Occasionally, companies offer proposals for shareholder vote that are not required to be submitted to shareholders. In such cases, the company must state the nature of such matter, the reasons for submitting it to a vote of security holders, and what action is intended to be taken by the registrant in the event of a negative vote on the matter by the security holders.

An example of such a matter is included in the TDS Telecom proxy statement:[3]

> We are not required to obtain shareholder ratification of the selection of PricewaterhouseCoopers LLP as our independent auditors by the Bylaws or otherwise. However, we have elected to seek such ratification by the affirmative vote of the holders of a majority of the votes cast by shares entitled to vote with respect to such matter at the annual meeting. Should the shareholders fail to ratify the selection of PricewaterhouseCoopers LLP as independent auditors, the audit committee of the board of directors will review whether to retain such firm for the year ending December 31, 2004.

Amendment of Charter, Bylaws, or Other Documents. If action is to be taken with respect to any amendment of the registrant's charter, bylaws, or other documents, the company must state the reasons for and the general effect of the proposed amendment. Such changes should also be rare, and the investor should evaluate the impact on future returns. This is particularly important for mutual funds as discussed below.

Voting Procedures. For each matter that is to be submitted to a vote of security holders, the company must disclose the vote required for approval or election and the method by which votes will be counted. TDS provides the following example:[4]

> To be approved, the Declassification Amendment must receive the affirmative vote of the holders of a majority of the votes entitled to be cast by holders of outstanding Common Shares, Series A Common Shares and Preferred Shares, voting together as a single group. In this vote, abstentions from voting on such proposal and non-votes will not represent affirmative votes and will, therefore, effectively constitute votes against the matter for purposes of such vote. In addition to the foregoing vote, Proposal 1 will require the affirmative vote of the holders of a majority of the votes entitled to be cast by the holders of Common Shares present in person or represented by proxy, voting separately as a class. A vote to abstain from voting on such proposal will be treated as a vote against such proposal. Non-votes with respect to such proposal will not be counted and, accordingly, will not affect the determination of whether such proposal is approved.

ADDITIONAL CONSIDERATIONS FOR AN INVESTMENT COMPANY PROXY STATEMENT

Unlike publicly traded corporations, investment companies do not issue annual proxy statements. A proxy statement is issued when something significant must be voted on such as a new investment advisory contract or distribution plan (12b-1). The investor should therefore pay close attention to these proxy statements. The items listed in the above section for proxy statements in general should be reviewed. In the case of fund trustees, the investor should examine how many of the trustees are independent of the fund company. The more independent trustees there are, the greater the likelihood that the trustees will act in the interest of investors rather than

Table 7.1: TIAA-CREF Proposed Agreement

Fund	Current Agreement	Proposed Agreement
International Equity Fund	0.09%	0.50% or less*
Large-cap Value Fund	0.08%	0.45% or less*
Small-cap Equity Fund	0.08%	0.48% or less*
Social Choice Equity Fund	0.04%	0.15%
Real Estate Securities Fund	0.09%	0.50% or less*
Bond Fund	0.08%	0.30% or less*
Inflation-linked Bond Fund	0.09%	0.30% or less*
Money Market Fund	0.04%	0.10%

* At the Board's request, the management fees of these Funds have modest breakpoints that may eventually gradually reduce the fee rates from the amounts indicated in the chart as each Fund's assets grow.
Source: TIAA-CREF Institutional Mutual Funds Proxy Statement, November 28, 2005, for Special Shareholder Meeting of January 25, 2006, page 11.

the fund company. Additionally, the investor should scrutinize the following key areas.

Investment Advisory and Fee Arrangements. If any changes are requested to the investment advisory agreement or other agreements that involve the fees and expenses of the fund, the proxy statement must provide a table showing the current and pro forma (expected) fees. This could include investment advisory fees, custodial fees, and transfer fees, among others. An example can be seen in a recent proxy solicitation for TIAA-CREF. TIAA-CREF requested an increase in fees for its funds stating that the adviser had originally set its fees at very low levels "making it difficult for the adviser to sustain the level and quality of management and service that shareholders expect in this competitive environment." Table 7.1 was included in the proxy statement:[5]

Table 7.1 shows that the fees were, indeed, very low, and the proposed change would raise them substantially. The trustees recommended as follows:[6]

> On January 25, 2006, the TIAA-CREF Institutional Mutual Funds will hold a special meeting of the shareholders of its International Equity, Large-Cap Value, Small-Cap Equity, Real Estate Securities, Social Choice Equity, Bond, Inflation-Linked Bond and Money Market Funds.
> The purpose of this meeting is to vote on a proposed new invest-

Understanding and Evaluating Prospectuses, Offering Documents, and Proxy Statements

Table 7.2: TIAA-CREF Expense Comparison

Fund	Proposed Total Expense Ratio	Median Peer Total Expense Ratio	Difference
International Equity Fund — Institutional	0.59%	1.19%	−0.60%
International Equity Fund — Retirement	0.80%	1.19%	−0.39%
Large-cap Value Fund — Institutional	0.50%	1.07%	−0.57%
Large-cap Value Fund — Retirement	0.75%	1.07%	−0.32%
Large-cap Value Fund — Retail	0.99%	1.05%	−0.06%
Small-Cap Value Fund — Institutional	0.55%	1.15%	−0.60%
Small-Cap Equity Fund — Retirement	0.78%	1.15%	−0.37%
Small-Cap Equity Fund — Retail	1.16%	1.26%	−0.10%
Social Choice Equity Fund — Institutional	0.25%	0.99%	−0.74%
Social Choice Equity Fund — Retirement	0.48%	0.99%	−0.51%
Real Estate Securities Fund — Institutional	0.59%	1.11%	−0.52%
Real Estate Securities Fund — Retirement	0.80%	1.11%	−0.31%
Real Estate Securities Fund — Retail	0.99%	1.18%	−0.19%
BOND FUND — Institutional	0.34%	0.69%	−0.35%
Inflation-linked Bond Fund — Institutional	0.35%	0.35%	0.00%
Inflation-linked Bond Fund — Retail	0.80%	0.72%	+0.08%
Money Market Fund — Institutional	0.15%	0.43%	−0.28%

Source: TIAA-CREF Institutional Mutual Funds Proxy Statement, November 28, 2005, for Special Shareholder Meeting of January 25, 2006, page 15.

ment management agreement with Teachers Advisors, Inc. (the "Advisor"), the current investment advisor to these Funds. This proposal is the same as the proposal for these eight Funds originally presented for shareholder approval in a proxy statement dated July 5, 2005, and voted on at a special shareholder meeting on August 31, 2005.

Because approval of the proposed agreement is vital to the future operation of these Funds, and because some shareholders have indicated a willingness to re-examine their vote if given more time to fully consider the proposal, the Advisor has recommended, and we have agreed, to provide a second opportunity to do so. *As before, we, the Funds' independent Board of Trustees, unanimously recommend that you vote "FOR" the new investment management agreement.*

As explained in the original proxy materials, the proposed new investment management agreement would help ensure that the Funds remain fairly and competitively priced and continue to serve shareholder needs, while also providing a sustainable fee and expense structure that enables the Advisor to continue managing the Funds. It's important for you to understand that although the new agreement would result in higher advisory fees, the Funds would remain *competitive with the lower-priced* offerings in the industry.

Note that this was the second time this issue was put to a vote of shareholders. It was defeated the first time. The proxy statement provides support for the claim that the new fee structure was competitive.[7] On this second occasion, the shareholders approved the new advisory agreement with the higher fee structure.

Changes to Permitted Investments or Strategy. If the investment company is proposing changes to the types of security transactions permitted and/or the fund's strategy, the investor should consider whether that is in line with his or her decision to invest in the fund. If not, he or she should vote against the proposal, and if the proposal passes, seek out a fund with a strategy more in line with the investor's objectives.

Distribution Plan. Distribution fees, also known as 12b-1 fees from the related SEC rule, may be paid for the marketing and selling of fund shares. Requested approval of or changes to a distribution plan must be disclosed in the proxy statement. The proxy statement must disclose the rate of the fee, to whom payments may be made, and the amounts of payments made during the most recent year to those affiliated with the fund or investment adviser. Institution of a new distribution plan or increases in rates should be scrutinized. Of course, termination of the plan or a reduction in fees should be welcome news.

CONCLUSION

Many investors take a quick look at proxy statements and either toss them away or quickly vote according to management's recommendation. It would be in the best interest of investors to take some time to understand the issues subject to a vote and deciding which are important to the interests of investors. You should advise the investor to review the proxy statement and

Understanding and Evaluating Prospectuses, Offering Documents, and Proxy Statements

vote their shares. You can assist the investor in identifying key issues. Some key points for investors to focus on in a proxy statement are:

- Conflicts of interests between investors, management, and directors, such as related party transactions or business transactions between management, directors, and the company
- Who is entitled to vote and which share classes may control the outcome
- The types and level of compensation of management and directors
- Changes in or disagreements with auditors and any fees paid for non-audit-related services
- Any significant changes to securities issued, mergers or acquisitions/dispositions
- Changes to investment advisory or other fee arrangements
- Institution of or changes to any mutual fund distribution plan

ENDNOTES

1 TDS Telecom 2004 Proxy Statement, May 28, 2004, page 4.
2 TDS Telecom 2004 Proxy Statement, May 28, 2004, page 36.
3 TDS Telecom 2004 Proxy Statement, May 28, 2004, page 24.
4 TDS Telecom 2004 Proxy Statement, May 28, 2004, page 5.
5 TIAA-CREF Institutional Mutual Funds, Proxy Statement, November 28, 2005, for Special Shareholder Meeting of January 25, 2006, page 11.
6 Ibid, cover letter.
7 Ibid, p. 15.

DISCUSSION QUESTIONS:

1. What are the key points to consider when reviewing a proxy statement for a corporation?
2. What might be some reasons for attending an annual meeting rather than voting shares by proxy?
3. What are the key points to consider when evaluating a proxy statement for an investment company?
4. Important disclosures in the proxy statement include stock and option grants to officers and directors. What are the pros and cons to these types of grants?

EXERCISE:

Examine the voting securities for TDS Telecom provided in Exhibit 7.2. What is the market value of the regular common shares? Are common shareholders' voting rights in line with their investment in the company? What inherent conflicts exist with this voting structure?

RECOMMENDED READING

United States Securities and Exchange Commission, "Proxy Rules: Regulation 14A—Solicitation of Proxies," www.sec.gov/divisions/corpfin/forms/14s.htm.
Unites States Securities and Exchange Commission, "Amendments to Rules on Shareholder Proposals," Release No. 34-40018, www.sec.gov/rules/final/34-40018.htm.

8 Hedge Funds

Over the last few, years there has been explosive growth in the number of hedge funds and the amount of assets managed by hedge funds. In 2005, the SEC reported that hedge fund assets had grown 260 percent over the prior five years and that hedge fund assets were growing faster than mutual funds.[1] The SEC also noted an increase in the number of fraud enforcement actions over that same period, numbering 51 cases and involving over $1 billion dollars.[2] Since most hedge funds and their advisers are not required to be registered with the SEC, investors and their advisers must take particular care in studying offering documents and performing due diligence on the fund and the fund's advisers. This chapter describes the regulatory requirements for hedge funds and key factors to examine in offering documents for hedge funds.

REGULATION AND OFFERING DOCUMENTS

Most hedge funds are not required to be registered with the SEC. Until recently, the managers running hedge funds also had no registration requirements. Beginning in 2006, some hedge funds managers are now required to register with the SEC and be subject to SEC oversight.

While most offerings of securities to the public are required to be registered with the SEC, Regulation D provides several exceptions to registration. Two of these exceptions relate to small offerings (less than $1 million or $5 million) of securities,

Understanding and Evaluating Prospectuses, Offering Documents, and Proxy Statements

but the third relates to offerings of unlimited amounts of money. This third exception, Rule 506 of Regulation D, permits hedge funds (private investment partnerships or other entities) to avoid registration with the SEC if they satisfy the following standards:[3]

- The company cannot use general solicitation or advertising to market the securities.
- The company may sell its securities to an unlimited number of "accredited investors" and up to 35 other purchasers. All nonaccredited investors, either alone or with a purchaser representative, must be sophisticated—that is, they must have sufficient knowledge and experience in financial and business matters to make them capable of evaluating the merits and risks of the prospective investment.
- Companies must decide what information to give to accredited investors, so long as it does not violate the antifraud prohibitions of the federal securities laws. *But companies must give nonaccredited investors disclosure documents that are generally the same as those used in registered offerings.* If a company provides information to accredited investors, it must make this information available to nonaccredited investors as well (emphasis added).
- The company must be available to answer questions by prospective purchasers.
- Audited financial statements must be provided.
- Purchasers receive "restricted" securities, meaning that the securities cannot be sold for at least a year without registering them.

Accredited investors include:[4]

- A bank, insurance company, registered investment company, business development company, or small business investment company
- An employee benefit plan, within the meaning of the Employee Retirement Income Security Act, if a bank, insurance company, or registered investment adviser makes the investment decisions, or if the plan has total assets in excess of $5 million

- A charitable organization, corporation, or partnership with assets exceeding $5 million
- A director, executive officer, or general partner of the company selling the securities
- A business in which all the equity owners are accredited investors
- A natural person who has individual net worth, or joint net worth with the person's spouse, that exceeds $1 million at the time of the purchase
- A natural person with income exceeding $200,000 in each of the two most recent years or joint income with a spouse exceeding $300,000 for those years and a reasonable expectation of the same income level in the current year
- A trust with assets in excess of $5 million, not formed to acquire the securities offered, whose purchases are made by a sophisticated person

The justification for permitting unregistered offerings to such accredited investors is that they should be sophisticated and able to look after themselves. Since hedge funds must provide offering documents equivalent to a prospectus for any nonaccredited investors, the same documents are typically provided to all investors. This will be in the form of a prospectus or private offering memorandum.

In the past, as long as fund managers had fewer than 15 clients, they were not required to register as investment advisers, and they were permitted to count the hedge fund as a single client rather than count all of the investors. Regulations now require that, in some cases, the hedge fund managers must count all investors in determining if they have fewer than 14 clients. This regulation was intended to require registration for virtually all hedge fund advisers so that the SEC would be able to better monitor the industry. Some private investment arrangements were not intended to be included. In particular, the SEC noted in its release requiring registration that venture capital funds and private equity funds structured as private investment entities were not intended to be captured by the registration requirements. Noting that most private equity and venture capital funds require a long lock-up period (initial period during which funds may be withdrawn by investors), the SEC determined that managers of private

Understanding and Evaluating Prospectuses, Offering Documents, and Proxy Statements

investment funds only need to count all fund investors in their number of clients if the investment fund permits investors to withdraw funds within two years. The consequence of this exception is that some hedge funds are revising their documents to insert a two-year lock-up period. As a result, many hedge fund managers will continue to be unregistered with the SEC. Due to the lack of oversight, let the buyer or investor beware. Investors and their advisers must read all of the fine print and perform thorough due diligence on the fund and its managers. Note that some hedge fund managers choose to register as investment advisers with the SEC. This enables an investor to review the manager's SEC filings to obtain additional information as discussed below.

Most hedge funds are structured as either limited partnerships or limited liability companies for several reasons. First, these structures permit a pass-through of income to the investors rather than imposing an entity-level tax. Second, these entities permit special allocation of income, gains, and losses. In a typical hedge fund, the manager receives not only a base fee for managing assets but also a disproportionate share of investment gains. Investors in hedge funds will therefore typically receive at least two key documents, a private offering memorandum (or prospectus) and a limited partnership agreement (or limited liability company operating agreement).

EVALUATING HEDGE FUND OFFERING DOCUMENTS

The private offering memorandum should contain information similar to that found in an equity (Chapter 3) or investment company (Chapter 5) prospectus. Investors and their advisers should read the offering memorandum in its entirety and apply the same techniques described in Chapters 3 and 5. Additionally, the evaluation of the offering documents including the partnership agreement should particularly focus on investment strategies, management, risk factors, fees, and partnership or LLC provisions.

Investment Objectives and Strategies. Since a hedge fund investment is part of an overall asset allocation decision, a key consideration is the investment strategies of the hedge fund and whether these fit into the investor's overall asset allocation. The term "hedge" in hedge funds implies the use of hedging with derivatives, short positions, or similar strategies. In reality, today, hedge funds come in all flavors. Some are effectively nothing more than unregistered long-investment-oriented investment companies (or hedge fund manager retirement plans); others use sophisticated hedging techniques or employ unique strategies that may not be easily replicable by others. In some cases, investment may be made in private, nonmarketable securities or employ strategies that are not permitted in mutual funds. While there is no comprehensive list of hedge fund strategies since they can use any conceivable strategy, some typical strategies include:

- Long-only funds with typical investment philosophies (value, growth, income).
- Long/short funds that may be net long in some periods and net short in other periods, depending upon the manager's view of the market.
- Market neutral funds where investments are simultaneously made both long and short. A directional market bet is not made. Instead, the manager seeks to sell securities that are perceived to be overvalued and buy those perceived to be undervalued.
- Other arbitrage-related funds.
- Special situations or distressed securities funds.

The hedge fund offering memorandum will disclose the fund's primary investment objective(s) and the strategies employed to reach the objective(s). Upon reviewing the objectives and strategies, the following questions should be considered:

- Are the objectives and strategies well defined (the preferred method) or is it totally open-ended as to what the fund will do and how (not as desirable)?
- Are the strategies ones that cannot be obtained elsewhere at the same or lower cost?
- Do the fund's objectives/strategies fit into the investor's overall asset allocation, or do they overlap with other holdings?
- If the fund has been operating, how is the prior performance compared to other funds utilizing a similar strategy?

Understanding and Evaluating Prospectuses, Offering Documents, and Proxy Statements

Management. The offering documents should provide information on the background of the fund managers. This information should be reviewed to determine if the managers have the appropriate experience, education, and other credentials (such as professional designations) to properly implement the fund's objectives and strategies. Due diligence of the fund managers should extend beyond the offering documents. Based on the information in the offering documents, the managers' histories should be scrutinized. If the manager is registered as an investment adviser, they must file a form ADV with the SEC or state. In the case of SEC-registered advisers and many state-registered advisers, the form ADV may be viewed online (www.adviserinfo.sec.gov). The ADV should be reviewed to make sure it is consistent with the offering documents and to determine if there have been any disciplinary problems in the past that required disclosure. If the fund manager was previously employed as a broker, a similar search should be performed with the NASD (http://pdpi.nasdr.com/PDPI). A simple Internet search may also reveal previous regulatory or legal problems. Additional research may be appropriate with prior employers or clients before substantial funds are invested if there are any questions concerning management's background.

Risk Factors. The offering documents should provide a discussion of risk factors involved with the fund. These should be examined to assess whether there are more risks with the fund under review than other similar funds or whether there is insufficient disclosure of risk factors. Typical risk factors include:

- Lack of operating history for new funds
- Concentration of investments/lack of diversification
- Use of leverage
- Short selling
- Use of derivatives (may add or reduce risk)
- Lack of liquidity/market prices for some investments
- Conflicts of interest
- Potential for loss of favored tax status

Note that if the fund is investing in illiquid nonmarketable securities, this is not only a risk factor but creates valuation issues. This may enable the manager to manipulate reported returns depending upon how these securities are valued for reporting to investors and computing fees. If these securities are used, the offering document should disclose the pricing process for nonmarketable securities. If it is not disclosed, ask for it.

Another risk in the hedge fund is the liquidity of the investor's investment in the fund. Often, funds can only be withdrawn on particular dates and after a lock-up period. The investor should determine the withdrawal provisions of the fund and consider whether this fits into their investment time horizon and liquidity needs.

Fees and Expenses. Relative to other investment vehicles, fees for hedge funds are high and should be carefully evaluated. A typical fee structure involves a base management fee of 1 percent plus an incentive fee of 20 percent of gains. Additionally, the fund must bear operating expenses such as legal and accounting costs. As the number of funds increases, though, it should be expected that fees may become more competitive, particularly with generic strategy funds. Fees should be compared with similar strategy funds to see if they are reasonable. For funds with an operating history, prior returns should be examined to see if the fee structure is justifiable. There are various fee arrangements and types such as:

- **Management fee**—A percentage of assets in the fund. Often 1 percent, but can be as high as 2 percent.
- **Performance/incentive fee**—A percentage of the return on the fund. Often 20 percent. So if the fund returned 10 percent, this fee would be effectively 2 percent of assets. A performance-based fee added to the management fee can cause total fees to be high (if returns are also high).
- **Performance/incentive fee with a hurdle rate**—In this case, a performance fee would only be payable if the return exceeds some predetermined amount or index. For example, with a hurdle rate of 5 percent, no performance fee would be paid. Read the fee disclosure carefully; the performance fee might be payable only on the excess of the return over the hurdle or payable on the entire return if the hurdle is surpassed.

Understanding and Evaluating Prospectuses, Offering Documents, and Proxy Statements

- **High water mark**—This provision protects investors by reducing the amount of performance fees after periods of losses. The fund has to pass the high water mark before performance fees are again charged.
- **Lookback provision**—This provision protects investors if an incentive fee is paid and then losses occur by looking back and rebating part of the incentive fee.

The fee disclosure should be examined carefully to see which of these provisions apply, and the amount of return to the shareholder should be computed for various assumed returns (for example, 4 percent, 6 percent, 8 percent, 10 percent, etc.) to see what the net return to the investor will be.

There has been an increase in the number of funds of funds. In a fund of funds, a hedge fund invests in other hedge funds. The "parent" hedge fund charges maintenance and performance fees in addition to fees charged by the underlying hedge funds. The fees therefore compound and can be quite high, as noted by the NASD in a 2002 Investor Alert.[5] There are potential advantages to a fund of funds such as diversification and, in some cases, a lower minimum investment. These structures should be reviewed carefully to see if the fees are worth the diversification benefits.

In addition to fees, the fund will incur various administrative expenses. If not disclosed, the investor should inquire about which expenses will be borne by the fund versus the fund manager and what the estimated level of expenses is.

Partnership/LLC Provisions. Funds organized as limited partnerships will be accompanied by a limited partnership agreement. Funds organized as limited liability companies will be accompanied by an operating agreement (or similarly named document). These agreements specify the profit- and loss-sharing arrangements, duties of the various partners or members, procedures of capital contributions and withdrawals, and which costs are to be borne by the fund. The agreement will also state the tax treatment of the entity and how the partnership would be dissolved if it were to be liquidated. These agreements should be read in detail and compared to the offering document and any oral representations made to ensure they are consistent. Particular attention should be paid to how withdrawals are handled:

- How often can withdrawals be made? (Note: Often withdrawals can only be made at year-end and, initially, only a portion of the requested withdrawal may be made, say 80 percent, with the balance paid after the annual audit.)
- Can partial withdrawals be made, and what is the minimum that must remain in the fund?
- Under what circumstances are withdrawals made in securities rather than cash?

Additional Considerations. There are a number of other parties involved with the operation of a hedge fund. The prime broker provided custodial and trading services. The audit firm audits the fund's financial statements. Other parties may provide administrative services, such as maintaining investor capital accounts and reporting to investors. These parties should be evaluated to determine if they are well known and reputable. Further, it is desirable that they do not have other relationships with the hedge fund manager such that conflicts of interest may arise.

CONCLUSION

Since most hedge funds are lightly regulated, if regulated at all, it is critical that the investor or his or her adviser carefully read the offering documents and understand the risks as well as the potential rewards of the investment. Some key points for investors to consider in evaluating these documents are:

- What are the investment objectives of the fund, and are they aligned with the portion of the investor's asset allocation under consideration?
- Are the fund's strategies and investments consistent with the fund's objectives?
- What risks are involved in the fund?
- Are the returns commensurate with the risks?
- Are the fund's fees and other expenses reasonable relative to comparable funds?
- How liquid are fund shares?
- What is the experience and past performance of the fund manager?

Understanding and Evaluating Prospectuses, Offering Documents, and Proxy Statements

ENDNOTES

[1] U.S. Securities and Exchange Commission, Registration Under the Advisers Act of Certain Hedge Fund Advisers, Release No. IA-2333, www.sec.gov.
[2] Ibid.
[3] U.S. Securities and Exchange Commissions, Rules 505 and 506 of Regulation D, www.sec.gov.
[4] U.S. Securities and Exchange Commission, Rule 501 of Regulation D, www.sec.gov.
[5] NASD Investor Alert, "Funds of Hedge Funds—Higher Costs and Risk for Higher Potential Returns," August 23, 2002.

DISCUSSION QUESTIONS:

1. Why are the limited partnership and limited liability company structures often used for hedge funds?
2. What are the key points to consider in evaluating a hedge fund?
3. What are some of the risks involved in a hedge fund?
4. What is the risk of having illiquid securities held by the fund?
5. What are types of fee arrangements found in hedge funds?
6. Recent years have seen an increase in the number of ETFs that invest in alternative assets such as commodities. ETFs can also be shorted. What is the potential impact of these trends on investments in hedge funds?

EXERCISE:

A recent hedge fund scandal involved Bayou Management, LLC. Do an Internet search on Bayou Management, LLC, and answer the following questions:
- What are the main known facts of the case?
- How much money was involved?
- What was the background of the principals?
- How did Bayou hide the problems at the fund?
- What steps, if any, could be taken to avoid investing in the next Bayou?

RECOMMENDED READING

NASD Investor Alert, "Funds of Hedge Funds—Higher Costs and Risk for Higher Potential Returns," August 23, 2002.

U.S. Securities and Exchange Commission, "Implications of the Growth of Hedge Funds," September 2003, www.sec.gov.

U.S. Securities and Exchange Commission, "Registration Under the

Advisers Act of Certain Hedge Fund Advisers," Release No. IA-2333, www.sec.gov.

U.S. Securities and Exchange Commission, "Hedging Your Bets: A Heads Up on Hedge Funds and Funds of Hedge Funds," www.sec.gov.

9 Specialized Private Equity Vehicles

Private equity funds provide total returns that are not significantly correlated to other investments, and which, if managed properly, have the potential to outperform stocks and bonds. Despite taking on potentially greater risk by investing in private companies, private equity funds are available to investors of any size thanks to the public offerings of business development companies (BDCs) and specialized acquisition companies (SPACs). Both BDCs and SPACs raise capital from the public and invest the proceeds according to uses specified in the prospectus. BDCs are a specialized form of publicly offered mutual funds, where investment funds are pooled and managed by professionals to invest in minority interests in private companies. SPACs are publicly offered corporate securities, where the proceeds are used to acquire controlling interests in a single, unidentified company. Regulations require that each investor be provided with a prospectus at the time of (or before) the purchase of these securities. There are potential risks and conflicts of interests specific to investing in these publicly traded private equity funds, so it is essential that an investor be made aware of these factors before deciding to invest. Advisers must thoroughly understand these investment structures and be able to advise the investor on the potential risks and rewards. This chapter discusses how to evaluate a BDC or SPAC prospectus.

Understanding and Evaluating Prospectuses, Offering Documents, and Proxy Statements

PRIVATE EQUITY INVESTMENTS

The key reasons for investing in private equities are to increase potential total return (dividends plus capital appreciation) and to reduce the volatility of an overall portfolio, selecting asset classes, that are not correlated over time. Fiduciary accounts with basic asset classes of stocks and bonds have been supplemented with private equity shares for decades when it is considered prudent to include less liquid and less predictable asset classes as part of overall portfolio planning. These fiduciary accounts are primarily large endowments and pension plans. The terms of the investment vehicles are negotiated by the large institutional investors and the management teams that will invest the capital. The size of these funds can be in the billions of dollars. Management deploys these funds by financing growth, recapitalization, or buyout of a portfolio of private companies.

Individual investors can gain the portfolio benefits of private equity by investing in publicly offered funds which, like institutional funds, invest in private companies for growth, recapitalization, or buyout. The managers of the public funds may also manage institutional funds. The terms of the publicly offered vehicles mirror those of institutional funds in several respects, but a key difference is that the public fund has an unlimited life, whereas the institutional fund is usually limited to a five- to six-year investment period and a ten-year limited life. Institutional fund managers must return the proceeds of investments to their fiduciary investors. Investors in a BDC do not receive their capital back. Rather, the publicly offered BDC stock trades in the public market, and is therefore subject to disclosure regulations similar to closed-end mutual funds discussed in Chapter 5. Investors desiring their money back can sell their shares through a broker.

One form of private equity investment is the SPAC. SPACs offer publicly traded common stock and are traded openly on the market after their initial public offering (IPO). However, since the issuer intends to use the offering proceeds to buy a company and to control the company it acquires, it is not subject to the same regulation as closed-end funds. SPACs are also called "blank check" or "blind pool" offerings, and pose special risks that must be evaluated. The BDC is a diversified way to invest in a strategy, while the

SPAC is a focused way to select an operating management team and a sector. In a SPAC, however, the management team must seek approval of its acquisition by a majority of its stockholders. The vote is requested through a proxy statement which details the characteristics of the target company, much like an IPO prospectus. If the investor wants to exit the investment, a market exists for the stock.

From the Web site of a BDC (www.americancapital.com):

> As a publicly traded company, we offer shareholders an opportunity to invest in privately held middle market companies through ownership of our stock. BDC Corp has paid $19.08 per share in dividends since going public in 1997 and has provided a 22 percent annualized return and a 430.5 percent total return over that time, assuming dividends are reinvested.

BUSINESS DEVELOPMENT COMPANY STRUCTURE AND REGULATION

The Investment Company Act of 1940 regulates the organization of all investment companies, including business development companies, and the disclosure of relevant information about the investment objectives, structure, and operations of investment companies. The Act regulates the BDCs' fee structure as one of its elements of investor protection. The managers are normally paid performance fees typical to those of institutional private equity fund managers. The BDC regulations permit the payment of these fees as long as conditions are met. These conditions are spelled out in the prospectus but primarily include the requirement that at least 70 percent of the assets of the BDC are invested in private companies.

BDCs may be operated by employees or by external management companies similar to mutual fund managers. Internally managed BDCs are more common, and some research analysts prefer this style due to perceived reduction of conflicts of interest. The fund stockholders are represented by a board of directors, a majority of which are required to be independent of the management of the BDC. The board oversees the fund and approves the terms of retention of the management team. One of the most important functions of the board is to oversee the valuation process for private company

Understanding and Evaluating Prospectuses, Offering Documents, and Proxy Statements

securities. Other parties associated with BDCs include the custodian that holds the funds' assets, transfer agents that process trades, and independent accountants that audit the funds' financial statements. Periodic reports on fund holdings and performance are required by the Exchange Act. Companies are subject to the same reporting requirements as other public companies, rather than mutual funds.

BDCs normally sell a fixed number of shares in an IPO. The offering is done as a firm commitment from a group of underwriters. After the IPO, these shares trade on a secondary market. The fund may trade at a discount or premium to net asset value. While these funds do not continuously sell new shares, they may offer new shares periodically in the form of a follow-on offering, provided that the price is at least equal to net asset value.

EVALUATING A BDC PROSPECTUS

Investors should obtain and read all available information including the prospectus before investing in a BDC. In this section, we discuss how to evaluate a potential investment in a BDC. Business development companies must file a registration statement with the SEC on Form N-2. This form contains the requirements for what must be provided to investors in the prospectus. In most cases, investors will be evaluating a prospectus in hard copy form obtained from a broker or financial consultant.

The Prospectus Cover. The cover of the prospectus will have valuable information that will assist in the overall assessment of the BDC. On the cover page of a mutual fund prospectus, you will find the fund's name, the date of the prospectus, and the size of the offering, represented in number of shares. The front also includes a statement of the investment goals of the company and a statement from the SEC that they have neither approved nor disapproved the fund shares. The cover also indicates whether there are selling shareholders, whether the fund is internally or externally managed, and where the shares will trade after the offering. An example of a BDC prospectus cover is shown in Exhibit 9.1.

Underwriters, Operations, and Market Information. The prospectus cover will also disclose the underwriters of the public offering. More information about the nature of the BDC's relationship with the underwriters is

Chapter 9 | Specialized Private Equity Vehicles

Exhibit 9.1: Prospectus Cover for a BDC

9,333,334 Shares: Patriot Capital Funding, Inc. Common Stock

We are offering 7,190,477 shares of our common stock and the selling stockholder named in this prospectus is offering 2,142,857 shares of our common stock. We will not receive any of the proceeds from the shares sold by the selling stockholder. This is our initial public offering and no public market currently exists for our shares. Our common stock has been approved for quotation on the Nasdaq National Market under the symbol "PCAP."

We are a specialty finance company that provides customized financing solutions to small- to mid-sized companies. Our ability to invest across a company's capital structure, from senior secured loans to equity securities, allows us to offer companies a comprehensive suite of financing solutions, including "one-stop" financing.

Our investment objective is to generate both current cash income and capital appreciation. We are an internally managed closed-end, non-diversified investment company that has elected to be treated as a business development company under the Investment Company Act of 1940.

Shares of closed-end investment companies, including business development companies, may trade at a discount to their net asset value. If our shares trade at a discount to our net asset value, it may increase the risk of loss for purchasers in this offering. The initial public offering price for a share of common stock in this offering is substantially higher than our as-adjusted pro forma net asset value per share of $10.67. As a result, investors purchasing stock in this offering will incur immediate dilution of $3.33 per share. See "Dilution" on page 31 for more information.

Investing in our common stock involves risks, including the risk of leverage.
See "Risk Factors," beginning on page 12.

	Per Share	Total
Public offering price	$14.00	$130,666,676
Underwriting discounts and commissions (sales load)	$0.91	$8,493,334
Proceeds, before expenses, to us(1)	$13.09	$94,123,344
Proceeds, before expenses, to the selling stockholder	$13.09	$28,049,998

(1) We estimate that we will incur approximately $1.8 million in offering expenses in connection with this offering, including a one-time advisory fee we have agreed to pay to A.G. Edwards & Sons, Inc., equal to 0.5% of the gross proceeds we receive in this offering.

Neither the Securities and Exchange Commission nor any state securities commission has approved or disapproved of these securities or determined if this prospectus is truthful or complete. Any representation to the contrary is a criminal offense.

Source: A.G. Edwards; Jefferies & Company, Inc.; Piper Jaffray; Harris Nesbitt
Filed Pursuant to Rule 497, Registration Statement No. 333-124831.
The date of this prospectus is July 27, 2005.

available in the pages of the prospectus.

Underwriters are important to an offering for a number of reasons. The identity and track record of the underwriters with previous BDCs is important to assess when making a determination about the investment. For each principal underwriter distributing securities of the fund, the fund must state the nature of the obligation to distribute the fund's securities and the aggregate dollar amount of underwriting commissions and the amount retained by the principal underwriter. Any payments made by the fund to an underwriter or dealer in the fund's shares during the last fiscal year must be disclosed along with the name and address of the underwriter or dealer, the amount paid and basis for determining that amount, the circumstances surrounding the payments, and the consideration received by the fund. This will highlight potential conflicts of interest by the underwriters and investors.

While not required, the lead underwriters may continue to provide investors with research reports about the BDC after the offering. These reports are important to investors because the operations of a BDC are not normally subject to daily net asset value (NAV) calculations like closed-end funds or open-end funds, and operating information about funds and their markets can be limited. Exhibit 9.2 is a table of publicly available BDC information derived from a brokerage report on the sector (source: Wachovia Securities).

These reports will not only give you insight into the individual BDC, but also the existence of a trading market within the sector, which is also an important investment consideration. The price paid by subsequent investors therefore depends on market conditions such as supply and demand.

Exhibit 9.2 provides insight into the relevant valuation metrics for the public companies within the market sector of the BDC, which are available as investment opportunities. These companies are primarily engaged in the "mezzanine" segment of the private equity asset class, which means that they make loans that are subject to greater risk than bank loans. They also have higher interest rates in exchange for the risk. These BDCs have fluctuating stock prices that could be impacted by events beyond performance of the fund, but the existence of a market for the shares creates a large potential

Chapter 9 | Specialized Private Equity Vehicles

Exhibit 9.2: Valuation Comparison

Ticker	Company	Rating	12/19/05 Price	52-Week Range High $	52-Week Range Low $	YTD Price Performance	Market Cap ($mm)	Div Yield	EPS Estimate FY2005E	EPS Estimate FY2006E	Price/EPS 2005E	Price/EPS 2006E	Price to Book Value
SP50	S&P 500		$1,278	$1,278	$1,136	4.0%	$12,599		$70.21	$75.00	17.9x	16.8x	NA
BDC-RICs													
Internally-Managed													
ALD	Allied Capital	NR	$29.10	$30.64	$24.02	12.6%	$3,966	8.4%	$1.08	$1.57	26.9x	18.5x	1.7x
ACAS	American Capital Strategies	Outperform	$36.98	$39.61	$29.51	10.9%	$4,008	8.5%	$3.10	$3.50	11.9x	10.6x	1.6x
HTGC	Hercules Growth Technology	NR	$11.15	$14.41	$9.71	1.4%	$109	10.8%	$0.39	$1.19	28.6x	9.4x	1.0x
MCGC	MCG Capital	Mkt Perform	$14.69	$18.57	$13.63	-14.2%	$777	11.4%	$1.40	$1.54	10.5x	9.5x	1.2x
PCAP	Patriot Capital	NR	$12.05	$14.80	$10.70	-13.9%	$146	9.0%	$0.64	$1.41	18.8x	8.5x	1.1x
	Average (Internal)							9.6%			19.4x	11.3x	1.3x
Externally-Managed													
AINV	Apollo Investment Corp	Outperform	$18.26	$20.74	$11.36	20.9%	$1,132	9.6%	$0.41	$1.45	44.5x	12.6x	1.3x
ARCC	Ares Capital Corporation	Outperform	$16.56	$20.00	$14.44	-14.8%	$383	8.2%	$1.15	$1.35	14.4x	12.3x	1.1x
GLAD	Gladstone Capital	Underperform	$21.61	$26.45	$19.80	-8.8%	$244	7.5%	$1.49	$1.60	14.5x	13.5x	1.6x
GAIN	Gladstone Investment	NR	$13.52	$16.30	$13.56	9.9%	$224	3.6%	$0.36	$0.97	37.6x	13.9x	1.0x
NGPC	NGP Capital Resources	NR	$13.45	$16.75	$13.22	-12.5%	$234	4.2%	$0.61	$1.11	22.0x	12.1x	1.0x
PSEC	Prospect Energy	NR	$15.29	$15.32	$10.56	27.4%	$108	7.3%	$1.12	$1.29	13.7x	11.9x	1.0x
	Average (External)							6.7%			24.4x	12.7x	1.2x
	All BDCs							8.0%			22.1x	12.1x	1.2x
TICC	Technology Investment Capital	Outperform	$14.66	$16.69	$14.10	-2.3%	$281	8.2%	$1.14	$1.40	12.9x	10.5x	1.1x

Source: FactSet Company Data and Wachovia Capital Markets, LLC, Estimates
Estimates for rated companies are Wachovia Capital Markets, LLC. All others are First Call consensus estimates.
ACAS & GLAD estimates are based on net operating income NOI (DNOI), and ARCC, AINV, and TICC are based on net investment income (NII).

investor pool for these companies. The attraction of this mezzanine segment includes the current coupon plus growth in company value due to equity participation in the private business.

The table shows the dividend yield and P/E ratios of the individual companies, which are common elements of valuation of private companies. The growth related to the equity appreciation of the portfolio, however, would neither be reflected in the dividend, nor in the earnings forming the basis of the P/E ratio. Rather, it is book value, or net asset value, which typically grows due to appreciation in value of the private company. The valuation metrics discussed in Chapter 3 may not be helpful in evaluating BDCs because they do not capture the appreciation of the equity component of the investment pool.

BDCs are operated to have higher total returns than the market in which they function; otherwise, the risk of investing in the private companies (inside the BDC portfolio) is not rewarded. There are three ways in which BDCs attempt to outperform the market:

- **Growth in capital value**, such as venture capital investments in young companies with limited operating history
- **Value investing**, where the companies are out of favor or have much lower growth targets and return potential, but commensurately less risk
- **Income focus**, which includes speculative lending to private companies in exchange for high current income and capital gains from warrants, options, or conversion features to the investment instrument

Additional Information Included in the Prospectus. The ways that a BDC can obtain equity upside participation are described in the prospectus and will help investors understand whether they should expect payouts of capital gains or increases of dividends as the primary way investors will receive their returns. The total return expectation of any investment to be made by a BDC is usually 10 percent or more above market averages, and can be from a combination of dividends or interest payments received by the BDC and capital gains realized on the value of the equity growth of the private company.

In its prospectus, the fund must discuss its principal investment strategies. This includes the types of securities in which the fund invests. Patriot Capital describes its investment strategy as follows:

> We are a specialty finance company that provides customized financing solutions to small- to mid-sized companies with annual revenues from $10 million to $100 million that operate in diverse industry sectors.... Our investments are principally in the form of senior secured loans, junior secured loans, and subordinated debt investments, which may include an equity component. We also offer a financial product that we refer to as "one-stop" financing, which typically includes a revolving line of credit, one or more term loans, and a subordinated debt investment.... Our investment objective is to generate both current cash income and capital appreciation.

The prospectus will then discuss the principal risks of investing in the fund. Here, risks are very similar to institutional private equity funds and primarily relate to management of the fund. The track record of the managers is the primary information tool investors can use to evaluate the expectations for success with the new fund. Since most BDCs are formed as blind pools, there is no operating history of the fund to review for performance purposes.

Management Fees, Compensation, and Expenses. The items for open-end investment companies, discussed in Chapter 5, will also be found in a prospectus for a closed-end company, and the key points to evaluate remain the same (investment objective, risks, fees, management, legal proceedings). There are additional considerations, however, for the prospectus of a BDC, which should be understood.

One of the potential conflicts of interest between management and stockholders relates to the valuation of the portfolio. Management fees are a combination of incentive fees based on capital gains and income, plus a base fee on total assets. This fee is normally around 2 percent of the value of total assets. The managers therefore have a theoretical incentive to increase asset value, even if there is not sufficient rationale to "mark up" the value of the

Understanding and Evaluating Prospectuses, Offering Documents, and Proxy Statements

investment. The board of directors is charged with evaluating management's proposed valuations. Recent regulatory actions have focused on the potential for conflict in this relationship. In response, independent valuation firms have been retained by the board in order to help assess the reasonableness of the manager's recommended valuations. The description of valuation methods in Exhibit 9.3 by Patriot Capital illustrates the methods used to value portfolio holdings. These methods are also commonly used by institutional investment funds.

Another risk factor related to management is the compensation structure. For internally managed funds, the managers typically receive equity options on fund stock as their way to participate in growth of the fund. For a fund with an income orientation, however, the fund manager is not compensated for the current pay portion of the total return. In 2003, a mezzanine fund was formed that had external management, with incentive fees based on both capital appreciation and on exceeding a current coupon threshold. This fund, Technology Investment Corporation, set off a wave of newly organized BDCs managed externally with an income orientation, some of which are noted in Exhibit 9.2. Commenting on the new BDCs, an established firm issued this press release in 2004:

> Bethesda, MD—April 16, 2004—American Capital Strategies Ltd. (NASDAQ:ACAS) announced today its views on new Business Development Companies (BDCs).
>
> "This is an appropriate time to welcome the new BDCs that have recently gone public and those that may follow. They will accelerate the growing investor interest in BDCs," said [American Capital's Chairman]. "We have long thought it inevitable that private equity and mezzanine partnerships would ultimately adopt the BDC structure. Compared to typical private equity and mezzanine partnerships, BDCs can retain their capital, enjoy greater access and lower cost of capital and offer investors greater transparency, control, and liquidity. BDCs can also offer debt and equity and longer term capital to companies. In addition, internally managed BDCs, like American Capital, are free of the many conflicts that exist between the general and limited partners of these partnerships... More importantly, we

Exhibit 9.3: Fair Value Calculation from Patriot Capital IPO Prospectus

Determination of Net Asset Value

We determine the net asset value per share of our common stock on a quarterly basis. The net asset value per share is equal to the value of our total assets minus liabilities and any preferred stock outstanding divided by the total number of shares of common stock outstanding.

Value, as defined in Section 2(a)(41) of the 1940 Act, is (i) the market price for those securities for which a market quotation is readily available and (ii) for all other securities and assets, fair value as is determined in good faith by the board of directors. Since there will typically be no readily available market value for the investments in our portfolio, we will value substantially all of our portfolio investments at fair value as determined in good faith by our board of directors pursuant to a valuation policy and a consistently applied valuation process. Because of the inherent uncertainty in determining the fair value of investments that do not have a readily available market value, the fair value of our investments determined in good faith by our board of directors may differ significantly from the values that would have been used had a ready market existed for the investments, and the differences could be material.

Our process for determining the fair value of our investments begins with determining the enterprise value of the portfolio company. There is no one methodology to determine enterprise value and, in fact, for any one portfolio company, enterprise value is best expressed as a range of fair values, from which we derive a single estimate of enterprise value.

To determine the enterprise value of a portfolio company, we analyze its historical and projected financial results. We generally require portfolio companies to provide annual audited and quarterly and monthly unaudited financial statements, as well as annual projections for the upcoming fiscal year. Typically in the private equity business, companies are bought and sold based on multiples of EBITDA, cash flow, net income, revenues or, in limited instances, book value. The private equity industry uses financial measures such as EBITDA in order to assess a portfolio company's financial performance and to value a portfolio company. When using EBITDA to determine enterprise value, we may adjust EBITDA for non-recurring items. Such adjustments are intended to normalize EBITDA to reflect the portfolio company's earnings power. Adjustments to EBITDA may include compensation to previous owners, acquisition, recapitalization, or restructuring related items or one-time non-recurring income or expense items.

In determining a multiple to use for valuation purposes, we look to private merger and acquisition statistics, discounted public trading multiples or industry practices. In estimating a reasonable multiple, we consider not only the fact that our portfolio company may be a private company relative to a peer group of public comparables, but we also consider the size and scope of our portfolio company and its specific strengths and weaknesses. In some cases, the best valuation methodology may be a discounted cash flow analysis based on future projections. If a portfolio company is distressed, a liquidation analysis may provide the best indication of enterprise value.

If there is adequate enterprise value to support the repayment of our debt, the fair value of our loan or debt security normally corresponds to cost plus the amortized original issue discount unless the borrower's condition or other factors lead to a determination of fair value at a different amount. The fair value of equity interests in portfolio companies is determined based on various factors, including the enterprise value remaining for equity holders after the repayment of the portfolio company's debt and other preference capital, and other pertinent factors such as recent offers to purchase a portfolio company, recent transactions involving the purchase or sale of the portfolio company's equity securities, or other liquidation events. The determined fair values of equity securities are generally discounted to account for restrictions on resale and minority ownership positions.

The fair value of our investments at March 31, 2005, December 31, 2004, and December 31, 2003, was determined by our then-existing board of directors. We received valuation assistance from our independent valuation firm, Duff & Phelps, LLC, on our entire investment portfolio at March 31, 2005, and December 31, 2004.

Source: Patriot Capital Prospectus, July 27, 2005.

Understanding and Evaluating Prospectuses, Offering Documents, and Proxy Statements

Exhibit 9.4: Expense Table for Technology Investment Capital Corp.

Stockholder Transaction Expenses

Sales load (as a percentage of offering price)	7.00% (1)
Offering expenses borne by the Company (as a percentage of offering price)	0.75% (2)(7)
Distribution reinvestment and cash purchase plan fees	None (3)
Total stockholder transaction expenses (as a percentage of offering price)	**7.75% (7)**

Estimated Annual Expenses (as a percentage of net assets attributed to common stock)

Management fees	2.00%
Incentive fees payable under Investment Advisory Agreement	0 (4)
Interest payments on borrowed funds	0 (5)(6)
Other expenses	1.67% (6)(7)
Total annual expenses (estimated) (6)(7)	**3.67%**

(1) The underwriting discount with respect to shares sold in this offering, which is a one-time fee, is the only sales load paid in connection with this offering.

(2) Amount includes estimated offering expenses of approximately $700,000.

(3) The expenses of the distribution reinvestment plan are included in "other expenses." We have no cash purchase plan.

(4) Based on our projected net operating income and net realized gains, and because we do not expect to fully invest the proceeds of this offering during our first year of operations, we would not anticipate paying any incentive fees in the first year after this offering. Based on our current business plan, we expect that we will not have any capital gains and only a small amount of interest income as we complete our investments during our first year of operations. In subsequent years, we expect the incentive fees to increase to the extent that we earn greater interest income on our investments in portfolio companies and, to a lesser extent, realize capital gains upon the sale of warrants or other equity investments in such companies. The incentive fee consists of two parts. The first part, which is payable quarterly in arrears, equals 20% of the excess, if any, of net investment income over an annual hurdle rate (equal to the interest rate payable on a five-year U.S. Treasury Note plus 5%). The second part of the incentive fee equals 20% of net realized capital gains, if any, less any net unrealized capital losses, payable at the end of each calendar year beginning on December 31, 2004. For a more detailed discussion of the calculation of this fee, see "Management—Investment Advisory Agreement," on pages 34–36.

(5) We do not plan to incur any indebtedness, or to pay interest in respect thereof, before the proceeds of this offering are substantially invested. See footnote (6) below. In addition, we do not currently plan to issue preference shares. The Company does not expect to borrow money in the first year of operations, and has not decided whether, and to what extent, it will finance investments using leverage thereafter.

Chapter 9 | Specialized Private Equity Vehicles

> (6) We have based estimates of other expenses ($1.6 million, including estimated organizational expenses of approximately $350,000) and total annual expenses on our projected operating expenses for our first year of operations divided by total net assets subsequent to this offering. Our estimated organizational expenses, which represent 0.37% of our total net assets, represent our initial start-up costs and will be treated as an expense in the year incurred. The percentage under "Other expenses" includes payments under the Administration Agreement based on our projected allocable portion of overhead and other expenses incurred by BDC Partners in performing its obligations under the Administration Agreement, including rent, and this percentage also assumes that we have not incurred any indebtedness. We expect that it will take at least one year to invest the net proceeds of this offering. See "Use of proceeds." Once the proceeds of this offering are substantially invested, we may borrow funds to the extent permitted by the 1940 Act and would, thereafter, make interest payments on borrowed funds which would increase our expenses. See "Regulation—Senior securities."
>
> (7) These amounts are estimates and may vary.

Source: Technology Investment Capital Corp. SEC Registration Statement, November 19, 2003.

also expect that the recent creation of new BDCs will accelerate the process of displacing many of the hundreds of traditional private equity and mezzanine partnerships that will no longer have access to capital..."

Exhibit 9.4 is Technology Investment Capital Corp's fee table, and it describes the fees and expenses that the investors may pay if they buy and hold shares of the fund. It discloses that 2 percent of the fund's assets are taken as management fees each year. Since fees reduce the investor's return, this information should be examined closely in comparison with other, similar funds to see if the fees are appropriate for the level of management involved in the fund and track record. It is also important to pay attention to any footnotes associated with fees and expenses, as more detail about expenses could be gained from reading the fine print.

Many funds are distributed (sold) via brokers, who are paid a commission for bringing new investors to the funds. Many funds thus include "loads," which are used to pay commissions and which create an obstacle to selling the shares quickly. In its prospectus, a fund must describe any sales loads. There is usually a risk factor related to the stock trading to a discount to the offering price shortly after the offering, as the cash is not yet invested and generating a return for investors. If an investor has a short time frame to invest, BDCs are generally not suitable due to short-term trading fluctuations such as the period immediately after an offering.

The sales load for Patriot Capital is set forth on the prospectus cover depicted in Exhibit 9.1. The sales load is not able to be invested. To provide a reward for the common stockholders despite the sales load, it is common for BDCs to incur leverage to enhance the fund level return. Of course, with leverage comes additional investment risk. Income-oriented funds are best able to generate current income with which to pay the interest costs, while growth funds relying on capital appreciation are least able to confidently repay interest and principal on the leverage. BDCs are limited by regulations to maintain an asset-to-leverage ratio of 2:1.

Investment Objectives, Principal Investment Strategies, Related Risk. This section takes a closer look at the fund's principal investment strategies and risks, with a more detailed discussion of the information in the risk/return summary. The following was disclosed in the Technology Investment Capital's recent secondary offering prospectus (December 7, 2005):

> We seek to continue to grow and manage a diversified portfolio that includes senior secured loans, junior secured loans, subordinated debt investments, and equity investments. We generally target investments of approximately $3 million to $20 million in companies with annual revenues between $10 million and $100 million. We also offer a financing solution that we refer to as "one-stop" financing, which typically includes a revolving line of credit, one or more term loans and a subordinated debt investment. Our loans may include both debt and equity components. The debt instruments provide for returns in the form of interest payments, including payment-in-kind or PIK interest, while the equity instruments, such as warrants and non-control, equity co-investments, provide us with an opportunity to participate in the capital appreciation of the portfolio company. We intend to generally target a total annualized return (including interest, fees, and value of warrants) on our individual debt investments of 6.5 percent to 19.0 percent.

Management. This section contains the name of the investment adviser of the fund and describes the investment adviser's experience. In this section,

Chapter 9 | Specialized Private Equity Vehicles

the fund is also required to describe any material pending legal proceedings, other than ordinary routine litigation incidental to the business, to which the fund or the fund's investment adviser or principal underwriter is a party. The prospectus for Apollo Investment Corporation, which is externally managed, provides the following:

About Apollo
Founded in 1990 by Leon Black, Michael Gross, John Hannan, and three other co-founders, Apollo is a recognized leader in private equity investing, having invested more than $10.6 billion in over 150 companies since its founding. Since its inception, Apollo has raised $13.2 billion in capital, primarily from institutional investors and six private investment funds. Apollo traditionally has focused on companies that it believes are undervalued yet have successful business models, strong cash flows, and prospects for value creation. The Apollo investment professionals' disciplined, value-oriented strategy has sought to identify opportunities in all investment environments, selecting from a range of approaches, such as corporate partner or traditional buyouts, distressed debt buyouts, or more liquid, non-control distressed debt investments. The Apollo investment professionals have sought, through this strategy, to provide investors with attractive returns while minimizing the risk of capital loss throughout economic cycles. Apollo actively manages its portfolio companies which, since 1990, have raised more than $80 billion in senior secured loans and more than $25 billion in high-yield bonds, including subordinated debt.

Apollo's active private investment funds focus on making either control-oriented equity investments of $100 million or more or distressed debt investments, either for control or non-control positions. In contrast, Apollo Investment will seek to capitalize on the significant investment opportunities emerging in the mezzanine segment of the lending market for middle-market companies, which it believes offers the potential for attractive risk-adjusted returns. Apollo Investment is currently the only Apollo-related investment vehicle focused primarily on investing in mezzanine and senior secured loans of middle-market companies, and currently the only publicly traded investment vehicle managed by an

Understanding and Evaluating Prospectuses, Offering Documents, and Proxy Statements

affiliate of Apollo.

Apollo Investment Management

Apollo Investment Management, our investment adviser, will be led by two managing partners with a combined 35 years of experience and will be supported by Apollo's team of 33 investment professionals. We expect that Apollo Investment Management will hire additional investment professionals. In addition, Apollo Investment Management expects to draw upon Apollo's 13-year history and to benefit from the Apollo investment professionals' significant capital markets, trading, and research expertise developed through investments in 23 different industries and over 150 companies in the United States and Western Europe.

In evaluating this section, the investor should examine the experience of the portfolio manager and their advisory firm. If they are new to this fund, their performance at other funds should be examined. Any pending legal proceedings or significant restrictions noted in this section should also be scrutinized, and consideration should be given to seeking out similar funds in the same asset class without such items. Allied Capital's disclosure contains the following red flag, which bears additional research before making an investment decision.

Legal Proceedings

On June 23, 2004, the SEC notified us that they are conducting an informal investigation of us. Based on the documentation requested by the SEC, the nature of the inquiry appears to pertain to matters related to our portfolio company, Business Loan Express, LLC, and allegations made by short sellers over the last two years. We have voluntarily agreed to cooperate fully with the SEC's investigation.

A sample of the Patriot Capital table showing selling stockholders and management investment is in Exhibit 9.5.

Beneficial ownership is the term used to describe an individual's or group's principal ownership of a specific security. Beneficial ownership is determined in accordance with the rules of the SEC and is usually defined as 5 percent or more of total shares of common stock. The following table sets forth certain information with respect to the beneficial ownership of shares of common stock immediately prior to the completion of this offering, and as adjusted to reflect the sale of the shares of common stock offered by this prospectus.

Taxation of the Fund. If applicable, the fund must state that it is qualified or intends to qualify under Subchapter M of the Internal Revenue Code. The consequences to the fund if it does not qualify under Subchapter M must also be disclosed. Failure to qualify will result in taxes at the fund level, as well as to individual fund holders. Like mutual funds and institutional private equity funds, BDCs do not pay federal or state taxes. Instead, the portfolio companies generally pay entity level taxes, and the stockholders of the BDC pay tax on dividends and distributed capital gains. The following disclosure from Patriot Capital addresses its tax status.

> We intend to elect, effective as of August 1, 2005, to be treated for federal income tax purposes as a regulated investment company, or "RIC" under Subchapter M of the Internal Revenue Code, or "Code." See "Material U.S. Federal Income Tax Considerations." As a RIC, we generally will not have to pay corporate-level federal income taxes on any net ordinary income or capital gains that we distribute to our stockholders as dividends if we meet

Exhibit 9.5: Sample Disclosure of Principal Holders

Name	Shares Beneficially Owned Immediately Prior to This Offering		Shares Offered Hereby	Shares Beneficially Owned Immediately After This Offering(1)(2)(3)	
	Number	Percentage	Number	Number	Percentage
Selling Stockholder:					
Compass Group Investments, Inc.	3,847,902 (2)	100%	2,142,857	1,603,357 (4)	14.5%
Interested Directors:					
Richard Buckanavage	—	—	—	48,302	*
Timothy W. Hassler	—	—	—	48,302	*
I. Joseph Massoud (5)					

Source: Source: Patriot Capital Prospectus, July 27, 2005.

Understanding and Evaluating Prospectuses, Offering Documents, and Proxy Statements

certain source-of-income and asset diversification requirements.

Business and Other Connections of the Investment Adviser. The fund should describe any other business relationship with each investment adviser, director, officer, or partner of the adviser during the last two fiscal years. You should carefully evaluate any such disclosures for conflicts of interest relative to investors.

CONCLUSION

When investors provide funds to an investment company, they are entrusting their wealth to others. Investors need to be comfortable that the investment company's managers are being good stewards of the investors' assets. You, as the adviser, provide an important role in educating the investor regarding these specialized investment vehicles. The prospectus and periodic reports provide important information to judge that stewardship. Some key points for investors to consider in evaluating these documents are:

- What are the investment objectives of the fund, and are they aligned with the portion of the investor's asset allocation under consideration?
- Are the fund's investments consistent with the fund's objectives?
- What industry risks are involved in the fund?
- Are the returns commensurate with the risks?
- Are the fund's fees, sales loads, and other expenses reasonable, relative to comparable funds?
- Do any conflicts exist that could benefit a few parties at the expense of other fund holders?
- How liquid are fund shares? Can they be sold easily in a secondary market?
- What is the experience and past performance of the investment advisory firm and individual fund managers?
- Are there sufficient outside directors or trustees to adequately monitor adequately the fund for fund holders?

DISCUSSION QUESTIONS:

1. Why might an investor want to include private equity in a portfolio?
2. What types of private equity vehicles are available for individual

investors?
3. What regulations apply to business development companies?
4. What metrics are important in evaluating an investment in a business development company?

EXERCISE:
Excerpt of Valuation Disclosure of a BDC:

Determination of Net Asset Value

We determine the net asset value per share of our common stock on a quarterly basis. The net asset value per share is equal to the value of our total assets minus liabilities and any preferred stock outstanding divided by the total number of shares of common stock outstanding.

Value, as defined in Section 2(a)(41) of the 1940 Act, is (i) the market price for those securities for which a market quotation is readily available and (ii) for all other securities and assets, fair value as is determined in good faith by the board of directors. Since there will typically be no readily available market value for the investments in our portfolio, we will value substantially all of our portfolio investments at fair value as determined in good faith by our board of directors pursuant to a valuation policy and a consistently applied valuation process. Because of the inherent uncertainty in determining the fair value of investments that do not have a readily available market value, the fair value of our investments determined in good faith by our board of directors may differ significantly from the values that would have been used had a ready market existed for the investments, and the differences could be material.

Consider the following questions:
- What are the components of return from an institutional fund or a BDC?
- What potential conflicts of interest do boards consider when approving valuations?
- What are the securities market implications of an overvaluation of the net assets of a BDC? Undervaluation?

Understanding and Evaluating Prospectuses, Offering Documents, and Proxy Statements

RECOMMENDED READING

Josh Lerner, Felda Hardymon, Ann Leamon, *Venture Capital and Private Equity: A Casebook*, John Wiley & Sons, 2004.

David Rubenstein, *Beyond Wall Street: The Rise of Private Equity and the Future of Investing*, Collins, 2005.

10 Real Estate Entities

Some of the most common types of prospectuses you can expect to encounter as a financial adviser are those for investments in real estate entities such as a real estate limited partnership (RELP) or initial offering of a real estate investment trust (REIT). Chapter 2 presented information on understanding financial disclosures in offering documents for equity investments, and Chapter 3 presented key points in evaluating equity offering prospectuses in general. This chapter extends the material in Chapters 2 and 3 to present particular financial metrics and considerations in evaluating real estate offerings. The first section of this chapter presents additional material relevant to evaluating a private real estate offering such as a limited partnership. The second section presents considerations in evaluating REIT offerings.

REAL ESTATE PRIVATE OFFERINGS

Private offerings related to real estate are quite common. Developers may seek additional equity from real estate investors to construct property for operation or resale. Investors may seek to invest in real estate without having the time or expertise to develop or manage property on their own. The developers or others, therefore, form a syndicate to raise capital from private investors. This is commonly structured as a limited partnership (or limited liability company).

In a general partnership, all partners have unlimited liability.

Understanding and Evaluating Prospectuses, Offering Documents, and Proxy Statements

While this form is used for joint ventures between experienced real estate developers, this is an unattractive arrangement for passive investors. Real estate limited partnerships, on the other hand, are a business form that allows investors to participate in professionally managed real estate investment activities while limiting liability. In a limited partnership, the limited partners are passive investors, and their liability is limited to their investment in the partnership. Like all limited partnerships, RELPs have at least one general partner and one or more limited partners. General partners control the operations and bear unlimited liability for any obligations undertaken by the partnership. Another advantage for limited partners is the ability to participate in a development venture that they may be unable to fund by themselves. If the RELP involves multiple properties, it also provides diversification within the investment. Low correlation with other investment classes also results in portfolio diversification benefits.

While limited liability and diversification are significant advantages to this investment structure, there are also disadvantages. Perhaps the most important of these is the lack of liquidity. Investors who need cash may not be able to liquidate their limited partnership ventures, or may incur substantial costs in doing so. Another disadvantage is that limited partners are passive investors with no control over the properties selected or how they are managed. If a limited partner exercises any function reserved for a general partner, the limitations on liability could be lost. Also, it is possible that the general partners could take other actions that eliminate the favorable tax treatment that limited partners expect. In addition, there are limitations on the deductibility of passive losses that may apply.

Regulations and Offering Documents. The Uniform Limited Partnership Act has been adopted in nearly every state, although some states have made considerable modifications. This act specifies the rights and responsibilities of general and limited partners. In order to qualify as a limited partnership, a certificate of limited partnership must be filed with the appropriate state agency. Otherwise, all partners will be treated as general partners and will be liable for all partnership obligations.

Limited partnership shares are considered securities and are potentially subject to both federal and state securities laws. If the partnership falls under the jurisdiction of the Securities and Exchange Commission (SEC), the syndicators must file a preliminary prospectus (red herring) prior to any advertising.

Real estate limited partnerships may be exempt from SEC registration if their partnership constitutes a private placement or an intrastate offering. In a private offering, securities can be sold only to qualified institutions, up to 99 accredited investors, and in some cases up to 35 nonaccredited investors.[1] While these private offerings are not registered with the SEC, they must still be accompanied by offering documents with disclosures similar to the documents for public offerings. In such cases, the partnership may still have to be registered with a state securities commission. States consider the size of the offering, the number of offices, the methods of advertising, and the fees paid to the promoter to determine whether to require registration. In certain cases, states may refuse registration if they believe an offering is too risky, if the promoter's fees are too large, or if the distribution of profits and losses between general and limited partners is unfair.

The basic evaluation of the prospectus for a real estate offering is the same as for other equity offerings as described in Chapter 3. However, in a private offering, the adviser and investor should exercise additional diligence in carefully reading the prospectus and investigating the history of those offering the securities. Key additional points to consider for private real estate offerings are:

- What is the experience of the developer and operator with similar real estate projects? If possible, talk to limited partners in prior deals.
- How many similar offerings have the syndicators put together in the past, and were they successful?
- What type of real estate (commercial, residential, etc.) project is involved, and is this attractive in the economic environment in which the property will be located?
- How diversified is the project? (Often, the answer is "not very diversified.")
- What is the use of proceeds from the offering?
- How much money are the general partners and/or syndicators putting into the venture?

Understanding and Evaluating Prospectuses, Offering Documents, and Proxy Statements

- What are the long-term plans for the property?
- When and how will investors be repaid?
- Does the project offer a sufficient return to justify the risk and illiquidity of such an investment?
- Are there any conflicts of interest/related party transactions? For example, will a company controlled by the general partner or syndicator provide services to the partnership venture?

Evaluating Financial Information in Private Real Estate Offerings. Real estate projects use some unique terms that must be understood to properly evaluate a real estate project. For example, real estate is often valued based on a multiple of net operating income (NOI) or, equivalently, capitalization of NOI. If a property has an NOI of $100,000 and similar properties sell for 12.5 times NOI, the value could be estimated at $1,250,000. Alternatively, an appropriate capitalization rate for a property might be 8 percent. Dividing NOI by 0.08 yields a value of $1,250,000. The capitalization rate is basically the desired return from the property, net of expected growth, and is based on current interest rates and the risk of the subject property compared to other properties. NOI is not the same as net income determined for most companies. Exhibit 10.1 shows an abbreviated computation of NOI.

Other income includes non-rental-related income, such as for laundry services. Reserve for replacements is the average annual amount expected

---

Exhibit 10.1: Computation of Net Operating Income

Rental Income at Full Occupancy
+ Other Income

Potential Gross Income
− Vacancy and Collection Losses

Effective Gross Income
− Operating Expenses
−Reserve for Replacements

Net Operating Income

to be paid for replacing long-term assets such as air-conditioning systems. To determine whether the purchase price of the investment is reasonable, the investor can calculate the "going-in cap rate." This can be determined by dividing the NOI by the total costs to acquire/develop the property. This can be compared to alternative real estate investments to see if the return is reasonable.

While NOI is important for valuation of the property and evaluating the operations of the property, it is not the cash flow available to the owners. Projections of cash flow would include payments for debt service and taxes. Projections in proposed real estate deals will normally include estimates of cash flow to the partners for several years and estimated net cash that would be available for distribution, assuming some future estimate of sales price. Investors can use any cash flow projections to compute the internal rate of return for the project.

Projections require many assumptions and estimates about such factors as vacancy rates. Investors should review these assumptions and compare them with other real estate projects in the same area to determine whether they are reasonable.

Evaluating Partnership Documents. In addition to the prospectus, potential investors are given a copy of the partnership agreement. This document defines the relationship between limited and general partners, as well as the rights and responsibilities of each. In the case of a limited liability company, the agreement is called an operating agreement, which defines the relationships among the "members." The operating agreement will contain similar types of provisions as the partnership agreement. These provisions should be carefully reviewed. In particular, the investor should examine all provisions related to the sharing of profits and losses during operations and upon sale of the property. Unlike corporations, partnership and limited liability companies permit special allocations of profits and losses. Some ventures provide for a special allocation of gains to the general partners that may be in excess of their normal profit- and loss-sharing percentage. The investor needs to be aware of how cash flow will be diverted to the general partners versus the limited partners.

Additionally, any provisions for salaries, management fees, and similar fees payable to the general partners or syndicators should be examined to determine whether they are reasonable for the work proposed or if this is just another vehicle to enrich the general partners and syndicators at the expense of the other investors.

Exhibit 10.2 presents common partnership agreement provisions.

Investors may also sign a subscription agreement that spells out the nature of the relationship between limited partners and the sponsoring general partner. In the case of private placements or intrastate offerings, investors may also be required to fill out a questionnaire designed to assess their ability to qualify as limited partners.

REAL ESTATE INVESTMENT TRUSTS (REITS)

Larger real estate investment ventures are commonly structured as publicly traded or private REITs. Similar to partnership investments, REITs are generally not subject to an entity-level tax. To qualify, a REIT must distribute at least 90 percent of its earnings. (There is no distribution requirement for a partnership.) REITs may invest in real estate (equity REITs), mortgages (mortgage REITs), or both (hybrid REITs). Within each category there are REIT subsectors. Exhibit 10.3 presents the REIT sector and subsector classification of the National Association of Real Estate Investment Trusts (NAREIT). As with any asset class, diversification within the asset classes is important, just as diversification across asset classes is important. REITs have been shown to provide diversification benefits to portfolios of stocks and bonds because they are not highly correlated with these other assets. In fact, a study by Ibbotson and NAREIT found that the correlation of REITs with stocks has declined over the period from 1970 to 2000 to about 0.25.[2] It is wise for a client to be diversified in different types of REITs as well as geographically diversified, as discussed further below.

REIT Offering Documents. REITs that are to be offered in the public market file a registration statement on SEC Form S-11, which also specifies the information that is required in a REIT prospectus. The main types of information required in a REIT prospectus parallel those for any other REIT, as discussed in Chapter 3. A REIT prospectus, however, must have an additional section describing the investment policies of the REIT. This section

Exhibit 10.2: Partnership Agreement Provisions

1. Name and business
   a. The name of the partnership and the principal office and place of business
   b. The state in which the partnership was formed
   c. That the partnership was formed for the purpose of investing in and operating real estate
   d. That the partnership may enter into any other investments, with respect to real estate, deemed prudent by the general partners
2. The term of the partnership
3. Contributions of general partners
   a. Cash
   b. Other (usually real property that the partnership will manage)
4. Capital contributions of limited partners
5. Profits and losses
   a. How the net profits and losses of the partnership are to be divided and borne by each of the partners
   b. Specifications of the order of treatment for capital disbursements among general and limited partners with respect to the recovery of initial capital investments and treatments of operating losses
   c. How the profitability of the partnership will be defined and determined
6. The procedures for distributing proceeds from mortgage refinancing
7. The procedures from allocating distributions following the sale of assets
   a. By returning the cash contributions made to the original capital of the partnership
   b. How additional proceeds are to be allocated among general and limited partners
8. Losses. The liability of any of the limited partners for partnership losses is normally limited to the aggregate amount of his or her contribution to the capital of the partnership. Any losses in excess of such amounts shall are borne by the general partners.
9. Whether any of the partners are entitled to salaries, drawings, and/or interest on capital contributions
10. Management, duties, and restrictions
    a. General partners have generally equal rights in the management of the partnership and must devote the time necessary to ensure its success. General partners are typically restricted from borrowing against partnership properties, or assigning partnership interests, without the consent of the other general partners.
    b. No limited partner can participate in the management of the business. Limited partners may withdraw their capital contribution upon the termination of the partnership provided all liabilities of the partnership have been paid. The agreement will specify whether limited partners may demand or receive property other than cash in return for the contribution. The limited partners consent to the decisions of the general partners with regard to business operations.
11. Where partnership funds will be held

> **Exhibit 10.2: Partnership Agreement Provisions, continued**
>
> 12. Any deed, bill of sale, mortgage, security agreement, lease, contract for sale and purchase, or other commitment purporting to convey or encumber the interest of the partnership in all or any portion of any real or personal property, must be jointly signed by the general partners, or by the survivor of them.
> 13. How the accounting books will be maintained
> 14. Provisions for termination/dissolution of the partnership

Source: Adapted from Revised Uniform Partnership Act — General Partnership Agreement and Articles of Limited Partnership at www.freelegalforms.net, July 7, 2006.

> **Exhibit 10.3: REIT Sectors and Subsectors**
>
> **Equity REITs**
> Industrial/Office
> • Office
> • Industrial
> • Mixed
> Retail
> • Shopping Centers
> • Regional Malls
> • Free Standing
> Residential
> • Apartments
> • Manufactured Homes
>
> **Equity REITs, continued**
> Diversified
> Lodging/Resorts
> Health Care
> Self Storage
> Specialty
>
> **Mortgage REITs**
> Home Financing
> Commercial Financing

Source: National Association of Real Estate Investment Trusts, www.nareit.com, July 7, 2006.

must disclose the types of real estate investments (equity, mortgages, or both) used and the percentage allocated to each. The policy must also disclose whether the allocation can be changed by the directors or requires a vote of security holders. The investment policy from the prospectus of Republic Property Trust states, in part:[3]

> We conduct all of our investment activities through our Operating Partnership and its affiliates. Our primary investment objectives are to maximize cash flow at our properties and provide quarterly cash distributions to our shareholders. We will seek to enhance the operating performance of our current portfolio of properties and acquire and

develop additional properties, including the acquisition of substantially-leased office and office-oriented mixed-use properties or properties where we have otherwise identified value creation opportunities. Our business will be focused primarily on Class A office and office-oriented mixed-use properties, although we will not be limited in the types of real estate in which we can invest. Additionally, we intend to provide, through our taxable REIT subsidiary, fee-based development services for all real estate asset classes where we believe we can identify value-added opportunities. We have not established a specific policy regarding the relative priority of the investment objectives, including the amount or percentage of assets which will be invested in any specific property or class of property. For a discussion of our properties, business and other strategic objectives, see "Business and Properties."

Note that the policy refers to an operating partnership. A common REIT structure, umbrella partnership REIT or UPREIT, is one in which the real estate is owned by an operating partnership which is, in turn, majority owned by the REIT. This structure facilitates nontaxable exchanges of real estate partnerships to initially acquire properties. Often, a REIT is formed by real estate developers who own the properties in their own operating partnership. If they exchanged their real estate partnership for REIT shares when the REIT was formed, a taxable event would occur. By using the UPREIT structure, the owner/developer can exchange one partnership interest for another and avoid a taxable event. As a result, the REIT will not own all of the shares of the operating partnerships. These types of complex capital structures can make analysis difficult, but, in most cases, the operating partnership unit holders are treated in the same manner as the REIT shareholders. The investor should be somewhat cautious with any structures for which the treatment is different.

For equity real estate investments, the policy must also disclose the following:[4]

- The geographic area or areas in which the entity proposes to acquire real estate or interests in real estate

Understanding and Evaluating Prospectuses, Offering Documents, and Proxy Statements

- The types of real estate and interests in real estate in which the entity may invest—for example, office buildings, apartment buildings, shopping centers, industrial and commercial properties, special purpose buildings, and undeveloped acreage
- The method or proposed method of operating and financing the registrant's real estate, including any limitations on the number or amount of mortgages that may be placed on any one piece of property
- Whether or not it is the registrant's policy to acquire assets primarily for possible capital gain or primarily for income
- The policy as to the amount or percentage of assets that will be invested in any specific property

In the case of mortgage investments, the policy must disclose:[5]

- The types of mortgages—for example, first or second mortgages, whether such mortgages are to be insured by the Federal Housing Administration or guaranteed by the Veterans Administration or otherwise guaranteed or insured; and the proportion of assets that may be invested in each type of mortgage or in any single mortgage
- A description of each type of mortgage activity in which the registrant intends to engage, such as originating, servicing, and warehousing of mortgages, and its portfolio turnover policy
- The types of properties subject to mortgages in which the registrant invests or proposes to invest—for example, single-family dwellings, apartment buildings, office buildings, bowling alleys, commercial properties, and unimproved land

If the REIT is to invest in securities such as other REITs, partnerships, stocks, or bonds, the types of securities and criteria for selection must be disclosed.

In the case of specific real estate properties held (or planned), the prospectus must disclose the location, nature, and use of the property. Additionally, disclosure must be made of material mortgages or liens and the terms of any leases or other contracts on the property. This information may be aggregated into classes of property and need not be detailed as to specific properties unless they constitute 10 percent or more of REIT assets or revenue.

These investment policies should be examined to determine whether they are consistent with the investor's intended asset allocation—for example, if the diversification or lack thereof is appropriate for the investor. You should pay particular attention to investment policies that may result in higher levels of risk (such as concentration of properties or high use of leverage on properties relative to other REITs).

Evaluating REIT Operating and Financial Data. In the prospectus, REITs will provide the standard financial statements described in Chapters 2 and 3 that should be analyzed as detailed in those chapters. REITs will also provide additional operating and financial data that are critical to understanding the REIT's operating effectiveness, profitability, and valuation. The SEC requires that the following data be provided for each material property:[6]

- Occupancy rate expressed as a percentage for each of the last five years
- Number of tenants occupying 10 percent or more of the rentable square footage and principal nature of business of such tenant
- Principal business, occupations, and professions conducted in the building
- The principal provisions of the leases between the tenants, including rental per year, expiration date, and renewal options
- The average effective annual rental per square foot or unit for each of the five years before the date of filing
- Schedule of the lease expirations for each of the ten years starting with the year in which the registration statement is filed, stating (1) the number of tenants whose leases will expire, (2) the total area in square feet covered by such leases, (3) the annual rental represented by such leases, and (4) the percentage of gross annual rental represented by such leases
- Each of the properties and components thereof upon which depreciation is taken, setting forth the (1) federal tax basis, (2) rate, (3) method, and (4) useful life

Understanding and Evaluating Prospectuses, Offering Documents, and Proxy Statements

- The realty tax rate, annual realty taxes, and estimated taxes on any proposed improvements

These metrics can be compared with other REITs operating in the same geographic area to determine if the prospective investment is operating more efficiently and more profitably than its peers. You should especially compare the occupancy rate and average effective rental per square foot with similar properties. The adviser should also determine if the types of tenants and lease terms involve a higher degree of risk (for example, concentration in a particular profession subject to a high degree of business variability or at risk in the current business environment). In the case of leases, long-term leases at favorable rental rates and rental escalation clauses would be desirable, whereas long-term leases at low rates or short-term leases with uncertainty over renewals should be viewed cautiously.

While not required by the SEC, REITs will normally disclose other metrics common to the industry, most commonly funds from operations (FFO) and adjusted funds from operations (AFFO). The computation of FFO and AFFO are shown in Exhibit 10.4. FFO is essentially the operating performance (profitability) of the REIT. Gains and losses on property sales are removed since they are not part of normal operations and may not occur each year. Depreciation on real estate (but not other assets) is added back, since real estate may appreciate or retain its value even though accounting

Exhibit 10.4: Computation of FFO and AFFO

Net Income
− Gains from Property Sales
+ Losses from Property Sales
+ Real Estate Depreciation

Funds from operations (FFO)
− Normalized Recurring Expenditures
− "Straight Lining of Rents"

Adjusted funds from operations (AFFO)

Source: National Association of Real Estate Investment Trusts, Investing In REITs, "Glossary of Terms," www.investinginreits.com, July 7, 2006.

rules require that depreciation be expensed in determining net income. AFFO is a measure of the normal cash available for distribution from the operations of the REIT for the period. The adjustment for normalized recurring expenditures reflects improvements that were capitalized by the REIT (for example, new carpeting) but which are necessary to maintain the property and result in a periodic cash outflow. Accounting principles require that rental income be reported on an even ("straight line") basis over the life of the lease even though the lease revenue received may be lower in the early years. The "straight lining" adjustment is therefore necessary to determine the cash flow as opposed to net income from the rental properties. In evaluating FFO and AFFO, numbers that are high and increasing are desirable.

FFO and AFFO are also used to assess the value of a REIT relative to its peers. Similar to the manner in which companies are compared based on P/E (price to earnings) ratios, REITS can be compared based on price per share/FFO per share or price per share/AFFO per share. This is a measure of whether the price of each REIT share is cheap (a low ratio) or expensive relative to FFO or AFFO by comparing ratios across REITS in the same sector or subsector. Often analysts will use an estimate of FFO for the coming year rather than the prior year in assessing relative value. Comparative data is readily available from NAREIT (www.nareit.com). Generally, a REIT with better future opportunities (higher expected growth) should be expected to have a higher P/FFO multiple than other peers. On the other hand, a REIT with higher risk should exhibit a lower P/FFO multiple relative to peers.

Since REITs must pay a high dividend, another common valuation metric is dividend yield (dividend per share/price per share). A high dividend yield indicates a better value, although some REITs with lower dividend yields may have better growth prospects.

Exhibit 10.5 presents some REIT valuation data as of March 31, 2006. Let's say that you are trying to determine if the shares of Archstone-Smith (ASN), an apartment REIT, are inexpensive or expensive relative to peers. The data in the exhibit indicates that ASN has a P/FFO multiple at the high end of the sector and a dividend yield at the low end. These both indicate that ASN is relatively expensive compared with other REITs in the sector. This could be due to better opportunities or lower risk. Judgment must be

Understanding and Evaluating Prospectuses, Offering Documents, and Proxy Statements

Exhibit 10.5: REIT Valuation Data as of March 31, 2006

Residential—Apartments REIT Name	Ticker	Price/Share 03/31/06	Dividend Yield	Price/FFO Estimates 2006
America First Apartment Investors	APRO	14.49	6.90	
American Campus Communities, Inc.	ACC	25.91	5.21	18.51
Apartment Investment & Management Company	AIV	46.90	0.22	16.40
Archstone-Smith	**ASN**	**48.77**	**3.57**	**22.27**
Associated Estates Realty Corporation	AEC	11.25	6.04	11.72
AvalonBay Communities, Inc.	AVB	109.10	2.86	26.29
BNP Residential Properties, Inc.	BNP	16.80	6.19	
BRE Properties, Inc.	BRE	56.00	3.66	23.93
Camden Property Trust	CPT	72.05	3.66	20.24
Education Realty Trust, Inc.	EDR	15.30	7.84	15.30
Equity Residential	EQR	46.79	3.78	19.33
Essex Property Trust, Inc.	ESS	108.73	3.09	22.84
GMH Communities Trust	GCT	11.64	7.82	14.37
Home Properties, Inc.	HME	51.10	5.01	17.26
Maxus Realty Trust, Inc.	MRTI	13.20	7.58	
Mid-America Apartment Communities, Inc.	MAA	54.75	4.35	16.74
Post Properties, Inc.	PPS	44.50	4.04	22.59
The Town and Country Trust	TCT	40.59	4.24	
United Dominion Realty Trust	UDR	28.54	4.38	16.89

Source: National Association of Real Estate Investment Trusts, www.nareit.com, June 15, 2006.

used in evaluating the relative opportunities and risks. The prospectus provides the disclosure necessary to evaluate the opportunities and risks.

CONCLUSION

When evaluating a real estate investment, the prospectus should be evaluated like any equity investment (explained in Chapter 3), and the financial statements should be evaluated to assess the profitability, financial position, and cash flow (described in Chapter 2) of the entity. In addition, the adviser or investor should consider the unique aspects of a real estate investment. In particular, the following key points should be considered:

- What is the structure of the entity (limited partnership, REIT, etc.), and how will profits and losses be allocated among the various parties? In particular, how much is expected to flow to the investor?
- What is the track record of the syndicator and management? Have they operated similar ventures (limited partnerships or REITs) in the past, and how did earlier investors fare?
- What type of real estate is involved, and how attractive is this in the current economic environment?
- How diversified is the project geographically and by sector, and how does this fit in to the investor's asset allocation?
- How are the proceeds of the offering to be used? Is the property already developed or yet to be built?
- How do operating measures compare with peer entities (net operating income, occupancy, FFO, etc.)?
- What are the opportunities and risks of the offering?
- Is the price of the offering reasonable compared with net operating income, FFO, or other metrics—particularly when compared with peer entities?

ENDNOTES

[1] See Chapter 1.
[2] NAREIT, "REITs' Low Correlation to Other Stocks and Bonds Is Key Factor for Portfolio Diversification," May 29, 1001, www.nareit.com.
[3] Republic Property Trust, Form S-11 filed September 26, 2005.
[4] United States Securities and Exchange Commission, Form S-11, Item 13, at www.sec.gov.
[5] Ibid.
[6] Ibid, Item 15.

Understanding and Evaluating Prospectuses, Offering Documents, and Proxy Statements

DISCUSSION QUESTIONS:
1. Why is the limited partnership structure often used in private real estate syndicates?
2. What are the key points to consider in evaluating a private real estate offering?
3. What is net operating income and how can it be used?
4. What are the advantages of a REIT structure for large public offerings of real estate investment?
5. What is an UPREIT?
6. What key metrics are used to compare REIT operating performance?
7. Explain FFO and how it can be used in REIT valuation.

EXERCISE:

The National Association of Real Estate Investment Trusts (NAREIT) provides extensive REIT data at www.nareit.com. From NAREIT's Web site:
- Select a REIT sector.
- Describe the types of REITs in this sector and the major public REITs in this sector.
- Evaluate the relative valuation of REITs in this sector.

RECOMMENDED READING

Ralph L. Block, Investing in REITs; *Real Estate Investment Trusts*, 3rd ed., Bloomberg Press, New York, 2006.

William B. Brueggeman and Jeffrey Fisher, *Real Estate Finance and Investments*, 11th ed., McGraw-Hill/Irwin, 2001.

Barry L. Cliff, "How to Evaluate a Real Estate Investment," *Journal of Financial Planning*, April 1990, pp. 58–61.

Investing in Real Assets

Investment advisers interested in creating a well-diversified portfolio might suggest that a portion be allocated to "real" assets, such as commodities and energy. These investments can be made directly, by purchasing and holding the actual asset, or through purchasing securities issued by companies holding these assets. This chapter discusses the key points to consider when examining offering documents of investment securities with real asset holdings: commodities, managed futures, and publicly traded partnerships.

Commodities are typically classified as consumable goods such as oil and grain, or raw materials such as copper. The value of a commodity depends on the supply and demand for the commodity around the world. Managed futures funds are pooled investments similar to hedge funds that allow investors to gain investment exposure to commodities and commodity-related futures through professional managers.

There are many types of commodities. The Goldman Sachs Commodities Index (GSCI®) tracks all futures contracts traded on the New York Mercantile Exchange, Inc. (NYM); the International Petroleum Exchange (IPE); the Chicago Mercantile Exchange (CME); the Chicago Board of Trade (CBT); the Coffee, Sugar, and Cocoa Exchange, Inc. (CSC); the New York Cotton Exchange (NYC); the Kansas City Board of Trade (KBT); the COMEX Division of the New York Mercantile Exchange, Inc. (CMX); and the London Metal Exchange

Understanding and Evaluating Prospectuses, Offering Documents, and Proxy Statements

Exhibit 11.1: Component Contracts of the GSCI®

Commodity	Weight January 2006	Market Symbol	Trading Facility
Crude Oil	30.05%	CL	NYM
Brent Crude Oil	13.81%	LCO	IPE
Natural Gas	10.30%	NG	NYM
Heating Oil	8.16%	HO	NYM
Gasoline	7.84%	HU	NYM
Gas Oil	4.41%	LGO	IPE
Live Cattle	2.88%	LC	CME
Aluminum	2.88%	IA	LME
Wheat	2.47%	W	CBT
Corn	2.46%	C	CBT
Copper	2.37%	IC	LME
Lean Hogs	2.00%	LH	CME
Soybeans	1.77%	S	CBT
Gold	1.73%	GC	CMX
Sugar	1.30%	SB	CSC
Cotton	0.99%	CT	NYC
Red Wheat	0.90%	KW	KBT
Primary Nickel	0.82%	IN	LME
Coffee	0.80%	KC	CSC
Feeder Cattle	0.78%	FC	CME
Zinc	0.54%	IZ	LME
Standard Lead	0.29%	IL	LME
Cocoa	0.23%	CC	CSC

Source: Form S-1 Registration Statement for the iShares GSCI Commodity-indexed trust offering, Feb 1, 2006, p.32

(LME). Exhibit 11.1 lists the futures contracts included in the GSCI® as of February 2006, their percentage dollar weights, their market symbols and the exchanges on which they are traded.[1]

Exhibit 11.1 illustrates that many commodity contracts are related to oil and gas. In fact, such commodities compose nearly 75 percent of the total index. As a result, many funds specialize in such energy-related commodities.

WHY INVEST IN COMMODITIES AND MANAGED FUTURES?

There are a number of benefits to investing in commodities and managed futures.

1. **Diversification.** Studies have shown that commodities futures tend to exhibit return characteristics that are completely unrelated to those of financial investments such as stocks and bonds. Because of the low correlation, portfolio risk is reduced for investors holding both financial assets and commodities.
2. **Potential for enhanced return.**
3. **Ability to profit in different economic environments.** This is a particularly important aspect of commodities futures. Although their long-term returns are similar to those of stocks and bonds, futures tend to perform well during times of economic crisis. Frequently, such crises either result from or cause temporary shortages in commodities. These shortages result in higher commodity prices, so the commodities futures do well.
4. **Global diversification.** Commodity prices are based on global supply and demand balances rather than regional concerns.
5. **House advantage.** Although futures contracts are a zero-sum game (any amount gained by one investor is lost by the investor taking the other side of the trade), not all participants in the futures market are in it to "win." Commodity producers (or their customers) may use futures markets to guarantee a price for their output (inputs), and thus be satisfied with that reduction of business risk rather than requiring that the futures trade itself be profitable. For commodities with imbalanced "natural" players, investors can earn a profit (similar to that earned by insurance companies or casinos) by taking the opposite side. Academic studies (Kritzman 1993, Spurgin 2003) have quantified this potential profit.

Diversification benefits from commodities futures can be significant. Commodities are a separate asset class from stocks or bonds and behave differently from such financial investments. When seeking diversification, the lower the correlation—or moving in the opposite direction—of investments the better. Commodities have low or even negative correlation with financial assets. One explanation for this is that commodity prices are influenced by short-term expectations, while stocks and bonds are influenced by longer-term expectations. Another explanation is that the three primary inputs to economic production are raw materials, labor, and capital. Since labor cost tends to be stable over the short term, for a given level of output, an increase in the return on capital should result in a decrease in the return on raw materials. By this measure, commodities and financial assets should move in opposite directions, and thus provide strong diversification benefits when used together.

Furthermore, commodities tend to perform well when there is inflation and when there are economic crises. They do well during inflationary times, partly because rising commodity prices are often the cause of overall inflation. They do well during economic shocks because shocks are usually the result of dramatic shifts in the supply (oil embargo or drought) or the demand (a cold snap increases demand for heating oil) of a commodity. Stocks and bonds tend to do poorly in inflationary or crisis periods, so having commodities offers protection during such periods.

There are also several ways to gain exposure to commodities in a portfolio. These include investing in the underlying commodities themselves, investing directly in commodity futures, investing in the equity of companies that produce commodities, or investing in a commodity futures index or managed futures fund. Direct investment in commodities or futures is either impractical or quite risky for most investors and beyond the scope of this book. The equities of commodity producers have not been shown to offer the same diversification benefits of commodity futures. Therefore, this chapter focuses on funds that invest in commodities, either by attempting to replicate a diversified index or by attempting to add manager skill through a managed futures fund.

WHO SHOULD NOT INVEST IN COMMODITIES AND MANAGED FUTURES?

Although many studies have confirmed the diversification benefits of commodities in general, the results are not as promising with regard to managed futures. Managers may charge high fees for their expertise, and after fees, the funds may perform no better than a simple index strategy. Unless investors are highly confident in the skill of their chosen managers, an index may be the better way to gain exposure to commodities.

As an example of the detrimental impact of fees, consider Quadriga Superfund, LP (Quadriga.) Quadriga is a managed futures fund that registered with the SEC. Its registration includes the break-even analysis presented in Exhibit 11.2. This analysis demonstrates that the managers must provide a return of 8.75 percent simply for investors to break even. After the break-even return has been achieved, the managers will take a performance fee of 25

Exhibit 11.2: Break-Even Analysis for Quadriga Superfund, LP

Break-Even Analysis

The following tables show the fees and expenses that an investor would incur on an initial investment of $5,000 in Quadriga Superfund and the amount that such investment must earn to break even after one year.

Series A

	Percentage Return Required Initial 12 Months of Investment	Dollar Return Required ($5,000 Initial Investment) Initial 12 Months of Investment
Routine Expenses		
Management Fees	1.85%	$92.50
General Partner Performance Fees (1)	25.00%	$0
Selling Commissions	4.00%	$200.00
Offering Expenses	1.00%	$50.00
Operating Expenses	0.15%	$7.50
Brokerage Fees (2)	3.75%	$187.50
Redemption Charts (3)	0%	$0
Less Interest Income	2.00%	$100.00
12-Month Break-Even	8.75%	$437.50

(1) No performance fees will be charged until breakeven costs are met.
(2) Assumes 1,500 round-turn transactionsper million dollars per year at a rate of $25 per transaction.
(3) No additional charges or fees are proposed on redemption of units.

Source: Form S-1 Registration Statement for Quadriga Superfund, LP, filed January 1, 2005, p. 5.

Understanding and Evaluating Prospectuses, Offering Documents, and Proxy Statements

percent of any further return. This compares to the 0.75 percent fee charged by the iShares GSCI Commodity-Indexed Trust (iShares GSCI).[2] Given that some studies have shown an average return on futures in the low double digits, the managers will have to provide substantial returns above those of the index for investors to fare better.

REGULATIONS AND OFFERING DOCUMENTS

Under most circumstances, funds that trade futures or commodities must register with the National Futures Association and/or the Commodity Futures Trading Commission. Registered persons must disclose fees and expenses, their backgrounds and past performance, and any material legal proceedings brought against them within the last five years.

Commodity funds will typically provide a prospectus or offering document when soliciting clients, whether they are registered with the SEC or with state agencies. These documents will be similar to the equity prospectus in terms of their content and significance to investors. See Chapter 3 for a thorough explanation of a prospectus.

When reviewing a commodity or managed futures prospectus, there are several important considerations specific to this type of investment. Perhaps the most important of these is a discussion of the types of futures that will be traded. The major benefit of investing in commodities is the low correlation to traditional asset classes such as stocks, bonds, and international financial instruments. Exhibit 11.3 contrasts the investment approaches of the Quadriga and the iShares GSCI, respectively.

The iShares GSCI fund should closely match the composition of the GSCI as disclosed in Exhibit 11.1. Approximately 75 percent of its return would be based on energy prices, with the remainder dependent upon the prices of metals and agricultural products. By contrast, Quadriga is only 13 percent exposed to energy and nearly half its returns are derived from futures contracts on currencies, interest rates, or stock indices—all of which are capital assets rather than consumable goods or raw materials. It is not clear whether the fund takes long or short positions on these capital asset futures. To whatever extent the fund's positions are long, the potential diversification benefits against portfolio financial assets could be lost.

Exhibit 11.3: Differences in the Investment Approach of Two Selected Commodities Funds

Quadriga Superfund, L.P.	iShares GSCI Commodity-Indexed Trust
Each series trades in approximately 100 futures and cash foreign currency markets globally, including both commodity and financial futures. The approximate allocation between sectors is currencies, 18%; livestock, 5%; agricultural, 10%; metals, 10%; interest rate, 12%; energy, 13%; stock indices, 18%; and grains, 14%. Each series will emphasize instruments with low correlation and high liquidity for order execution.	The investment objective of the trust is to seek investment results, through the trust's investment in the investing pool, that correspond generally, but are not necessarily identical, to the performance of the Index, before the payment of expenses and liabilities of the trust and the investing pool. The investing pool will hold long positions in CERFs, which are futures contracts listed on the CME that have a term of approximately five years after listing and whose settlement at expiration is based on the value of the GSCI ® Excess Return Index, or GSCI-ER, at that time. The Investing Pool will also earn interest on the assets used to collateralize its holdings of CERFs. The GSCI-ER is calculated based on the same commodities included in the Goldman Sachs Commodity Index, or GSCI®, which is a production-weighted index of the prices of a diversified group of futures contracts on physical commodities.

Sources: Form S-1 Registration Statement for Quadriga Superfund, LP, filed January 1, 2005, p. 1, and Form S-1 Registration Statement for iShares GSCI Commodity-indexed Trust, filed February 1, 2006, p. 3.

Similar concerns may be raised when considering alternative means of obtaining commodity exposure. For example, investors commonly invest in the common stock of oil producers such as Exxon Mobil or in publicly traded partnerships related to oil infrastructure or pipelines as a means of diversifying into commodities. However, these may not provide the desired exposure. For example, the value of Exxon is partly based on its current cash flow from oil production and partly from the value of the oil reserves it can access. If oil prices rise, the company earns higher cash flow, and the value of its reserves rise, but it may be more difficult to acquire additional reserves.

Taxes are another important consideration. The offering documents should disclose how the fund and its investors will be taxed. For example, the iShares GSCI fund explains that "the Trust will not be treated as an association taxable as a corporation for U.S. federal income tax purposes, and the investing Pool will be treated as a partnership and not as an association taxable as a corporation for U.S. federal income tax purposes. Accordingly, the Trust and the Investing Pool will not be taxable entities for U.S. federal income tax purposes and will not incur U.S. federal income tax liability. Instead, you will be taxed as a partner in a partnership, which means that you generally will be required to take into account your allocable share of the Trust's and Investing Pool's items of income, gain, loss, deduction, expense, and credit in computing your U.S. federal income tax liability."[6]

Many commodity funds are set up as limited partnerships, trusts, or other nontaxable entities. In addition to the tax consequences, this may result in other differences compared with equity positions in a corporation. For example, shareholders may not be entitled to the same rights as owners of shares issued by a corporation. "By acquiring Shares, you are not acquiring the right to elect directors, to receive dividends, to vote on certain matters regarding the Trust, or to take other actions normally associated with the ownership of common shares."[7]

Finally, such structures may imbed a higher potential for conflicts of interest between the managers and shareholders than those of a corporation. "The Sponsor is an affiliate of the Trustee and therefore may have a conflict of interest with respect to its oversight of the Trustee. In particular, the Sponsor, which has authority to remove the Trustee in its discretion, has an incentive not to exercise this authority, even when it is in the best interests of the Shareholders to do so, because of the affiliation between the entities."[8]

PUBLICLY TRADED PARTNERSHIPS

Another security with real asset diversification benefits is the common units of a publicly traded partnership, commonly referred to as either a master limited partnership (MLP) or publicly traded partnership (PTP), which is publicly offered to investors and trades on an exchange. They pay out to investors all operating cash flow, which provides investors with relatively stable distributions.

The operations of MLPs must relate to natural resources or real estate (generally energy, timber, real estate, and mortgage securities investments) in order for the company to be publicly traded and retain partnership tax status. There are nearly 50 such issuers, about half of which are in the energy sector—primarily energy infrastructure. These energy infrastructure MLPs are used to transport, process, and store energy commodities, but investment results are not correlated highly to other energy investments. Rather, the investment characteristics are more similar to equity income securities such as REITs and utilities. The types of companies formed as energy MLPs are described in Exhibit 11.4.

As for the commodity diversification potential of MLPs, most issuers have a low level of direct commodity exposure. The primary commodity exposure is based on volumes shipped or processed, not on commodity prices. This is due to the fee-based contract terms with energy producers and end users, where the MLP is paid a fee for services and does not take title to the underlying commodity. For example, consider the following statement in the prospectus for MarkWest Energy Partners, LP.[9]

> In these three areas, we provide midstream services to our customers under four types of contracts. On a pro forma basis for the nine months ended September 30, 2003, we generated approximately 69 percent of our gross margin (revenue less cost of gas purchases) from contracts under which we charge fees for providing midstream services. Gross margin from these fee-based services is dependent on throughput volume and is typically less affected by short-term changes in commodity prices. The remainder of our gross margin is generated pursuant to percent-of-index, percent-of-proceeds, and keep-whole contracts, and is more affected by changes in commodity prices.

In 2006, there was a newly issued MLP, which included an additional commodity opportunity for investors: Linn Energy, LP was the first "upstream" MLP to be traded in the public market for decades. In the oil and gas industry, upstream refers to exploration and production

Understanding and Evaluating Prospectuses, Offering Documents, and Proxy Statements

> **Exhibit 11.4: Types of Energy MLPs**
>
> Energy infrastructure MLPs in which Tortoise Energy invests can generally be classified in the following categories:
>
> - Pipeline MLPs are common carrier transporters of natural gas, natural gas liquids (primarily propane, ethane, butane and natural gasoline), crude oil or refined petroleum products (gasoline, diesel fuel and jet fuel). Pipeline MLPs also may operate ancillary businesses such as storage and marketing of such products. Revenue is derived from capacity and transportation fees. Historically, pipeline output has been less exposed to cyclical economic forces due to its low cost structure and government-regulated nature. In addition, pipeline MLPs do not have direct commodity price exposure because they do not own the product being shipped.
>
> - Processing MLPs are gatherers and processors of natural gas as well as providers of transportation, fractionation and storage of natural gas liquids (NGLs). Revenue is derived from providing services to natural gas producers, which require treatment or processing before their natural gas commodity can be marketed to utilities and other end user markets. Revenue for the processor is fee based, although it is not uncommon to have some participation in the prices of the natural gas and NGL commodities for a portion of revenue.
>
> - Propane MLPs are distributors of propane to homeowners for space and water heating. Revenue is derived from the resale of the commodity on a margin over wholesale cost. The ability to maintain margin is a key to profitability. Propane serves approximately three percent of the household energy needs in the U.S., largely for homes beyond the geographic reach of natural gas distribution pipelines. Approximately 70 percent of annual cash flow is earned during the winter heating season (October through March). Accordingly, volumes are weather dependent, but have utility type functions similar to electricity and natural gas.
>
> - Coal MLPs own, lease and manage coal reserves. Revenue is derived from production and sale of coal, or from royalty payment related to leases to coal producers. Electricity generation is the primary use of coal in the U.S. Demand for electricity and supply of alternative fuels to generators are the primary drives of coal demand. Coal MLPs are subject to operating and production risks, such as: the MLP or a lessee meeting necessary production volumes; federal, state and local laws and regulations which may limit the ability to produce coal; the MLPs' ability to manage production costs and pay mining reclamation costs; and the effect on demand that the Clean Air Act standards have on coal end-users.

Source: 2005 Annual Report, Tortoise Energy Infrastructure Corporation.

activities while downstream refers to refining and marketing. The business of the partnership was ownership and exploitation of natural gas reserves. The assets of the partnership were hedged such that prices were locked in for a number of years. This provides a hybrid type of commodity exposure, since investors will receive steady cash flows until the hedges reset, plus the potential for management to grow the reserve base by conducting drilling activity funded with internal cash flow and borrowing.

We enter into hedging arrangements to reduce the impact of natural gas price volatility on our cash flow from operations....[A]pproximately 94 percent of our total expected production volume [for 2006 is hedged]...By removing price volatility from a significant portion of our natural gas production, we have mitigated, but not eliminated, the potential effects of changing natural gas prices on our cash flow from operations....[10]

As partnerships, the taxes are also flow-through in character, like the iShares discussed above. Investors receive a tax reporting Form K-1 (rather than a Form 1099) indicating their share of ordinary taxable income and deductions, which must be transferred to their tax return. The amount to taxable income tends to be around 20–30 percent of the cash distribution, and for some issuers the distribution grows with growth of the economy and population trends. The remainder of the distribution reduces basis in the stock, deferring ordinary taxable income until the security is sold.

MLP common unit holders have typical limited partner rights, including limited management and voting rights. MLP common units have priority over convertible subordinated units upon liquidation. Common unit holders are normally entitled to minimum quarterly distributions (MQD), prior to any distribution payments to convertible subordinated unit holders or incentive distribution payments to the general partner.

For some investors, the taxation of investing in individual MLPs is not suitable (such as qualified retirement plans). For these investors, there are a limited number of publicly traded, closed-end investment companies that invest in MLPs. These funds provide their shareholders with diversification, professional management, and a simpler tax structure. Tortoise Energy Infrastructure Corporation (NYSE: TYG) was the first such fund, launched in 2004. Closed-end funds are discussed in Chapter 5.

CONCLUSION

Investments in real assets such as energy provide diversification benefits. Since the investment vehicles are often organized as limited partnerships and are sometimes not publicly traded, you must review the offering documents carefully. You must consider the risks as well as the potential rewards of the investments as with any new investment. Some key points for investors to focus on are:

- What is the structure of the entity (limited partnership, PTP, etc.), and how will profits and losses be allocated among the various parties? In particular, how much is expected to flow to the investor?
- What is the fee structure, and how profitable must the venture be in order for investors to receive an adequate return on their investment?
- What is the track record of management? Have they operated similar ventures in the past, and how did earlier investors fare?
- What type of underlying assets are involved, and how attractive is this in the current economic environment?
- How diversified is the project geographically and by sector, and how does this fit in to the investor's asset allocation?
- What are the opportunities and risks of the offering?

ENDNOTES

[1] Form S-1 Registration Statement for the iShares GSCI Commodity-indexed Trust offering dated February 1, 2006, p. 32.
[2] Form S-1 Registration Statement for iShares GSCI Commodity-indexed Trust, filed February 1, 2006, p. 2.
[3] Form S-1 Registration Statement for Quadriga Superfund, LP, filed January 1, 2005, p. 5.
[4] Form S-1 Registration Statement for Quadriga Superfund, LP, filed January 1, 2005, p. 1.
[5] Form S-1 Registration Statement for iShares GSCI Commodity-Indexed Trust, filed February 1, 2006, p. 3.
[6] Form S-1 Registration Statement for iShares GSCI Commodity-Indexed Trust, filed February 1, 2006, p. 5.
[7] Form S-1 Registration Statement for iShares GSCI Commodity-Indexed Trust, filed February 1, 2006, p. 19.
[8] Form S-1 Registration Statement for iShares GSCI Commodity-Indexed Trust, filed February 1, 2006, p. 20.
[9] Form S-1 Registration Statement for MarkWest Energy Partners, LP, filed December 18, 2003, p. 1.
[10] Form S-1 Registration Statement for Linn Energy, LLC, filed January 12, 2006, p. 3.

DISCUSSION QUESTIONS

1. What are the advantages of investing in real assets through securities versus direct ownership?
2. If economists predict an increasing chance of deflation, should an investor increase or decrease exposure to commodities? Why?
3. What could happen that would award performance-based fees to commodities investment managers that is not a result of their expertise? What are the short- and long-term effects on investor returns in that case?
4. Review the suitability information in Chapter 1. What factors would influence your decision to invest in commodities if your age was 45, 65, or 85? Would the type of security matter (such as MLPs or index funds)?

EXERCISE

Find the most recent SEC filings for the following funds, and compare their investment strategy, NAV, and total return since inception, along with their management fee calculation. Which provides greater commodity diversification to a portfolio of stocks and bonds? Which do you believe would have lower volatility? These filings can be viewed on the SEC's EDGAR filing system.

1. Scudder Global Commodities Stock Fund, Inc. (NYSE: GCS)
2. Kayne Anderson MLP Investment Company, Inc. (NYSE: KYN)

RECOMMENDED READING

Center for International Securities and Derivatives Markets, The Benefits of Managed Futures: 2005 Update, CISDM Research Department, June 2005, www.cisdm.org.

Mark Kirtzman, "The Optimal Currency Hedging Policy with Biased Forward Rates," *The Journal of Portfolio Management*, Summer 1993, pp. 94–100.

George Kleinman, *Trading Commodities and Financial Futures: A Step by Step Guide to Mastering the Markets*, 3rd ed., Financial Times Prentice Hall, 2004.

Richard Spurgin, "Sources of Return in Managed Futures," Working Paper, CISDM, 2003, www.cisdm.org.

Appendix A: Suggested Solutions to End of Chapter Questions and Exercises

Chapter 1: Investor Protections: Legal and Regulatory Framework

DISCUSSION QUESTIONS
1. Private securities offerings are made to a limited number of "accredited" investors under securities laws. These accredited investors are assumed to be more sophisticated and capable of making appropriate inquiry and analysis to evaluate an investment. For this reason, private securities offerings are less heavily regulated than public offerings, which are made available to a wider investor base, including less experienced investors.
2. Under a partnership structure, investors are usually treated as limited partners. Since many states have limits on how many limited partners may participate, this may not be appropriate for large numbers of investors. Corporations, meanwhile, are taxed at both the corporate and the investor level. The LLC framework allows for an unlimited number of investors while preserving the favorable pass-through tax treatment of a partnership.

Understanding and Evaluating Prospectuses, Offering Documents, and Proxy Statements

3. The separation of ownership from control can result in situations where owners and managers have conflicting interests. Agency costs result from these conflicts of interest between managers and owners. Examples of agency costs can include areas where managers increase their personal wealth at the expense of owners, such as lavish expense accounts, other perquisites, engaging in mergers to increase management's compensation, and retaining cash rather than paying dividends.
4. Agency and other costs can be lowered by investors effectively monitoring hired managers through oversight of the board of directors, external auditors, and the assistance of financial advisers who can point out potential conflicts.
5. State and federal regulation contribute to lower agency costs. Federal requirements, such as the Sarbanes-Oxley Act, increase the effectiveness of internal controls and decrease the risk of fraud by management. The SEC also requires that shareholders be provided with a proxy statement allowing shareholders to cast informed votes. By increased shareholder involvement, it becomes important for managers to work for the shareholders.

EXERCISE

There is no one answer for this exercise. The SEC Web site will provide more than 40 pages listing various forms. The forms related to prospectuses begin with Form S-1. Additionally, the listing will include proxy statements as from DEF-14. To find a form S-1, under the Search for Company Filings click on Latest Filings and then enter "S-1" in the form type box. A list of recently filed prospectuses will appear. One can be printed and discussed.

Chapter 2: Understanding and Analyzing Financial Statements

DISCUSSION QUESTIONS

1. Working capital provides an investor with a dollar amount equal to current assets minus current liabilities. The current ratio is current assets divided by current liabilities. Ratios allow for easier comparisons over

time and across companies of different sizes. Note that a growing company would require growing working capital in dollar terms to maintain a level ability to meet its obligations. Using the current ratio instead provides an automatic adjustment.

2. The Defensive Interval Ratio results in the number of days of costs that can be met with quick assets on hand. It determines the length of time a firm can sustain normal operations with minimal profit or even revenue. This ratio can be important to investors in start-up companies that do not expect to generate any profit immediately, or for a firm in financial distress.

3. The historical cost convention of accounting is supported by the accounting principles of objectivity and conservatism. Asset acquisition and disposal, revenues and expenses are all accounted for at the actual amount paid or received under historical cost-based accounting. An advantage is that this removes any subjectivity, estimates, or appraisals from the process. Historical cost accounting is the only method that produces definite values; any other method would be subjective. The disadvantage is that assets that appreciate in value (such as land) will be recognized at less than their fair value on the balance sheet. Industries such as retail or railroads that have large amounts of land that has been owned for a long time are most affected.

4. A firm that capitalized $50 million of R&D expenditures in its most recent year provides an analyst with a few inferences. First, the firm will have higher income because the amount was not expensed when incurred. Next, the firm will have higher assets because the capitalization creates an asset that is then reduced in future periods. Finally, the analyst could infer that this company is a foreign company, because U.S. GAAP does not allow R&D expenses to be capitalized. It is considered more conservative for a firm to expense development expenditures, as it results in lower net income and assets in the year the expenditure is incurred.

5. The only way a firm can have a debt-to-asset ratio exceeding 1.0 is in the presence of negative equity. Companies that have cumulative net losses since inception can have negative equity. Negative equity can also incur

during recession when value of assets drops below the amount remaining on a loan for the asset.
6. Holding earnings and all other characteristics (for example, growth and risk) constant, investors would always prefer to buy a security with a lower P/E ratio. An above-market P/E therefore implies that investors believe the stock has higher growth potential or lower risk (and therefore requires a lower return.) Alternatively, it could indicate that the security is overpriced relative to other investments.

EXERCISE

Dell's ROE declined between 1999 and 2001, primarily due to lower profit margins and asset turnover. Although these only partially recovered in 2002 and 2003, the ROE grew to exceed its prior peak. The remaining improvement was due not to operating factors but to higher leverage and lower tax burden.

Chapter 3: The Prospectus: Equity IPOs

DISCUSSION QUESTIONS

1. There are many requirements a company must meet before going public. They can be both time-consuming and costly. However, there are many reasons a company undergoes this process to go public.
    - Companies want to raise additional capital to expand operations and debt or who have insufficient private equity.
    - Founders, venture capitalists, and other investors desire to "cash out" all or some of their investment.
    - The company may wish to make acquisitions using public securities as payment.
    - The company may wish to establish an external value measure for the firm.
    - The company may wish to have a liquid market for shares that can be issued to employees and others for services provided to the firm.
2. In a firm commitment, the underwriter buys the entire issue at a discounted

price and resells it. The markup, or discount, is typically around 7 percent. In a best efforts offering, the underwriter does not buy the securities, but pledges to make their "best effort" to sell the offering. Under this arrangement, the underwriter makes a commission.

3. A "red herring" is the preliminary prospectus that must be filed with the SEC. It may be updated and changed several times before being called the final prospectus. It is called a "red herring" because of the passage in red that states the company is not trying to sell any shares before it receives SEC approval.

4. Companies provide investors with a large amount of information that can help an investor's decision. When looking at the prospectus summary and risk factors, an investor should be sure they fully understand how the company generates profit, how much of the profit is from operating activities, who the company's competitors are, how serious and likely the potential risk factors are, and how the company compares to other potential investments.

5. Dilution occurs during an IPO as the result in the change in the net tangible book value per share before and after the offering, and the disparity between existing stockholders' price per share and the new stockholders' price per share. Existing shareholders benefit greatly from this dilution. The stock price as well as the tangible book value per share often increases dramatically with an IPO.

6. Because GPI is a new offering, the price of an IPO tends to be a little undervalued to induce investors and reflect the dilution that will occur. Additionally, if GPI will be growing with its IPO, it must prove it is capable of performing successfully at a higher level. If GPI is going public because it cannot afford to take on any more debt, then the value of the company will be lower due to its high debt. GPI's P/E ratio may increase after the IPO; higher earnings growth is expected to result from investment of the proceeds. Compared to its peers, the stock will trade at a higher price and the P/E will increase. P/E ratios are also a function of risk and growth. A company with a high level of risk or a low level of expected growth should trade at a lower P/E than other companies in the same industry.

Understanding and Evaluating Prospectuses, Offering Documents, and Proxy Statements

7. If there are family or business relationships among officers and directors, the directors may have interests more aligned with management than with outside investors. Directors may be inclined to vote in favor of management on key issues, to the detriment of outside investors.

EXERCISE

Most IPOs are priced by the underwriters based on the level of interest in the shares. A higher valuation is assigned to companies that have greater investor desire to own shares. However, in most cases, the underwriters will price the shares somewhat below what the market is likely to bear to guarantee that all of the shares are sold. This frequently results in a strong first day's performance as the shares adjust to the market-based price. Google's auction process was intended to more closely match the market-clearing price.

Since an auction-based IPO is not intentionally underpriced in order to guarantee that all the shares are sold, it might be expected not to do as well in the first day's trading than a typical IPO.

In actual trading, Google's first day closing price was quite close to its opening price, which is unusual for an IPO and suggests that the auction met its intended purpose. The shares also traded within a relatively tight range for the first month. After that time, investors enjoyed very strong returns.

Chapter 4: The Prospectus: Secondary Offerings and PIPEs

DISCUSSION QUESTIONS

1. Companies generally issue new equity in order to raise additional capital for growth.
2. The securities sold in a PIPE are not unregistered and therefore cannot be traded on an exchange after the offering. They are typically offered at a discount to the public value of similar securities to compensate for this lack of liquidity and to complete the deal quickly.
3. Investors in PIPEs tend to be skeptical that the new capital will help earnings grow faster. As a result, they tend not to be strategic investors

but are looking instead for the superior investment return that can be had by forfeiting liquidity.
4. The reasons a company may turn to a PIPE offering are:
   - The need for a small equity infusion of perhaps $5 million to $50 million that would otherwise fail to attract underwriters
   - Time constraints that prohibit the lengthy process of a public offering
   - Small market capitalization relative to the amount being raised
   - Limited interest from institutional investors
   - The need for confidentiality during the offering process
5. Because the securities sold in a PIPE are usually offered at a discount to the publicly traded securities, the existing shareholders will have their ownership diluted. This contrasts with an IPO, wherein the new proceeds increase the book value per existing shareholder while leaving the new shareholders with a book value below their contribution.
6. The appropriate P/E ratio for a company is a function of its risk profile and growth potential. These would need to be known to compare the relative attractiveness of the company to its peers. Given that the P/E multiple is higher than that of the peers, the company would probably prefer a straight common stock offering to a structured offering.

EXERCISE

This exercise is intended to stimulate discussion about evaluating such a secondary offering, While there is no "correct" answer, it would be useful for readers to examine Google's subsequent financial statements to evaluate how the cash was used, if at all.

Chapter 5: The Prospectus: Mutual Funds

DISCUSSION QUESTIONS
1. The SEC categorizes investment companies into three main types:
   - Open-end companies (mutual funds)
   - Closed-end companies (closed-end funds)
   - Unit investment trusts (UITs)

Understanding and Evaluating Prospectuses, Offering Documents, and Proxy Statements

2. Registered investment companies must provide investors the following documents:
   - Prospectus
   - Fund profile (upon request)
   - Statement of additional information (SAI) (upon request)
   - Annual and semiannual reports
3. Taxation of mutual fund returns can be complicated, and investors should understand them. They include:
   - That fund distributions may be taxed as ordinary income and capital gains
   - That distributions, whether received in cash or reinvested, may be subject to federal income tax
   - That an exchange of the fund's shares for shares of another fund will be treated as a sale and any gain on the transaction may be subject to federal income tax.
4. The financial statements and management's discussion of its performance are found in the statement of additional information (SAI).
5. When investors consider a fund's financial statements, they should consider not only the performance, but whether any performance advantage (disadvantage) relative to the benchmark could be a result of taking more (less) risk. In addition, the level of fees should be considered, regarding whether they are justified by superior performance. Finally, the turnover of funds should be reviewed (particularly in taxable accounts) because it can cause higher taxes to be levied.
6. The fund's registration statement includes the following information investors may find useful:
   - Articles of incorporation
   - Bylaws
   - Instruments defining rights of security holders
   - Investment advisory contracts
   - Underwriting contracts
   - Bonus or profit-sharing contracts
   - Custodian agreements
   - Other material contracts

Appendix A | Suggested Solutions to End of Chapter Questions and Exercises

7. This question is intended to stimulate open discussion regarding mutual fund conflicts. There is no "correct" answer.

EXERCISE

The answer will depend upon the date of the *ICI Fact Book*. This solution is based upon the 2006 edition.

Over the period 1985 to 2005, total U.S. registered investment company assets increased from $602 billion to $9,518 billion. The 2005 data broken down by type of investment company are (in billions):

Mutual Funds	$8,905
Closed-End Funds	$276
ETFs	$296
UITs	$41

Mutual funds and ETFs have shown the greatest increase over time. UITs have actually declined in use. The ICI attributes some of the growth in total to investment performance. The growth in ETFs can be attributed to the desire to invest in particular asset classes, some of which were not previously available in an investment company format (for example, commodities).

ICI reports that fees and expenses for stock funds have declined from 2.32 percent in 1980 to 1.13 percent in 2005 (includes annualized loads). Fees and expenses for bond funds have declined from 2.05 percent to 0.90 percent over the same period.

Chapter 6: The Prospectus: Principal Protected Securities

DISCUSSION QUESTIONS

1. PPSs are considered hybrid securities because they purport to offer equity-like return without the corresponding downside risk. Thus, they have characteristics of both equity and fixed-income securities.
2. Unlike equity mutual funds, PPSs are not continuously offered and may not have an active secondary market. Between issuance and

maturity, the investor has no assurance of receiving the net asset value or even anything approaching it.
3. To deliver on the hybrid features of a PPS, issuers may use one or more of the following approaches:
   - Options
   - Futures
   - Zero-coupon bonds
4. To balance the principal protection component against the upward return potential, the issuer must vary the equity proportion of total assets invested. If equity markets suffer considerable losses, the fund may be required to allocate more to fixed income to guarantee the principal protection. This would limit subsequent upside potential.
5. Two approaches investors can use to estimate expected return are to compare the instrument to historical market returns (backtesting) and to simulate potential market behavior.

EXERCISE

1. PPSs returned an average of 2 percent and 5 percent in 2003 and 2004, respectively. The equity markets posted far greater returns of 12 percent and 33 percent, respectively. Given that many PPSs purport to deliver 70–80 percent of the equity market return, the performance was likely disappointing to investors.
2. Investors could receive near-zero returns if market returns are volatile and the PPS has a cap to periodic returns. For example, some PPSs cap returns at 15 percent quarterly. If the market rose by 30 percent in one quarter, the PPS would rise only 15 percent. A 15 percent decline in the next quarter would leave the investor with no return, although the market was up 15 percent in total.

Appendix A | Suggested Solutions to End of Chapter Questions and Exercises

Chapter 7: The Proxy Statement

DISCUSSION QUESTIONS

1. Key points to consider when reviewing a corporation's proxy statement include:
   - Conflicts of interests between investors, management, and directors, such as related-party transactions or business transactions between management, directors, and the company
   - Who is entitled to vote and which share classes may control the outcome
   - The types and level of compensation of management and directors
   - Changes in or disagreements with auditors and any fees paid for non-audit-related services
   - Any significant changes to securities issued, mergers, or acquisitions/dispositions
2. Rather than vote shares by proxy, investors may want to attend the annual meeting in order to participate in discussion related to certain of the issues being voted, or to propose issues to be voted on in future meetings.
3. Key points to consider when reviewing an investment company's proxy statement include (in addition to those for corporations):
   - Changes to investment advisory or other fee arrangements
   - Institution of or changes to any mutual fund distribution plan
4. This question is intended to stimulate open discussion and there is no "correct" answer. Some pros will likely include aligning officer and director interests with those of shareholders. Cons could include encouraging managers to have a short-term focus.

EXERCISE

TDS Common shareholders have a disproportionately low share of voting rights relative to their share of the equity capital provided. Although they constitute nearly 90 percent of the capital provided, their voting power is less than half.

Conflicts related to this voting structure include the inability to remove ineffective management or oversee management.

Understanding and Evaluating Prospectuses, Offering Documents, and Proxy Statements

Chapter 8: Hedge Funds

DISCUSSION QUESTIONS

1. Hedge funds often use the limited partnership or limited liability company structures because they allow income to pass through to investors (avoiding taxation at the corporate level) and because they permit special allocation of income, gains, and losses (with a disproportionate share going to the manager).
2. Investors evaluating a hedge fund should consider:
   - Are the objectives and strategies well-defined or open-ended?
   - Are the strategies unique or are they available elsewhere at lower cost?
   - Do the fund's objectives/strategies diversify the investor's current holdings?
   - How has the fund performed compared to others employing a similar strategy?
3. Hedge fund risk factors include:
   - Lack of operating history for new funds
   - Concentration of investments/lack of diversification
   - Use of leverage
   - Short selling
   - Use of derivatives
   - Lack of liquidity/marketability for some investments
   - Conflicts of interest
   - Potential for loss of favored tax status
4. Hedge funds holding illiquid issues may be unable to sell them if necessary, and the lack of a market requires that the value of such securities be estimated. Management therefore has the potential to estimate the value in a way that shows stronger performance.
5. Hedge funds typically have one or more of the following fees:
   - A management fee, set as a percentage of assets
   - A performance incentive, set as a percentage of total return
   - A hurdle rate that must be cleared before performance incentives are awarded
   - A high water mark, which reduces fees following a period of losses until the mark is surpassed

- Look-back provisions that return previously awarded incentives if performance reverses
6. This question is intended to stimulate discussion and there is no "correct" answer. Potential implications include the ability to create hedge fund-type investments using long and short positions in ETFs.

EXERCISE

1. Court documents allege that Israel and his chief financial officer, Daniel Marino, disguised trading losses from Bayou's early investors by lying about the fund's performance and padding the results with infusions of cash from Bayou Securities, a stock-trading subsidiary that racked up heavy commissions from Israel's frenetic trading.
2. Two hundred million dollars in investments remain missing of a total of $440 million invested. About $100 million was recovered.
3. Simon Israel III, founder of Bayou Hedge Funds, has maintained from the start that he is a third-generation trader, coming from a family of successful commodities traders dating back to the 1890s. However facts suggest that he was indeed a low-level order taker who bounced from one obscure firm to another.
4. Court documents allege that Israel and his chief financial officer, Daniel Marino, disguised trading losses from Bayou's early investors by lying about the fund's performance and padding the results with infusions of cash from Bayou Securities, a stock-trading subsidiary that racked up heavy commissions from Israel's frenetic trading.

    The SEC alleges that since it was impossible to hide this manipulation from Grant Thornton, the fund's auditors, Israel and Marino fired them and replaced them with a new entity, Richmond-Fairfield Associates.

    According to prosecutors, Richmond-Fairfield was a sham company, established by Marino to make it appear as though Bayou's financials had been audited. Marino was the sole principal and the firm had no other clients.
5. For fees ranging from $1,000 to several thousand dollars, a growing number of hedge fund "sleuths" will conduct background checks on these secretive partnerships and their managers by searching for such

red flags as bad credit histories and padded résumés. And thanks to the dissemination of information on the Internet, individual investors can tap into some of the same tools the professionals use, such as searches of court documents.

Chapter 9: Specialized Private Equity Vehicles

DISCUSSION QUESTIONS
1. Because private equity funds tend to have low correlation with other asset classes, they can provide investors with reduced risk and enhanced returns.
2. Individual investors can invest in publicly offered funds such as business development companies (BDCs) and specialized acquisition companies (SPACs).
3. Business development companies are regulated under the Investment Company Act of 1940.
4. Important metrics for investors considering a BDC are presented in Exhibit 10.2 and include dividend yield, price/earnings ratio, and price/book ratio.

EXERCISE
Private equity funds generate return primarily through capital appreciation. This value cannot be realized until the investment is sold (or often, written off). Since interim values must be estimated, there is a potential conflict of interest, since it is in the manager's interest to assign as high a value as possible. This could, in turn, overstate the value of the BDC. It could also unduly influence investors to allocate too many assets to private equity as a class. Undervaluation of net assets could hurt exiting shareholders when they sell their shares.

Appendix A | Suggested Solutions to End of Chapter Questions and Exercises

Chapter 10: Real Estate Entities

DISCUSSION QUESTIONS

1. Real estate syndicates often use the limited partnership structure so that passive investors can get the benefit of experienced managers while limiting their liability.
2. Key points to consider in evaluating a private real estate offering include:
   - The experience of the developer and operator
   - Number and success of past deals by the syndicator
   - The type of real estate project and the attractiveness of such real estate
   - How diversified the project is
   - How offering proceeds will be used
   - How much money the general partners and syndicators are investing
   - Long-term plans for the property
   - When and how investors will be repaid
   - If the return is sufficient to justify the risks
   - If there are conflicts of interest, such as related-party transactions
3. Net operating income is gross potential income, less vacancy costs and uncollectible rent, less operating expenses and reserves for replacements. It can be used as a valuation metric (NOI yield).
4. The advantage of a REIT for large offerings is that, unlike an LP, there is no limit to the number of investors. Like an LP, the income is passed through to investors for tax purposes, under most circumstances.
5. An UPREIT is a REIT in which the real estate is owned by an operating partnership that in turn is owned by the REIT. The structure facilitates nontaxable acquisitions of partnerships.
6. Key metrics used to compare REIT operating performance include:
   - Occupancy rate
   - Number of tenants occupying 10 percent or more of the space
   - Principal businesses of tenants
   - Major lease provisions
   - Average effective annual rent per square foot
   - Schedule of lease expirations

Understanding and Evaluating Prospectuses, Offering Documents, and Proxy Statements

- Depreciable assets and remaining lives
- Realty tax rate

7. FFO, or funds from operations, is a cash flow measure used to evaluate REIT performance. It is calculated as net income excluding depreciation, gains, and losses. Similar to net operating income, it can be used as a capitalization or yield measure when comparing valuations of multiple REITs.

EXERCISE

An Excel table of the REITs by property type is available on the NAREIT site at www.nareit.com/newsroom/charts.cfm. As an example, the industrial/office REIT sector, which consists primarily of office buildings and industrial buildings, is dominated by Equity Office Properties and Boston Properties. These two companies combined have a third of the total market cap of the 24 companies in this sector.

Chapter 11: Investing in Real Assets

DISCUSSION QUESTIONS

1. Securities vs. direct ownership not covered in chapter. Some of the benefits to investing in commodities include:
   - Diversification against financial assets
   - Potential for enhanced return
   - Strong downside protection during crises
   - Global diversification
   - House advantage from providing liquidity
2. Commodities tend to perform best in inflationary times rather than deflationary times. However, financial assets such as stocks and bonds fare poorly during deflation and certain commodities, such as gold, should hold their value.
3. Commodities could turn in average performance (low double-digit) and still result in performance fees if the manager is awarded bonuses based on total return rather than relative return. In such cases, managers must have markedly superior skill for investors to benefit on an after-fees basis.

4. Given the diversification benefits commodities provide, an allocation may be appropriate for investors of any age. Unless the investor had high confidence in the active manager, the lower fees of an index fund would probably be the safer bet.

EXERCISE

Although the Scudder fund consists primarily of stocks, it would likely provide the greater diversification to a broad portfolio of stocks and bonds due to its exposure to commodity producers. The pipeline income of the MLP, however, should prove more stable. However, the fees on the MLP are much higher than those of the Scudder fund.

Index

Accounting, 13, 14, 42–44, 99, 100, 197
Accounts receivable turnover ratio, 53
Accredited investors, 16, 17, 117, 206, 207
Activity ratios, 52–54
Adjusted funds from operations (AFFO), 248, 249
Advisory agreements, 138, 156, 158, 199–201
Advisory board, 149, 156, 160
American Stock Exchange, 24
Analytical tools, summary of, 3–5
Annual meetings, 184, 197
Annual report, mutual funds, 130, 132, 138, 164
Auctions, 75, 76, 78, 79, 81, 88

Balance sheet, 35–39
Benchmarks, mutual funds, 134, 161
Best efforts underwriting, 73, 79, 92
Blank check offerings, 218
Blind pool offerings, 218
Blue Sky laws, 14–18
Board of directors
    compensation, 190–192
    duties, 18, 19
    election of, 187, 188, 190
    and equity IPOs, 92, 93, 96, 100–102
    indemnification, 101, 102
    mutual funds, 128, 129, 149, 150, 152, 153, 156
    and state law, 79
Book value, 56
Brokers
    business development companies, 229
    hedge funds, 213
    mutual funds, 128, 138, 140–143, 153, 159, 161, 162
    NASD requirements, 19, 20
    public offerings, 22, 23

Business development companies (BDCs), 217–219
    discussion questions, 234, 235, 280
    exercise, 235, 280
    prospectus, evaluating, 220–234
    recommended reading, 236
    structure and regulation of, 219, 220
    summary of key issues, 234
Business entities, 10–12, 28, 267, 268

Capital structure, mutual funds, 137–139
Capital structure ratios, 49–51
Cash flow statement, 40–42, 66
Chicago Board of Trade (CBT), 253
Chicago Mercantile Exchange (CME), 253
Closed-end companies, 128, 130, 144, 146, 263, 264
Coffee, Sugar, and Cocoa Exchange, Inc. (CSC), 253
COMEX (CMX), 253
Commodities
    advantages of investments in, 255, 256
    discussion questions, 265, 282, 283
    entity structure, 260
    exchanges, 253, 254
    exercise, 265, 283
    fees, impact of, 256–258
    index funds, 256
    prospectus, evaluation of, 258–260
    recommended reading, 265
    summary of key issues, 264
Commodity Futures Trading Commission, 258
Common size data, 45–46
Compensation
    board of directors, 190–192
    business development companies, 225–230

Understanding and Evaluating Prospectuses, Offering Documents, and Proxy Statements

executive, 3, 192, 194
mutual fund advisers and managers, 137–139, 146, 149, 150, 153, 155, 158, 160, 161, 163
and proxy statements, 188–195, 202
Conflicts of interest, 3, 19, 174, 184, 186, 187, 202, 213, 225, 226, 260
Conservatism accounting principle, 42
Control persons, 155, 156
Corporations, 11, 12, 197, 198
Cost-based accounting, 42
Cover page
    business development company prospectus, 220, 221
    Google IPO, 9, 10, 75, 76
    initial public offering prospectus, 9, 10, 72, 74, 75, 77–81
    mutual fund prospectus, 132, 133
Coverage ratios, 51, 52
Current ratio, 46–48

Days inventory, 53
Days receivable, 53
Debt ratio, 50–51
Defensive interval ratio, 49
Delaware, 19, 79
Depreciation, 43, 44, 66
Dilution
    earnings per share, 35
    equity IPOs, 88–91, 104
    secondary offerings, 114, 122, 123
    warrants and options, exercise of, 81
Direct participation programs, 20–22
Disclaimers, 9, 10
Disclosures
    and aftermarket trading, 24
    conflicts of interest. *See* Conflicts of interest
    equity IPOs, 74, 78, 86, 89, 96, 98, 99, 101–103
    public offerings, 22, 74, 109
    real estate investment trusts, 245–247
    and scope of regulations, 9
Distribution arrangements, 142, 143
Distribution fees. *See* Rule 12b-1
Distributions, 12
Diversification
    master limited partnerships, 261
    publicly traded partnerships, 260
    REITs, 242, 247, 251
    RELPs, 238, 239, 251
Dividend yield, 249
Dividends, 11
Due diligence, 3
    hedge fund managers, 210
    NASD guidelines for brokers, 20, 21

PIPEs, 121, 123
public offerings, 9, 22, 23
Dutch auction, 81, 88
Duty of care, 18, 19

Earnings before interest, tax, depreciation, and amortization (EBITDA), 65
Earnings before interest and taxes (EBIT), 51, 52, 55, 60
Energy-related MLPs, 261–263
Enterprise value/EBITDA, 65
Equity IPOs. *See* Initial public offerings (IPOs)
Exchange-traded funds (ETFs), 128, 131
Exemptions from SEC registration, 23, 24, 117, 205–207
Experts and counsel, identification of, 93

Fairness opinion, 88, 93
Financial adviser, role of, 7, 8
Financial data, REITs, 247–250
Financial statements
    accounting conventions, 42–44
    annual, 23
    audited, 12, 13
    balance sheet, 35–39
    cash flow statement, 40–42, 66
    compilation, 13
    discussion questions, 68, 268–270
    equity IPOs, 73, 81, 85, 95, 98–100
    exercise, 69, 270
    generally, 67
    hedge funds, 213
    income statements, 33–35
    issuer-prepared statements, 13, 14
    mutual funds, 128, 145, 147, 164, 165
    pro forma, 120
    ratios, use of. *See* Ratios
    real estate investment trusts, 247, 251
    recommended reading, 69
    review or verification of, 12, 13
    statement of owners' equity, 40, 42
    use of, 31
Firm commitment underwriting, 73, 79, 92, 110, 116
Form ADV, 210
Form K-1, 263
Form N-1A, 132
Form S-1, 72, 74, 111
Form S-3, 111, 113
Fund description, 148, 149
Fund history, 147, 148
Fund profile, 129, 130
Funds from operations (FFO), 248, 249

Index

General partnership, 11
Generally accepted accounting principles (GAAP), 13, 14, 43
Generally accepted auditing standards (GAAS), 14
Goldman Sachs Commodities Index (GSCI), 253, 254
Google, Inc.
    balance sheet, 35–37, 39
    cash flow statement, 40–42
    common size data, 45, 46
    debt ratio, 51
    general and administrative expenses, 46
    income statement, 33–35
    interest coverage ratio, 51
    IPO, evaluation of, 74–103
    IPO prospectus cover page, 9, 10, 75, 76
    liquidity ratios, 46–49
    net profit margin, 54
    return on assets, 55, 58, 59
    return on equity, 55, 59, 60
    secondary offering, 112–114
    total asset turnover, 53
Governance, 3, 18, 19, 24, 197, 198

Hedge funds
    business structure, 208
    discussion questions, 214, 278, 279
    exercise, 214, 279, 280
    offering documents, evaluation of, 208–213
    recommended reading, 214, 215
    registration requirements, 205–208
    summary of key issues, 213

Income statements, 33–35
Indemnification of officers and directors, 101, 102
Independent public accountants, 192
Initial public offerings (IPOs)
    closed-end companies, 130
    discussion questions, 105, 270–272
    exercise, 105–107, 272
    prospectus, evaluation of, 73–103
    reasons for going public, 71, 72
    recommended reading, 107, 108
    research, 102, 103
    summary of key issues, 103, 104
    types of, 71
Insiders, 3
Intangible assets, 43
International Accounting Standards Board (IASB), 43
International Petroleum Exchange (IPE), 253
Intrastate offerings, 23
Inventory turnover ratio, 52, 53
Investment advisers
    business development companies, 230, 231, 234
    evaluation of investment, 8
    hedge funds, 207, 208, 210
    mutual funds, 128, 129, 137, 139, 149, 153, 154, 156–160, 162, 163, 165, 166
Investment banks, 72, 110. *See also* Underwriting
Investment companies
    prospectus, evaluation of, 144, 145
    proxy statements, 198–201
    types of, 127–131
Investment Company Act of 1940, 127, 131, 148, 154, 219
Investment objectives
    business development companies, 230
    hedge funds, 208, 209
    mutual funds, 133, 134, 137, 144, 158, 165, 166
Investment strategy
    business development companies, 224, 225, 230
    changes to, 201
    mutual funds, 133, 137
iShares GSCI Commodity-Indexed Trust, 258–260
Issuer-prepared financial statements, 13, 14

Janus Twenty Fund, 132–137, 143, 145
Jurisdiction, 14, 15

Kansas City Board of Trade (KBT), 253

Limited liability company (LLC), 12
    hedge funds, 208, 212, 213
    real estate, 237. *See also* Real estate limited partnership (RELP)
Limited partnership, 11
    hedge funds, 208, 212, 213
    real estate. *See* Real estate limited partnership (RELP)
Liquidity
    exit from investment, evaluating, 17, 24
    hedge funds, 211
Liquidity ratios, 46–49
Loads. *See* Sales loads
London Metal Exchange (LME), 253, 254

Managed futures funds, 253
    advantages of investments in, 255, 256
    prospectus, evaluation of, 258–260
    recommended reading, 265
    regulation of funds, 258
    summary of key issues, 264
Management
    business development companies, 225–233
    hedge funds, 210
    mutual funds, 128, 137–139, 143, 144, 149, 150, 152, 153, 160, 161

Understanding and Evaluating Prospectuses, Offering Documents, and Proxy Statements

Management's discussion and analysis (MD&A)
    equity IPOs, 99
        financial statements, 14
        mutual fund financial statement, 164, 165
Master limited partnership (MLP), 11, 260–265
Mixed model accounting, 42, 43
Money market funds, 133, 134, 164
Mortgage investments, REITS, 246
Mutual funds
    discussion questions, 167, 273–275
    exercise, 167, 168, 275
    fees, 129, 134, 136, 138, 143, 144, 156, 159
    investment companies, 127, 128
    management, 128, 137–139, 143, 144, 149, 150, 152, 153, 160, 161
    open-end companies, 127–130
    prospectus, evaluation of, 131–146
    recommended reading, 168
    registration statement, 165, 166
    sales loads. *See* Sales loads
    statement of additional information, 129–133, 138, 140, 146–165
    summary of key issues, 166
    tax consequences, 138, 142–144, 163, 164
    transaction fees, 128
    trustees, 128, 138, 146, 149–153, 158, 166
    underwriters, 139, 141, 148, 153, 154, 159, 163–166

NASDAQ, 24, 25, 78
National Association of Securities Dealers (NASD), 19–22
National Futures Association, 258
Net asset value (NAV)
    business development companies, 222, 227
    mutual funds, 128, 130, 140, 143, 145, 165
Net profit margin, 54
New York Cotton Exchange (NYC), 253
New York Mercantile Exchange, Inc. (NYM), 253
New York Stock Exchange (NYSE), 24, 25
Nontraditional investments, 1

Offering price
    equity IPOs, 77, 78, 81, 86–88, 93, 102–104
    private placements, 114, 115
    secondary offerings, 114, 115
Officers
    compensation. *See* Compensation
    and equity IPOs, 88, 92, 96, 100–102
    indemnification, 101, 102
Operating cash flow, 66, 67
Operating data, REITs, 247–250
Ownership and control, separation of, 26. *See also* Proxy statements

P/E ratio. *See* Price-to-earnings (P/E) ratio
Partnerships, 11, 12. *See also* Limited partnership
Performance data, mutual funds, 130, 132–134, 139, 143–146, 161, 164–166
PIPE. *See* Private investments in public securities (PIPEs)
Plan of distribution, 92, 93
Portfolio manager, 138, 139, 160, 161
PPS. *See* Principal protected securities (PPSs)
Price-to-book (P/B) ratio, 63–64
Price-to-cash flow (P/CF) ratio, 64–66
Price-to-earnings (P/E) ratio, 61–62
    business development companies, 224
    equity IPOs, 73, 88
    secondary offerings, 123
Price-to-sales (P/S) ratio, 62–63
Pricing
    and disclosure of risk, 2, 23
    initial public offerings, 73
    mutual fund shares, 139–142
    secondary offerings, 110, 112–116, 120–123
Principal protected securities (PPSs), 169, 170, 181
    advantages and disadvantages of, 171–173
    categories of, 174–181
    discussion questions, 182, 275, 276
    exercise, 182, 276
    expected return, 172, 176–178, 181
    recommended reading, 182
    risk factors, 173
Private equity funds
    business development companies. *See* Business development companies (BDCs)
    discussion questions, 234, 235
    exercise, 235
    reasons for investing in, 218
    recommended reading, 236
    specialized acquisition companies (SPACs), 217–219
Private investment entities, 207, 208
Private investments in public securities (PIPEs)
    evaluation of, 114–123
    private placement memorandum, 112–123
    reasons for, 113, 114, 116
    registration exemption for, 117
    regulation of, 109, 110, 112–114
    terminology, 121
Private offerings
    discussion questions, 28, 267, 268
    generally, 8, 9, 16
    hedge funds. *See* Hedge funds
    limitation to accredited investors, 15–17
    market for and liquidity, 17
    multi-state, SEC regulation of, 16, 17

Index

NASD rules, 19–22
recommended reading, 28, 29
and state regulation, 15–18
Private placement memorandum, 9, 112–123
Proceeds, use of
    equity IPOs, 85–87
    secondary offerings, 119–121
Profitability ratios, 54–56
Proprietorships, 10, 11
Prospectus
    defined, 8
    equity IPOs. *See* Initial public offerings (IPOs)
    mutual funds. *See* Mutual funds
    preliminary (red herring), 72, 74, 75, 77–79, 114
    principal protected securities. *See* Principal protected securities (PPSs)
    publicly-traded offerings, 22
    secondary offerings. *See* Secondary offerings
Proxy statements, 7, 8, 26, 27, 183, 201
    discussion questions, 202, 277
    evaluating, 184–198
    exercise, 203, 277
    investment companies, 198–200
    recommended reading, 203
    SPACs, 219
    summary of key issues, 202
Proxy voting, 154
Public offerings, generally, 8, 9
Publicly traded partnership (PTP), 260–265
Purchaser representative, 17

Qualified institutional buyers, 117
Quick ratio, 48

Ratios
    activity ratios, 52–54
    analysis, 45, 46, 56
    common size data, 45, 46
    debt ratio, 50, 51
    earnings to fixed charges, equity IPOs, 80, 85
    liquidity ratios, 46–49
    price-to-book (P/B) ratio, 63, 64
    price-to-cash flow (P/CF) ratio, 64–66
    price-to-earnings (P/E), 61, 62, 73, 88, 123, 224
    price-to-sales (P/S) ratio, 62, 63
    profitability ratios, 54–56
    solvency ratios, 49–52
    valuation ratios, 61–67
Real estate investment trust (REIT), 237, 242
    discussion questions, 252, 281, 282
    diversification, 242, 247, 251
    exercise, 252, 282
    investment categories, 242, 244
    investment policies, 242, 244–247
    prospectus, 242, 244–250
    registration, 242
    umbrella partnership (UPREIT), 245
Real estate limited partnership (RELP)
    advantages and disadvantages of, 238
    discussion questions, 252, 281, 282
    diversification, 238, 239, 251
    financial information, 240, 241
    general partners, 238
    liability issues, 237, 238
    partnership documents, 241–244
    prospectus, evaluation of, 239–250
    recommended reading, 252
    regulation of, 238, 239
    summary of key issues, 251
Red herring, 72, 74, 75, 77–79, 114
Redemption, mutual fund shares, 128, 136, 140–144, 146, 162–164
Registration
    exemptions, 23, 24, 117, 205–207
    hedge funds, 205–208
    initial public offering, 72, 74–102
    mutual funds, 131, 132
    new securities offerings, 22
    secondary public offerings, 110–112
Regulation A, 23
Regulation D, 23, 117, 205, 206
Regulation S-K, 72
Regulatory framework, 7–29
Restatement of accounts, 197
Return on assets (ROA), 55–59
Return on common equity (ROCE), 55
Return on equity (ROE), 55–60
Return on sales, 54
Risk and reward, evaluation of, 2, 5, 71, 74
Risk factors
    business development companies, 224–226, 229, 230
    disclosure of, 3
    equity IPOs, 74, 78–85, 88, 97, 104
    hedge funds, 210, 211
    mutual funds, 133–137
    secondary offerings, 110, 121, 123
Road shows, 73, 111
Rule 504, 23
Rule 505, 23, 24
Rule 506, 24, 206
Rule 12b-1, 140, 143, 159, 160, 198, 201

S corporation, 11, 12
Sales loads
    business development companies, 229, 230

Understanding and Evaluating Prospectuses, Offering Documents, and Proxy Statements

mutual funds, 128, 134, 142, 143, 146, 149, 153, 160, 163, 166
Sarbanes-Oxley Act (SOX), 24, 25, 192
Scandals
   corporate scandals, 19, 83, 84
   mutual funds, 129
Secondary offerings
   disclosure protections, 109–112
   discussion questions, 124, 272–274
   exercise, 124, 273
   pricing, 110, 112–116, 120–123
   private offerings, 112–114
   prospectus, evaluation of, 114–123
   public, 109–112
   recommended readings, 125
   risk factors, 110, 121, 123
   summary of key issues, 123
Securities Act of 1933, 22, 23, 72, 109
Securities and Exchange Commission (SEC)
   accredited investors, 16, 17, 117, 206, 207
   electronic filing, 28, 268
   equity IPOs, regulation of, 73, 74, 81, 98, 101, 102. *See also* Initial public offerings (IPOs)
   investment companies, regulation of, 127, 128. *See also* Mutual funds
   and private offerings, 16, 17
   proxy statement requirements, 26, 27
   registration with. *See* Registration
   regulations, 22–24
   and requirements for issuers of securities, 2
Securities Exchange Act of 1934 (Exchange Act), 22, 109, 111, 220
Security offerings, types of, 8–10
Shareholder information, mutual funds, 139–141
Shares
   allocation of IPO shares, 103. *See also* Auctions
   classes of, 77, 80, 81, 86, 100, 101
   description of security being offered, 115, 116
   dilution. *See* Dilution
   offered by corporation, 77, 78
   offered by existing shareholders, 77, 78, 91, 92, 114, 115
   offering price. *See* Offering price
   plan of distribution, 92, 93
Small order execution system (SOES), 25
Solvency ratios, 49–52
Sophistication of investors, private offerings, 15, 16, 23, 117. *See also* Accredited investors
Specialized acquisition companies (SPACs), 217–219
State regulation of securities, 14–18, 78, 79
Statement of additional information (SAI), 129–133, 138, 140, 146–166, 178
Stock exchange listings, 78

Stock exchange requirements, 24–26
Stock options, 81, 194, 195

Tax consequences
   business development companies, 233
   commodities and managed futures funds, 260
   corporations, 11, 12
   limited liability company, 12
   master limited partnerships, 263
   mutual funds, 138, 142–144, 159, 163, 164
   partnerships, 11
   proprietorship, 11
   real estate investment trusts, 245
   S corporations, 11, 12
Total asset turnover ratio, 53, 54
Trustees
   investment companies, 198
   mutual funds, 128, 138, 146, 149–153, 158, 166

Umbrella partnership real estate investment trust (UPREIT), 245
Underwriting
   business development companies, 220, 222
   and due diligence, 9
   Google IPO, 77–79, 86, 88, 92, 93, 106
   initial public offerings, 22, 23, 72, 73
   mutual funds, 139, 141, 148, 153, 154, 159, 163–166
   secondary public offerings, 110–112, 114, 116, 117
Unit investment trusts (UITs), 128, 130, 131, 144, 146
UPREIT, 245

Valuation ratios, 61–67
Venture capital funding, 16, 207
Voting, 187, 198. *See also* Proxy statements

Warrants and options, 81, 194